Market and Technical Knowledge Integration in R&D-Intensive Companies

Market and Technical Knowledge Integration in R&D-Intensive Companies explores the integration of market and technical knowledge within R&D-intensive companies.

The crux of the book's theoretical premise is the importance of integrating market and technical knowledge within organisations. Drawing from the resource-based view (RBV) and the knowledge-based view (KBV) of organisations, this premise stresses the need for knowledge integration. After an analysis of the literature on R&D, the book presents qualitative evidence from interviews of R&D professionals who elucidate knowledge integration methods.

The book provides theoretical as well as practical insight on market and technical knowledge integration. Presenting a new approach to understanding how R&D-intensive companies operate, the book gives researchers and practitioners practical advice on improving market and technical knowledge integration. It explains the critical role of efficient market and technical knowledge integration in innovation. It also examines how knowledge management contributes to the superior business performance of R&D-intensive companies.

Dr. Marcin Soniewicki works as an assistant professor at Poznań University of Economics and Business (PUEB), Poland. In his research, he focuses on issues related to knowledge, knowledge management, market orientation, competitiveness of companies and innovation. He has authored almost 50 scientific papers.

He has been the lead researcher in two projects financed by Poland's National Science Centre and has participated in many other research projects. He is a reviewer for a number of journals, including the *Journal of Knowledge Management*, *Journal of Knowledge Management Research and Practice*, and *Journal of Marketing Intelligence and Planning*.

In addition to the doctoral degree, he holds two master's degrees: one in international economics from PUEB and the other in international accounting from the Royal Holloway, University of London.

Market and Technical Knowledge Integration in R&D-Intensive Companies

Marcin Soniewicki

Routledge
Taylor & Francis Group
NEW YORK AND LONDON

Cover: www.shutterstock.com

First published 2025
by Routledge
605 Third Avenue, New York, NY 10158

and by Routledge
4 Park Square, Milton Park, Abingdon, Oxon, OX14 4RN

Routledge is an imprint of the Taylor & Francis Group, an informa business

ISBN: 978-1-032-63500-2 (hbk)
ISBN: 978-1-032-64234-5 (pbk)
ISBN: 978-1-032-64235-2 (ebk)

DOI: 10.1201/9781032642352

Typeset in Adobe Garamond Pro
by Apex CoVantage, LLC

Contents

Acknowledgements

Reviewers:
Prof. Dr. Fatih Çetin, Baskent University, Turkey
Prof. Dr. hab. Jerzy Gołuchowski, University of Economics in Katowice, Poland

Translation:
Grzegorz Grygiel

This monograph is the effect of a research project no. 2016/23/D/HS4/02527 entitled *"The role of integrating market and technical knowledge in the process of innovation undertaken by high and medium-high tech companies in a globalised economy: the network approach"*, which was financed by the National Science Centre, Poland.

Introduction

The importance of knowledge in the creation of competitive advantage by companies is nowadays commonly accepted in the literature (e.g. Sopińska, 2008; Mikuła & Oczkowska, 2009; Ujwary-Gil, 2012; Skrzypek, 2013a; Levallet & Chan, 2016; Mikuła & Stefaniuk, 2018; Antunes & Pinheiro, 2020; Piñeiro-Chousa et al., 2020). Knowledge is the foundation of business development, and in the conditions of global economy and fierce competition, companies need to innovate if they want to survive. Theories of knowledge and innovation are closely related, which has been emphasised by many authors (e.g. Popadiuk & Choo, 2006; Delgado-Verde et al., 2011; Urbancová, 2013; Ritala et al., 2015; Ode & Ayavoo, 2020). Until recently, however, the literature of the subject has focused on more general aspects associated with knowledge in the context of its impact on innovativeness, competitive advantage or business performance, with knowledge management being the dominant concept in this area (Inkinen, 2016; Gaviria-Marin et al., 2019), involving a number of processes regarding knowledge, such as acquisition, creation, sharing, application and implementation (Sun, 2010; Skrzypek, 2013b; Tan & Wong, 2015; Intezari et al. 2017). However, to gain a better understanding of how knowledge-related activities affect innovativeness and business performance and how they can become more effective, the problem should be analysed in more detail by applying other approaches. One of them consists in identifying what types of knowledge are the most important and investigating processes that take place in business entities[1] in connection with these resources in order to improve their effectiveness. Currently, when analysing knowledge-related activities, many authors do not focus on specific types of this resource (e.g. Durmuş-Özdemir & Abdukhoshimov, 2018; Mardani et al., 2018; Ferraris et al., 2019; Shujahat et al., 2019), as a result of which it is frequently treated as a monolithic resource, which it certainly is not. Many types of knowledge are distinguished in the literature (e.g. Sapienza et al., 2004; Fletcher & Harris, 2011; Moos et al., 2011; Sáenz et al., 2012; Deligianni et al., 2015; Suseno & Pinnington, 2018), which could be more frequently used for the purpose of modelling and analysis. This monograph concentrates on market and technical knowledge, which are among the most commonly mentioned types of knowledge in the literature (e.g. Fletcher & Harris, 2011; Sáenz et al., 2012). What is more, many authors agree that market and technical knowledge is necessary for successful innovation (e.g. Shang et al., 2017; Spigel & Harrison, 2018). It should be emphasised that knowledge and its creation are particularly important for R&D-intensive companies (e.g. Coff, 2003), where research and development (R&D) are used to create knowledge which later generates profits (Hall & Lerner, 2009). This is why this monograph focuses on R&D-intensive companies, which are particularly important for the economy because of their activity in the field of research and development. Such investments are associated with a high level of private (20–30%) and social (30–80%) rates of return (Fraumeni & Okubo, 2005). R&D activities contribute to the growth of productivity in society (Verbič et al., 2011) and are important for economic growth (Sokolov-Mladenović et al., 2016). There is no single commonly accepted definition of R&D-intensive companies in the literature. In this monograph, they are defined according to the classification created by Galindo-Rueda and Verger (2016). This relatively recent classification was chosen on account of its numerous benefits, particularly because it includes non-manufacturing companies, which are often excluded by other authors. The analysis focuses on firms operating in medium-high and high R&D intensity industries, the two categories of R&D-intensive industries proposed by Galindo-Rueda and Verger (2016); hence, such entities are further referred to as R&D-intensive companies. Both groups are commonly analysed jointly by authors who use this classification (e.g. Bakhtiari, 2021; Mulier and Samarin, 2021).

This monograph is based on the resource-based view (RBV).[2] The main assumption underlying this theory is that organisations differ in terms of their resources, which cannot be fully transferred between companies (Barney, 1991). One special category of non-transferrable resources are capabilities (Makadok, 2001), which enable organisations to make use of other resources (Barney & Hesterly, 2012). According to the RBV, in order to gain competitive advantage, a company must have resources that are defined by the acronym VRIN: valuable, rare, imperfectly imitable and non-substitutable (Barney, 1991). At the end of the 20th century, as a result of changes and the emergence of post-industrial economies, there was a growing interest in the role of knowledge (Grant, 2002). This new focus had an effect on the RBV, which started to emphasise the importance of intangible resources, particularly knowledge (e.g. Grant, 1996a; Rouse & Daellenbach, 2002). This led to the creation of the knowledge-based view (KBV), which is based on the RBV (Nieves & Haller, 2014).

The KBV recognises that knowledge is the primary resource underlying the creation of new value and the main factor of production and that the company's main role consists of integrating this resource (Grant, 1996b). It should be stressed that rather than being a theory of the firm, the KBV is a series of unified insights concentrating on the role of knowledge in the organisation of production and as a factor of production (Grant, 2002). According to Grant (1996a), value creation is connected with various kinds of specialist knowledge. In his opinion, there is a need for employees with more specialised skills, that is with deeper knowledge, which is, necessarily, narrower. In this case, if the store of the organisation's knowledge is split between highly specialised employees, then the company's main task is to integrate it (Grant, 1996a), which is why the integration of all kinds of specialist knowledge plays a key role in gaining competitive advantage (Grant, 2002).

The RBV was also the basis of another concept, which is very popular nowadays, namely that of dynamic capabilities, one of which includes knowledge integration capability (e.g. Chirico & Salvato, 2008; Villar et al., 2014; Martinelli et al., 2018). It should be pointed out, however, that this capability has not always been perceived in the same way. It is usually understood as the company's capability of integrating any kind of knowledge (e.g. Verona & Ravasi, 2003; Martinelli et al., 2018).

Many authors confirm the importance of knowledge integration in the organisation and its role in the creation of innovation, competitive advantage or improving business performance (e.g. Malik et al., 2020; Yang et al., 2021; Acharya et al., 2022). Nonetheless, instead of concentrating on the integration of particular types of specialist knowledge, they adopt a more general approach to the knowledge integration in a company. However, research into activities aimed at integrating such a complex resource requires a more fine-grained perspective. Moreover, a more comprehensive approach is needed, which takes into account not only knowledge integration but also the development of different kinds of knowledge that are being integrated. In the case of a particular company, failure to account for this factor may lead to an excess of one kind of knowledge and an insufficient stock of another kind. In practice, this could mean having knowledge about the needs of a given customer but no technical possibilities of satisfying them or investing in the development of products or services for which the company will not be able to find customers.

As already mentioned, this monograph concentrates on market and technical knowledge. It should be emphasised that gaps in the literature regarding analyses of integration of these two types of knowledge have been recognised by some authors (e.g. Azari et al., 2020). While market and technical knowledge are just two of the many different kinds of knowledge that exist and are integrated in modern companies, the author of this monograph also believes that they deserve special attention because of their importance for the effectiveness of business operations, a fact emphasised, among others, by Deligianni et al. (2015) and Suseno and Pinnington (2018).

So far, research on the integration of market and technical knowledge has been fragmentary and mostly limited to the concept of R&D-marketing integration (e.g. Fain & Wagner, 2014; Shin & Roh, 2015; Li & Chen, 2016; Boles & Link, 2017; Yongsheng & Jinjie, 2019). The main idea behind this concept is to foster closer cooperation between employees involved in R&D activities (those with technical knowledge) and those responsible for marketing (equipped with market knowledge). The author of this monograph has chosen to use a more general term, namely "market and technical knowledge integration", because he believes the problem in question requires a broader perspective. There are a number of arguments in favour of this approach. Firstly, the term "R&D-marketing integration" can imply a limitation of the scope of investigation. Studies on this topic have mostly focused on the integration of R&D and marketing departments. It should be pointed out, however, that market and technical knowledge does not reside exclusively in specific departments but is distributed throughout the organisation. Moreover, for years authors have stressed that knowledge and innovation are not created only in R&D departments (e.g. Baldwin & Hanel, 2003; Probst et al., 2004; Klincewicz, 2012), which is why activities relating to knowledge integration should not be limited to these two departments. Secondly, many companies implement modern frameworks of project management, such as Scrum, which enable people with market knowledge (e.g. about the needs of customers) to cooperate with those responsible for technology as part of one team. Thirdly, while drawing on the insights derived from research on R&D-marketing integration, this monograph also relies on the KBV and the concept of dynamic capabilities. Authors investigating R&D-marketing integration tend to focus on integration practices aimed at facilitating cooperation between employees of the two departments while practically ignoring market and technical knowledge resources as such. Since this monograph takes into account not only market and knowledge integration practices but also knowledge resources that companies have, it seems that in this case it is better to speak about "market and technical knowledge integration". It should be stressed, however, that so far, the biggest contribution to the study of market and technical knowledge integration has been made precisely by authors interested in the concept of R&D-marketing integration. That said, the fact remains that this approach still has a number of gaps or even contradictions, which could be filled or eliminated by applying the KBV and the concept of dynamic capabilities. This *research gap* (see Section 4.3 for a more detailed description of the *research gap*) covers six different aspects: five of them concern existing research on R&D-marketing integration, while the sixth has to do with the lack of a comprehensive approach to the topic, which can be addressed by combining all the three concepts mentioned so far—R&D-marketing integration, the KBV and dynamic capabilities.

Firstly, there are a number of studies on R&D-marketing integration whose results are contradictory. Most authors in this group report that activities designed to foster R&D-marketing integration have a positive effect on business performance (e.g. Song & Song, 2010; Yao et al., 2014). However, according to some studies, such activities bring negative effects (e.g. Brettel et al., 2011; Rubera et al., 2012).

Secondly, most publications on R&D-marketing integration focus on the exchange of information, relationships and cooperation between R&D and marketing departments (e.g. Shim et al., 2016; Homburg et al., 2017; Nijssen & Ordanini, 2020). It should be pointed out, however, that nowadays people involved in R&D (with technical knowledge) and those dealing with marketing (with market knowledge) often work together, for example within the same project teams.

Thirdly, one major problem of many studies on R&D-marketing integration is the fact that they are based on samples of firms representing various industries, which differ greatly in terms of how much they spend on research and development, according to the classification proposed by Galindo-Rueda and Verger (2016); as a result, these companies differ considerably with respect to the nature of their business activity (e.g. Sanzo et al., 2012; Homburg et al., 2017; Yongsheng & Jinjie,

2019). Results of such analyses can be misleading because the importance of integration practices and the role of knowledge may vary depending on the industry in which a given company operates.

Fourthly, there are very few recent publications on R&D-marketing integration. This shortage is particularly evident if one looks for comprehensive studies on R&D-intensive or high-tech companies. Available studies address this topic in a very fragmentary manner: for example, articles by Li and Chen (2012, 2016) focus only on the semiconductor industry, whereas those by Boles and Link (2017) focus on the selected aspects of R&D-marketing integration among high-tech manufacturing companies.

Fifthly, even the few recent studies on R&D-marketing integration often rely on approaches and measurement methods used in the 1980s or 1990s (e.g. Eng & Ozdemir, 2014; Ali & Matsuno, 2018; Nijssen & Ordanini, 2020). They are not very compatible with modern business realities, since, as already mentioned, over the years, the way companies operate, especially in R&D-intensive industries, has changed considerably.

The sixth and final aspect has to do with the fact that the literature on R&D-marketing integration lacks comprehensive studies involving analyses of market and technical knowledge as well as the question of the development of these two knowledge resources. The problem of integrating different kinds of knowledge has, however, been addressed in the context of the KBV (Grant, 1996a, 1997) and the concept of dynamic capabilities (Verona & Ravasi, 2003). Both approaches originate from the RBV and, consequently, focus on resources, one factor which is usually overlooked in research on R&D-marketing integration. It can therefore be argued that the resource-based approaches—the KBV and the concept of dynamic capabilities—complement R&D-marketing integration. Another important thing to keep in mind is the fact that many authors who regard market and technical knowledge as crucial for the company's effectiveness do not take into account their integration (e.g. Atuahene-Gima, 2005; Giuliani, 2008; Bohlmann et al., 2013). As a result, valuable insights from R&D-marketing integration research with respect to practical strategies aimed at integrating people with technical and market knowledge can be analysed together with ways in which these two resources can be developed. It is important to note that these knowledge resources need to be constantly developed as up-to-date knowledge is crucial for companies (e.g. Hitt et al., 2009) and without them even the most effective strategies of integrating both resources will not serve its purpose and may not help companies to improve their operations.

In order to fill this *research gap*, it is necessary, above all, to analyse knowledge integration activities which companies operating in R&D-intensive industries employ to integrate market and technical knowledge. This requires a comprehensive approach to integration, which not only involves analysing current strategies of integrating both kinds of knowledge in the selected group of companies but also takes into account the development of these resources, including the identification of sources of market and technical knowledge used by R&D-intensive firms.

In view of the above, the main objective of the monograph is twofold: *to identify factors that determine the integration of market and technical knowledge in R&D-intensive companies and to evaluate the effect of market and technical knowledge integration on innovativeness and business performance of these firms.*

To achieve this goal, the following five research questions have been put forward:

RQ1: What sources of market and technical knowledge are used by R&D-intensive companies?
RQ2: How does the development of market and technical knowledge affect integration of these knowledge resources in R&D-intensive companies and their innovativeness and business performance?
RQ3: How do R&D-intensive companies integrate market and technical knowledge?
RQ4: How does the integration of market and technical knowledge affect business performance and innovativeness of R&D-intensive companies?
RQ5: What recommendations should be made to managers so that they can facilitate the integration of both kinds of knowledge in R&D-intensive companies and, consequently, improve their business performance and innovativeness?

Taking into account Grant's view (1996a, 1997) regarding the key role of knowledge integration in the company, which is one of the tenets of the KBV, and restricting the scope of knowledge to its two kinds that are particularly important for any business (e.g. Deligianni et al., 2015; Suseno & Pinnington, 2018), it can be assumed that the development of market and technical knowledge has a positive impact on knowledge integration activities. This is because these two kinds of knowledge need to be constantly updated to ensure that knowledge integration is really effective. Following Grant's view (1996a, 1997), it can also be assumed that knowledge integration activities have a mediating effect between the development of market and technical knowledge and innovativeness and business performance of R&D-intensive companies. It should be pointed out, however, that the existence of this mediating effect does not rule out the possibility that the development of market and technical knowledge can directly affect the two response variables. As already noted, the effect of both kinds of knowledge on innovativeness and business performance has been emphasised in the literature (e.g. Li & Cavusgil, 1999; Atuahene-Gima, 2005; Giuliani, 2008; Bohlmann et al., 2013). Nonetheless, it is necessary to conduct additional studies to investigate these effects in more detail in order to determine if they are direct, indirect, mediated through knowledge integration, or both effects exist in parallel. It can also be assumed that the development of market and technical knowledge and their integration are particularly important for firms operating in R&D-intensive industries, which are under constant pressure to innovate (Wang & Li, 2017; Pham et al., 2019), as they need to compete with innovative rivals (Avsar, 2018).

In view of the above and the research gap described, 12 hypotheses of this monograph have been formulated as follows:

H1: The development of market knowledge has a direct positive effect on market and technical knowledge integration activities.
H2: The development of technical knowledge has a direct positive effect on market and technical knowledge integration activities.
H3: Market and technical knowledge integration activities have a positive mediating effect between the development of market knowledge and innovativeness of R&D-intensive firms.
H4: Market and technical knowledge integration activities have a positive mediating effect between the development of technical knowledge and innovativeness of R&D-intensive firms.
H5: Market and technical knowledge integration activities have a positive mediating effect between the development of market knowledge and business performance of R&D-intensive firms.
H6: Market and technical knowledge integration activities have a positive mediating effect between the development of technical knowledge and business performance of R&D-intensive firms.
H7: The development of market knowledge has a direct positive effect on innovativeness of R&D-intensive companies.
H8: The development of technical knowledge has a direct positive effect on innovativeness of R&D-intensive companies.
H9: The development of market knowledge has a direct positive effect on business performance of R&D-intensive companies.
H10: The development of technical knowledge has a direct positive effect on business performance of R&D-intensive companies.
H11: Market and technical knowledge integration activities in R&D-intensive firms have a direct positive effect on innovativeness of these companies.
H12: Market and technical knowledge integration activities in R&D-intensive firms have a direct positive effect on business performance of these companies.

The theoretical underpinnings of this monograph are drawn from management sciences and the RBV, and the author's ambition is to make a contribution to this field. Frequent reference is also made to the KBV, the concepts of dynamic capabilities and R&D-marketing integration.

In order to achieve the objectives specified above and answer the research questions, the author opted for a mixed-method approach, which is defined as "research in which the investigator collects and analyses data, integrates the findings, and draws inferences using both qualitative and quantitative approaches or methods in a single study or a program of inquiry" (Tashakkori & Creswell, 2007, p. 4). More specifically, an exploratory sequential design was adopted, which is used, among other things, to create new quantitative research tools that are based on qualitative data. Tools created in this way are rooted in the culture of the studied group, which increases the likelihood of them being perceived as relevant (Creswell & Plano Clark, 2018). The choice of an exploratory sequential design was motivated by the lack of up-to-date measurement tools designed to study the problem investigated in this monograph. In effect, the first stage of the empirical study involved qualitative interviews with representatives of 16 companies. During the second stage, a quantitative survey of 520 firms was conducted. All stages of the research process conducted for the purpose of this monograph are shown in Figure I.1.

The goal of the qualitative study was to collect information about activities currently undertaken by R&D-intensive firms to integrate and develop market and

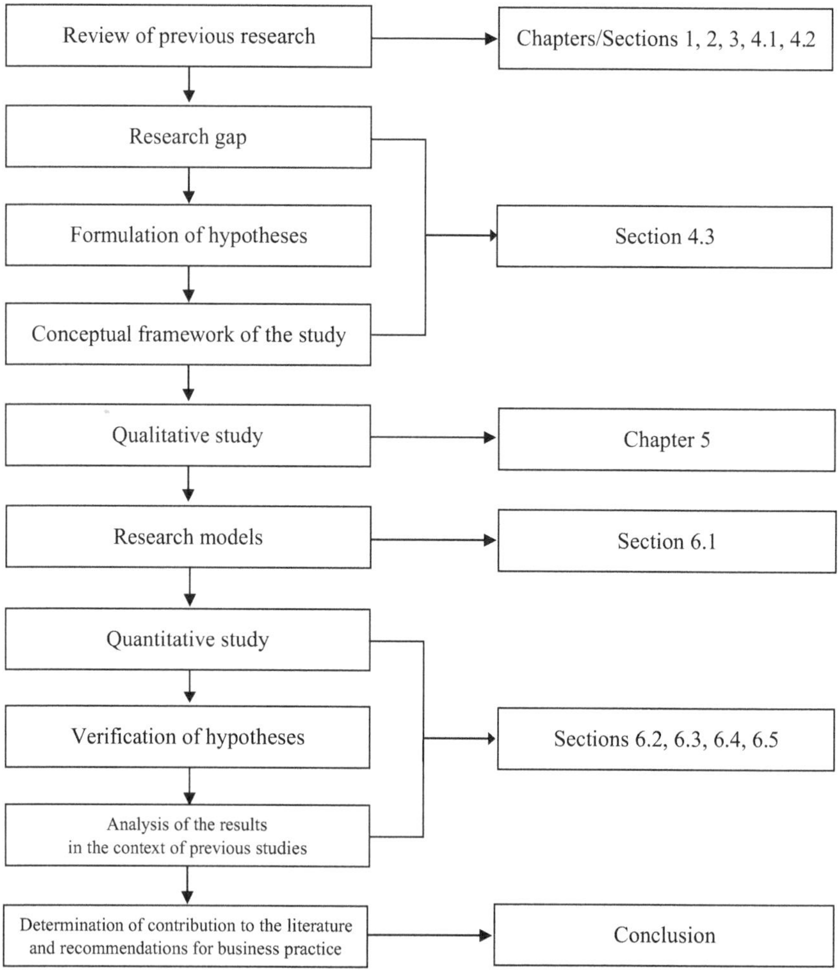

Figure I.1 Steps of the research process described in the monograph

technical knowledge, which was then used to formulate questions for the quantitative survey. The goal of the quantitative survey was to collect data from a bigger sample of companies that could be used in a statistical verification of insights from the literature and findings from the qualitative study by applying the method of partial least squares structural equation modelling (PLS-SEM).

The qualitative study conducted during the first stage of empirical research relied on semi-structured in-depth interviews consisting of open-ended questions, which had been designed according to recommendations made by different authors (e.g. Cook, 2008; Yin, 2016; Leavy, 2017). The question format enabled respondents to describe the phenomenon of interest using their own words. The questions were formulated on the basis of the conceptual framework of the study (presented in Chapter 4), the research questions set at the beginning and a review of the literature. They were particularly concerned with the integration of market and technical knowledge in the company, including such aspects as the importance of integration, the respondent's thoughts about the topic and activities undertaken by the company in this area. There were also questions about the sources of market and technical knowledge and respondents' opinions about the impact of such activities on their companies' innovativeness and business performance. To ensure comparability of results, the interviews were conducted using a questionnaire developed by the author.

Qualitative interviews were carried out in Poland with representatives of 16 companies between May and September 2019. To select a sample of R&D-intensive firms, the author used the classification developed by Galindo-Rueda and Verger (2016). Respondents included company representatives with a good knowledge of their respective organisations: presidents, CEOs, board members, managers of different levels and heads of R&D departments. Each interview was personally conducted by the author of this monograph, who had the most comprehensive knowledge of the subject and was able to adequately engage the respondents in conversation and thus elicit more detailed information. All interviews were recorded, except one, which was conducted on the phone and could not be recorded for technical reasons.[3] The interviews lasted from 1.5 to 2 hours. Some of the responding business entities agreed to reveal their names, while others chose to remain anonymous. The companies in the sample were quite diverse, though most of them were large firms employing over 250 people. They were selected from different R&D-intensive industries since the intention of the qualitative study was to gain the broadest possible understanding of processes that take place in different kinds of R&D-intensive firms and to identify the differences between them. The sample was also diverse in terms of ownership status: half of them were owned by Polish-based entities and the other half by foreign entities.

The purpose of the quantitative survey was to collect data that could be used to verify the previous findings using statistical methods. With this goal in mind, on the basis of the hypotheses, the conceptual framework of the study and a review of the literature, two research models were created. In the first model, the goal was to investigate the influence of the studied phenomena on innovativeness of

R&D-intensive companies; and in the second, it was to analyse their impact on business performance of such companies. Each model consisted of 5 latent variables (constructs) and 17 indicators. 3–4 indicators were used for each of the latent variables. The survey was commissioned by the author and conducted by the Indicator company using computer-assisted telephone interviewing (CATI) between April and May 2020. Respondents were informed that survey questions concerned 2019, which is important given the impact of the Covid-19 pandemic on the business sector in 2020. The Bisnode database was used as the sampling frame. According to information provided by Indicator, the database has a smaller coverage error than databases maintained by Statistics Poland. A total of 3528 entities were selected and information about them was transferred into the CADAS software, which used a randomisation algorithm to ensure that each company had an equal probability of being sampled. Fifteen interviewers were employed to conduct the survey, which was stopped after 520 interviews were completed. 798 entities refused to participate and 12 interviews were interrupted. As in the case of the qualitative study, only R&D-intensive firms, according to the classification proposed by Galindo-Rueda and Verger (2016), were included in the sample. Both empirical studies were conducted as part of a research project no. 2016/23/D/HS4/02527 entitled "*The role of integrating market and technical knowledge in the process of innovation undertaken by high and medium-high tech companies in a globalised economy: the network approach*", which was financed by the National Science Centre, Poland. In addition to the author of this monograph, who acted as the project leader, the project team consisted of Joanna Paliszkiewicz, Aleksandra Hauke-Lopes and Grzegorz Grygiel.

The monograph consists of six chapters, introduction and conclusion. Four chapters are devoted to theoretical considerations and two contain empirical analyses. The introduction presents the goal and main assumptions of the monograph. The first chapter presents a number of classifications and typologies of technology industries, where categories depend on the intensity of R&D activities conducted by companies. The presentation also includes classifications and typologies based on other criteria. The chapter provides a justification for why the author chose the classification of industries created by Galindo-Rueda and Verger (2016) to identify R&D-intensive companies, which this monograph focuses on. A list of features that characterises this group of companies is given, along with a description of their role in the economy. The last part of the chapter explains the importance of market and technical knowledge and their integration for R&D-intensive companies.

The second chapter focuses on the concept of knowledge and presents its various definitions and characteristics, including factors taken into account in each case. This part is followed by an overview of knowledge typologies, with emphasis on the division into market and technical knowledge, including their definitions, importance and dimensions. Market and technical knowledge sources used by companies are also analysed.

The third chapter concentrates on the theoretical consideration of two measures of effectiveness used in the assessment of R&D-intensive companies, namely innovativeness and business performance. Various definitions of innovation are provided and compared in terms of key words they contain. This is followed by a review of innovation typologies. Much attention is devoted to the analysis of "organisational innovativeness", which is one of the key concepts used in the monograph. This includes an overview of different definitions of organisational innovativeness and the author's own typology of these definitions. The second part of the chapter, devoted to the analysis of business performance, includes an overview of its definitions and key words used in them and provides a justification for the use of this concept in the monograph.

The fourth chapter is the most important element of the theoretical part of the monograph. It explains the importance of market and technical knowledge integration in an organisation. Drawing on insights from the RBV and the KBV, the author highlights the role of knowledge and the need to integrate this resource, which, according to Grant (1996a, 1997), is one of the main tasks that companies should strive to achieve. After analysing the problem of knowledge integration from the perspective of dynamic capabilities, the author offers a comprehensive, critical analysis of R&D-marketing integration, including his own classification of publications representing this strand of research, which is followed by a thorough discussion. The chapter ends with a number of conclusions regarding previous research on the integration of market and technical knowledge including the existing research gap and presents the main objective of the monograph, research questions, 12 hypotheses and the conceptual framework of the study.

The empirical part of the monograph starts with the fifth chapter, which presents the results of qualitative interviews carried out by the author with representatives of 16 R&D-intensive firms. The findings provide information about ways in which such companies integrate market and technical knowledge and the origin of these resources. This information was used to expand and update an inventory of activities used by R&D-intensive companies to foster the integration of market and technical knowledge, which are mentioned in the literature. The inventory of activities supporting knowledge integration served as the basis for two research models used in the quantitative study.

The sixth chapter, the crucial element of the empirical part of the monograph, presents the two research models. The first one focuses on the impact of activities aimed at developing and integrating market and technical knowledge on the innovativeness of R&D-intensive companies. The second model concentrates on how these activities affect these companies' business performance. The research models are a detailed representation of the conceptual framework of the study created on the basis of the literature review and the findings of the qualitative study. The hypotheses are analysed using research models and data from the quantitative survey of 520 R&D-intensive companies. The analysis is performed by applying the PLS-SEM method, which is described in detail. The chapter ends with a summary of hypotheses validation, including a number of conclusions drawn from the quantitative analysis and a discussion of the results in the context of previous studies.

The monograph ends with a conclusion, containing a summary of all results and a list of theoretical contributions resulting from the monograph as well as several recommendations for business practitioners. The section ends with a list of limitations of the quantitative survey and suggestions regarding directions for future research.

Notes

1 Throughout the monograph, words like "company", "firm", "business entity" and "organisation" are used interchangeably to avoid repetition, although the author realises that they are not, strictly speaking, exact synonyms.
2 In the monograph, the resource-based view is treated as a theory, as is the case in many other publications (e.g. Lavie, 2006; Ketchen Jr et al., 2007; Czakon, 2010; Barney & Mackey, 2016; Raguseo & Vitari, 2018; Beamish & Chakravarty, 2021; Gueler & Schneider, 2021; Lanzolla & Markides, 2021; Battisti et al., 2022; Ferreira et al., 2022; Chatterjee et al., 2023).
3 According to Ward et al. (2015), a qualitative interview conducted over the telephone can also yield valuable information, which is comparable to that obtained through face-to-face interviews.

Chapter 1

R&D-Intensive Companies: Characteristics and the Importance of Market and Technical Knowledge Integration

The purpose of this chapter is threefold. Firstly, it aims to present and compare typologies and classifications of industries taking into consideration the intensity of R&D activities and other classification criteria with a view to choosing the most optimal way of determining R&D-intensive industries. Secondly, it identifies the key characteristics of R&D-intensive companies and their significance for the economy. Thirdly, it explains the reasons why R&D-intensive companies need knowledge resources, particularly market and technical knowledge, and need to implement effective ways of integrating these two types of knowledge.

1.1 Classifications and typologies of technology industries according to R&D expenditure

There are a number of typologies and classifications of industries according to the intensity of R&D activity, which is frequently treated as equivalent to the technological level of particular industries and is most used to distinguish high-tech

DOI: 10.1201/9781032642352-1

Table 1.1 Selected industrial classifications

ISIC	*NACE*	*NACIS*	*JSIC*
1948—creation 1958—1st revision 1968—2nd revision 1989—3rd revision 2008—4th revision	1970—creation 1990—1st revision 2002—revision 1.1. 2006—2nd revision 2023—2nd revision update 1 (NACE revision 2.1)	1997—creation 2002—1st revision 2007—2nd revision 2012—3rd revision 2017—4th revision 2022—5th revision	1949—creation 1951—1st revision 1953—2nd revision 1954—3rd revision 1958—4th revision 1963—5th revision 1968—6th revision 1972—7th revision 1977—8th revision 1985—9th revision 1994—10th revision 2002—11th revision

Source: Department of Economic and Social Affairs Statistics Division, United Nations (2008); Executive Office of the President Office of Management and Budget (2022); Eurostat (2023); Ministry of Foreign Affairs and Communications (n.d.).

companies (e.g. Ortega-Argilés et al., 2009). In some cases, however, authors who categorise industries based on the intensity of their R&D activity point out that the term "technology" should be avoided (e.g. Galindo-Rueda & Verger, 2016). This question is discussed in more detail later in the chapter.

Such divisions are based on general industry classifications, such as International Standard Industrial Classification (ISIC), Nomenclature statistique des activités économiques dans la Communauté européenne (NACE), North American Industry Classification System (NAICS) or Japan Standard Industrial Classification (JSIC), which are regularly updated (see Table 1.1).

On the basis of ISIC Rev. 2, Hatzichronoglou (1997) published the High-Technology Sector and Product Classification, which was described as groundbreaking by Galindo-Rueda and Verger (2016). It served as the basis for the creation of OECD's classification of manufacturing industries based on technology, which was published in its 1999 report (OECD, 1999). Two years later, the OECD published an updated version of this classification, which was based on ISIC Rev. 3 (OECD, 2001).

As part of their report for the Milken Institute, DeVol et al. (1999) created a typology which distinguishes only high-technology manufacturing and high-technology service industries. The report focuses on the United States and is based, among other sources, on data from the U.S. Bureau of Labor Statistics. According to this typology, industries are classified as high-tech sectors when they spend a large part of their revenue on R&D and employ more than an average number of specialists that rely on technology, such as engineers, programmers, scientists or mathematicians (DeVol et al., 1999).

A similar approach was adopted by Hecker (1999), who created a typology including only high-technology industries, which was based on criteria such as the share of technical, scientific and engineering staff as well as personnel engaged in R&D activities. According to the U.S. Occupational Employment Statistics survey, the percentage of such employees in industries categorised as high-technology sectors was at least twice as high as the national average. Hecker also distinguished a subset of high-tech industries, which he called high-tech intensive, where the level of employment in the above-mentioned categories was five times as high as the average (Hecker, 1999).

In their article reviewing the main approaches to classifying industries by levels of technology, Carroll et al. (2000) used data from the second innovation survey conducted by Australian Bureau of Statistics in 1996/97 and created three classifications of manufacturing industries using just two categories: high-tech and low-tech. In one case, where R&D intensity was measured in terms of R&D spending, they classified industries that spent at least 3% of their sales on R&D as high-tech industries (Carroll et al., 2000).

In its 2003 report, the OECD updated Hatzichronoglou's classification (1997) by relying on more recent data. In comparison with the earlier version, however, the main difference was the exclusion of R&D expenditures and the resulting changes were relatively small. Moreover, Hatzichronoglou's original classification was created using data from 10 OECD countries. The following classifications published by the OECD in 1999 and 2001 were based on data from 13 OECD countries, while the 2003 classification was based on data from 12 OECD countries. Hatzichronoglou's classification and its later versions published by the OECD are still very popular and frequently used in the literature (e.g. Silva & Lima, 2017; Li & Bathelt, 2018; Peretz et al., 2018; Campi et al., 2019; Lee et al., 2019; Garavan et al., 2020; Nikiforou et al., 2020). Some authors simplify it by combining certain categories, for example high with medium-high and medium-low with low (e.g. Liu & Daly, 2011; Antonelli & Crespi, 2012; Kato & Honjo, 2015).

Ortega-Argilés et al. (2009) developed a classification of companies based on data from the UK's Department of Trade and Industry (DTI), which collects information on R&D investment and value added from major European firms operating in the service and manufacturing sector. The classification, based on data for 2000–2005 from 532 European firms, includes three categories: high-tech, medium-tech and low-tech. The inclusion of the service sector is certainly an advantage. The main drawback, however, is that the underlying data come exclusively from bigger companies representing only 14 European countries, with an overrepresentation of British firms (Ortega-Argilés et al., 2009).

In 2016, Galindo-Rueda and Verger (2016) created a new version of the OECD classification taking into account R&D intensity in relation to gross value added (GVA). Among the key changes was the inclusion of non-manufacturing industries, the use of ISIC Rev. 4 and the addition of a fifth category, namely medium R&D intensity industries. The classification was based on data from 27 OECD countries and 2 partner countries: Chinese Taipei and Singapore. It has been used by a number of authors, including Wojan and Parker (2017), Fleury et al. (2018), Lampón and González-Benito (2019), Becker et al. (2020), Carrillo-Carrillo and Alcalde-Heras (2020) and Herrero and Rial (2023).

The most important characteristics of the above-mentioned industrial classifications and typologies in terms of R&D intensity are summarised in Table 1.2.

One of the most crucial differences between the divisions listed in Table 1.2 is the fact that some of them can be regarded as classifications—they include all economic sectors (e.g. Carroll et al., 2000; Galindo-Rueda & Verger, 2016), while the others should rather be called typologies since their objective is to distinguish high-tech industries (e.g. DeVol et al., 1999; Hecker, 1999). It should be noted, however, that even the classifications that include other groups of business entities (e.g. Hatzichronoglou, 1997; Ortega-Argilés et al., 2009) focus on high-technology industries.

One of the main advantages of Hatzichronoglou's classification (1997), together with its later versions published by the OECD (1999, 2001, 2003) as well as the one created by Galindo-Rueda and Verger (2016) is the fact they are based on data from many countries: as many as 29 in the case of the latter one. In contrast, the typologies created by DeVol et al. (1999) and Hecker (1999) are based mainly on U.S. data, while the classification proposed by Ortega-Argilés et al. (2009) relies on data from European countries; the classification created by Carroll et al. (2000) is based on data from the Australian Bureau of Statistics.

Although R&D intensity is the main criterion of all of these divisions, one can notice big differences: for example Galindo-Rueda and Verger (2016) take into account R&D expenditures in relation to gross value added (GVA), while Carroll et al. (2000) take R&D in relation to sales. The other divisions account for other factors, such as the use of technology (e.g. DeVol et al., 1999). Unlike the other typologies, the one created by Hecker (1999) is not based on direct R&D spending but takes into consideration the level of R&D employment, which is also an important factor that determines R&D intensity.

Regardless of which criterion is adopted, a key decision in every classification is which cut-off points are used to distinguish one category from another. For Galindo-Rueda and Verger (2016), it was mostly not a problem, except for the borderline between medium and medium-low categories, which is rather blurred. However, in the other classifications, cut-off points are chosen in a more subjective manner, as in the case of the one by Ortega-Argilés et al. (2009), where the thresholds between the groups are set at 5% and 15%. A similar criticism is levelled against the OECD classification, which is considered somewhat arbitrary by Goldschlag and Miranda (2016).

Another subjective aspect associated with the classifications in Table 1.2 is the number of groups distinguished by their authors. It ranges from two (DeVol et al., 1999; Hecker, 1999; Carroll et al., 2000) to five (Galindo-Rueda & Verger, 2016), although in the case of Hecker's, one of the groups (high-technology intensive) is

Table 1.2 Classifications and typologies of industries by level of technology in terms of R&D intensity

No.	*Classification/ typology*	*Number of categories*	*Division criterion*	*Number of industries*	*Classification/ typology includes non-manufacturing industries*
1.	Hatzichronoglou (1997)	4	Direct R&D and indirect R&D expenditures (purchase of technology)	22	No
2.	DeVol et al. (1999)**	2	R&D spending and technology use	14	Yes
3.	Hecker (1999)**	2	R&D employment and in all technology oriented occupations	29	Yes
4.	Carroll et al. (2000)	2	R&D/sales	20	No
5.	OECD (2003)*	4	Direct R&D expenditures	19	No
6.	Ortega-Argilés et al. (2009)	3	Overall R&D intensity	28	Yes
7.	Galindo-Rueda and Verger (2016)	5	R&D intensity in relation to Gross Value Added (GVA)	44	Yes

Source: Based on publications referenced in the table.

Notes:

* The updated version of Hatzichronoglou's (1997) classification was based on ISIC Rev. 3 and included only information on direct R&D expenditures.

** The typology only distinguishes high-technology industries.

actually a subset of the main group, which includes high-technology industries. In the case of the remaining divisions, all groups are disjoint. It is worth noting that a classification with a greater number of categories is more useful as an analytical tool. On the other hand, different categories can be combined, which is often the case in the literature (e.g. Dawid & Mitkova, 2020).

It should be noted that Hatzichronoglou's (1997) classification and its later versions published by the OECD (1999, 2001, 2003) as well as the one created by Carroll et al. (2000) are classifications of manufacturing industries. This is a limitation given the fact that the role of the services sector in the modern economy is growing, so the inclusion of non-manufacturing industries is important.

The last difference between the divisions presented in Table 1.2 is the number of industries included in the classification, which results from differences between the underlying general industrial classifications and depends on whether a given division is a classification or merely a typology, which only includes high-technology industries, such as the one mentioned by DeVol et al. (1999) or whether it is limited to manufacturing industries, such as OECD (2003). As a result, the number of industries ranges from 14 (DeVol et al., 1999) to 44 (Galindo-Rueda & Verger, 2016).

1.2 Other classifications and typologies of industries by level of technology

In addition to the divisions discussed in Section 1.1, there are also other related typologies and classifications, which were excluded from the above analysis because they are not based on the criterion of R&D intensity. Nonetheless, they are also used to distinguish high-tech companies and some of them are sometimes discussed in the literature alongside the divisions presented in the previous section (e.g. Goldschlag & Miranda, 2016). Among them are typologies created by Carroll et al. (2000), Chapple et al. (2004), Hecker (2005) and Census ATP.

Carroll et al. (2000), in addition to the classification of high-tech manufacturing industries based on the ratio of R&D expenditures of an industry to its total sales, created two other unidimensional classifications of manufacturing industries. One of them is based on the criterion of innovation rate, that is an industry is categorised as high-tech if a certain minimum percentage of companies in that industry have undertaken technological innovation activities in a given period. The authors set the cut-off point at 26% after finding that only 26% of Australian manufacturing firms had undertaken one or more innovation activities over the three-year reference period. The other classification is based on the product approach proposed by Hatzichronoglou (1997). However, the authors proposed their own criterion of "the technological endowment of the final product", defined as follows: an industry is classified as high-tech if products manufactured by companies in that industry are categorised as "technologically equipped", that is "made up of raw materials and endowed with intelligent devices" (Carroll et al., 2000, p. 424). Moreover, the authors tested the empirical consistency (one-to-one correspondence) between the three unidimensional classifications mentioned above. An industry was regarded as robust, that is passed their robustness test, if it was included in the same level of technology regardless of which criterion was applied. One can raise certain reservations regarding the criteria analysed by Carroll et al. (2000), especially with respect to the technological endowment of the final product. Some technologically simple products (e.g. manufactured by pharmaceutical companies) may actually require high R&D input, which should also be taken into consideration when developing classifications. In the case of robustness test, out of 20 industries analysed in the study, only 2 high-tech industries passed the test (satisfied all three criteria), 14 did not pass at least one of the criteria (were classified as "intermediate", and 4 satisfied the three criteria for low-tech industry. The authors use their results to argue that unidimensional classifications make clear distinctions between high- and low-tech industries at the extremes but are not entirely adequate tools for the majority of industries, where the dividing line between the two groups is blurred. However, their main tool their conclusion is based on, namely, the robustness test, is questionable as it is based on very different criteria, one of which is definitely controversial.

Another typology was created by Chapple et al. (2004) who use the share of science and technology occupations in a given industry as the criterion of division: an industry is categorised as high-technology if the share of people employed in these occupations is at the least three times the national average. The resulting typology consists of 30 high-technology industries (Chapple et al., 2004).

The second typology in this group is a newer version created by Hecker (2005). It is discussed at this point because unlike the earlier version (1999), it no longer takes into account the level of R&D employment, but instead relies on the percentage of science, technician and engineering (technology-oriented) occupations. This change is due to the lack of data: the Occupational Employment Statistics survey conducted by the U.S. Bureau of Labor Statistics, which is the basis for the typology, no longer includes information about R&D employment (Hecker, 2005). Because of the change in methodology, the typology can be regarded as a different tool. Hecker himself admits that the new version (2005) is similar to the typology created by Chapple et al. (2004). According to this new division, an entity is categorised as a high-technology company if the total percentage of people employed in these occupations is at least twice as high as the 4.9% average for all industries. The typology distinguishes three levels, which contain 46 industries in total (Hecker, 2005):

- Level I—14 industries where the percentage of technology-oriented occupations is at least five times the average for all industries
- Level II—12 industries where the percentage of technology-oriented occupations is from 3 to 4.9 times the average for all industries
- Level III—20 industries where the percentage of technology-oriented occupations is from 2 to 2.9 times the average for all industries

According to Goldschlag and Miranda (2016), the big advantage of Hecker's typology is its replicability. Although it was created in 2005, it can easily be updated using data from the U.S. Bureau of Labor Statistics, which is exactly what they did in their study.

The third typology frequently discussed together with those based on the criterion of R&D intensity is the classification scheme developed by the U.S. Census Bureau in 1989 to categorise advanced technology products (ATP). The classification consists of 10 high-technology fields, which are developing quickly and have seen many breakthroughs thanks to new ideas (Abbott et al., 1989; McGuckin et al., 1992; Ferrantino et al., 2010). The classification, with minor changes in the names of its categories, has been used by the U.S. Census Bureau (United States Census Bureau, n.d.) until today. It is also used in the literature (e.g. by Goldschlag & Miranda, 2016).

In summary, the exclusion of the R&D component, whether in the form of expenditures or employment, affects the position of some industries in the above classifications/typologies. This is particularly evident in the service sector. For example, companies providing services connected with electricity, gas and water supply are classified into the group of low R&D intensity industries by Galindo-Rueda and Verger (2016) and into the group of high-technology industries by Chapple et al. (2004). Another example, namely telecommunications, is classified as low technology by Ortega-Argilés et al. (2009), as medium-low R&D intensity industry by Galindo-Rueda and Verger (2016) and as high-technology by Chapple et al. (2004) or Hecker (2005). Differences can also be observed in manufacturing sectors, although they are smaller. For example, petroleum products manufacturing is classified as high-technology activity by Chapple et al. (2004) and Hecker (2005), as low technology by Ortega-Argilés et al. (2009) and as medium-low R&D intensity industry by Galindo-Rueda and Verger (2016).

The authors of these classifications/typologies use the term "technology" to distinguish groups of industries, such as low-technology or high-technology, with the exception of Galindo-Rueda and Verger (2016), who use the term "R&D intensity". According to these authors, the term "technology" should not be used because R&D expenditure, which is the basis for calculating R&D intensity, is not an adequate indicator for the use of technology, especially in service industries. This is a valid point, considering that Hatzichronoglou determines the use of technology in terms of "the ratio of R&D expenditure to value added" and "the technology embodied in purchases of intermediate and capital goods" (Hatzichronoglou, 1997, p. 3). It should be noted, however, that the term "technology" is sometimes also used in classifications based exclusively on R&D intensity. As an example of this practice, Galindo-Rueda and Verger (2016) mentioned the updated version of Hatzichronoglou's original classification, created by the OECD (2003, p. 156).

Analyses conducted in this monograph are based on the classification created by Galindo-Rueda and Verger (2016). Its main advantage is the inclusion of non-manufacturing industries, such as scientific research and development, software publishing and IT and other information services. With regard to manufacturing industries, this classification is not much different from the one created by

Table 1.3 R&D-intensive industries

Manufacturing
1. Air and spacecraft and related machinery
2. Pharmaceuticals
3. Computer, electronic and optical products
4. Weapons and ammunition
5. Motor vehicles, trailers and semi-trailers
6. Medical and dental instruments
7. Machinery and equipment n.e.c.
8. Chemicals and chemical products
9. Electrical equipment
10. Railroad, military vehicles and transport n.e.c.
Non-manufacturing
1. Scientific research and development
2. Software publishing
3. IT and other information services

Source: Based on Galindo-Rueda and Verger (2016).

Hatzichronoglou (1997) and its later versions published by the OECD (1999, 2001, 2003). Another point worth noting is that most non-manufacturing activities are classified as medium-low and low R&D intensity industries. While this may be surprising, for example, in the case of telecommunications, it must be remembered that that many firms in these industries are good at adopting technologies they have not developed (Galindo-Rueda & Verger, 2016). As a matter of fact, thanks to this classification, the following study could focus on companies that are the real source of new technologies and innovation in the economy.

The monograph focuses on firms operating in industries originally classified by Galindo-Rueda and Verger (2016) as high- and medium-high R&D intensity industries, where R&D expenditures as a percentage of gross value added exceed 5%. A similar approach in the case of this classification has also been adopted by other authors (e.g. Brandt, 2018;, Carbonara et al., 2019; Dawid and Mitkova, 2020). In the rest of the monograph, industries listed in Table 1.3 are referred to as R&D-intensive industries, while firms operating in these industries are referred to as R&D-intensive companies.

1.3 Characteristics and the significance of R&D-intensive companies

R&D-intensive companies[1] share a number of unique characteristics that differentiate them from other economic entities. These differences are mainly related to the nature of R&D activities.

First of all, a large part of R&D expenditure is used to pay salaries of employees involved in the creation of knowledge, which is usually not codified. Consequently, such knowledge can be lost when such employees leave the firm (Hall & Lerner, 2009). Moreover, R&D investment carries an element of risk since potential rewards are uncertain (Hall, 2002; Hall & Lerner, 2009; Pham et al., 2019); this uncertainty is usually the highest at the start of research projects (Hall & Lerner, 2009). In addition, the R&D process itself is difficult to control (Ilyina & Samaniego, 2011) and outcomes can only be expected after a longer period of time and may require a considerable initial investment (Ilyina & Samaniego, 2011). The path from an idea to a commercial product is usually long (Hall & Lerner, 2009), and, according to Stevens and Burley (1997), only one out of 3,000 ideas becomes a market success.

R&D-intensive companies have to innovate (Wang & Li, 2017; Pham et al., 2019), but, above all, have to deal with innovative competitors, who often surprise them with their ideas that have been working on in secret (Avsar, 2018). R&D-intensive firms, more than any other entities, are under pressure from foreign competitors (Legler et al., 2000). As a result, changes of market leaders are more common in R&D-intensive industries (Honjo et al., 2018). To meet market demand and, above all, to compete more effectively, R&D-intensive companies forge alliances with other entities (Fu et al., 2020). Many companies of this kind benefit from being part of industrial clusters (Gerlach et al., 2009).

One challenge faced by many firms operating in R&D-intensive industries are greater difficulties in securing sources of external financing (Gur & Avşar, 2016; Avsar, 2018), especially in countries where financial systems are less developed (Ilyina & Samaniego, 2011). For one thing, as already mentioned, their activities are harder to control (Gur & Avşar, 2016). As a result, it is more expensive for R&D-intensive firms to obtain external funding and, consequently, they are more vulnerable to financial problems (Avsar, 2018).

Another problem associated with R&D-intensive firms results from different ways in which they account for their R&D expenditures; consequently, indicators generated on the basis of their financial reports are not always comparable, which makes it more difficult to assess their activities. This is particularly problematic in the case of comparisons involving firms from different industries, where the manner in which R&D spending is treated for accounting purposes depends on what accounting principles are applied and on individual judgement (Austin, 2006; Popa et al., 2018).

Despite these problems, R&D-intensive firms usually record higher rates of return compared to those operating in low R&D-intensive industries (Pham et al., 2019). In their analyses of pharmaceutical and chemical companies (R&D-intensive industries), Hsieh et al. (2003) found that R&D intensity was correlated with all performance indicators they considered in their study, namely sales growth, market value, operating margin and net margin. According to Pham et al. (2019), higher profits earned by R&D-intensive firms are mainly associated with higher risk that they incur. However, as noted by Triantis (2019), these companies need to have higher profit margins to account for this risk.

Table 1.4 Characteristics of R&D-intensive firms

No.	*Characteristic*
1.	Salaries account for a large part of expenditure
2.	A high level of uncertainty and investment risk
3.	A long time required to commercialise an idea
4.	Strong competitive pressure
5.	The pressure to innovate
6.	Frequent changes of market leaders
7.	Frequent alliances with other entities
8.	A big role of industrial clusters
9.	Problems with obtaining external funding
10.	Lower comparability of financial reports
11.	High profit margins
12.	High rates of return

Source: Based on Hall (2002); Gerlach et al. (2009); Hall and Lerner (2009); Gur and Avşar (2016); Wang and Li (2017); Avsar (2018); Honjo et al. (2018); Popa et al. (2018); Pham et al. (2019); Triantis (2019); Fu et al. (2020).

All the above characteristics of R&D-intensive firms are summarised in Table 1.4.

In order to identify differences regarding profitability and risk between R&D-intensive and non-R&D-intensive firms, Pham et al. (2019) analysed the following groups:

1. Low-profit companies from non-R&D-intensive industries
2. High-profit companies from non-R&D-intensive industries
3. Low-profit companies from R&D-intensive industries
4. High-profit companies from R&D-intensive industries

As can be expected, companies in the last group had the highest profits. In addition, the profit difference between high-profit and low-profit companies from non-R&D-intensive industries was smaller than that observed between firms from R&D-intensive industries. Interestingly, in the group of low-profit companies, higher profits (or lower losses) could be observed in firms from non-R&D-intensive industries. It can therefore be concluded that if successful, R&D-intensive firms can generate higher profits; but in case of failure, their losses are bigger (Pham et al., 2019).

In spite of the risk involved, R&D activities undertaken by enterprises are an important driver of economic development. This is mainly due to the fact that social rates of return are much higher than private rates of return (Griffith, 2000; Fraumeni & Okubo, 2005; Sveikauskas, 2007). There are a number of studies concerning average rates of return on R&D investment. In the case of private rates of return, estimates range from 20 to 30%, in contrast to 30–80% for social rates of return (Fraumeni & Okubo, 2005).

Recognising the importance of R&D activities, many international institutions publish information about countries' R&D expenditure as a percentage of their GDP (e.g. OECD, 2020; World Bank Group, 2021). Many countries try to increase the level of this indicator. In the Lisbon Strategy, the European Union set the target of increasing the total R&D expenditure to 3% of GDP, with two thirds of that contribution coming from this business sector (Helmers et al., 2009; Uppenberg, 2009). Failure to achieve this objective has demonstrated that such ambitions are a big challenge.

In general, the role of research and development is well recognised in the literature. R&D activities enable technological changes (Guellec & Van Pottelsberghe de la Potterie, 2004; Gao & Jefferson, 2007). Some authors point out that R&D investments lead to higher wages in the economy (Sheehan & Wyckoff, 2003) and a higher standard of living (Sheehan & Wyckoff, 2003; Gao & Jefferson, 2007). Such achievements are possible thanks to higher productivity in various sectors of the economy (Guellec & van Pottelsberghe de la Potterie, 2002; Park, 1995; Lichtenberg, 1992; Zachariadis, 2004; Cameron et al., 2005; Verbič et al., 2011). Other authors emphasise the importance of R&D activities conducted by companies from the private sector (Lichtenberg, 1992; Park, 1995). Moreover, R&D activities are important for economic growth (Guellec & Van Pottelsberghe de la Potterie, 2004; Silaghi et al., 2014; Freimane & Bāliņa, 2016; Sokolov-Mladenović et al., 2016; Hill, 2020).

As can be seen from the above overview, R&D-intensive enterprises are an important element of every country's or region's economy.

1.4 The need for market and technical knowledge integration in R&D-intensive companies

As shown in the previous section, R&D-intensive companies are characterised by highly specific conditions of operation, such as strong competitive pressure (Legler et al., 2000; Avsar, 2018) or pressure to innovate (Pham et al., 2019). It is therefore reasonable to determine what such companies should do to maintain their innovativeness and a high level of competitiveness. This in turn requires a very good understanding of how they operate. Many authors emphasise that knowledge is particularly important for R&D-intensive companies (e.g. Coff, 2003). Enterprises of this kind utilise R&D to create new knowledge that can later bring profits (Hall & Lerner, 2009). There is also a consensus in the literature that knowledge is the basis of innovation (e.g. Urbancová, 2013; Ritala et al., 2015; Ode & Ayavoo, 2020). Nowadays, knowledge management is the most popular concept concerning the use of knowledge in companies (Inkinen, 2016; Gaviria-Marin et al., 2019). It has a lot of advantages, as it is practical, explicit and relatively easy to implement by distinguishing clear knowledge-related processes, such as acquisition, creation, sharing, application or implementation (Sun, 2010; Skrzypek, 2013b; Tan & Wong, 2015; Intezari et al. 2017).

However, in order to examine the impact of knowledge on innovation and business performance of R&D-intensive companies and identify what can be improved in this area, a more detailed perspective should be adopted. Currently, when analysing knowledge-related issues in companies and how they influence their innovativeness and business performance, authors often do not distinguish between the different types of this resource (e.g. Durmuş-Özdemir & Abdukhoshimov, 2018; Mardani et al., 2018; Ferraris et al., 2019; Shujahat et al., 2019). As a result, knowledge is treated as a monolithic resource, which it is not. Various typologies or classifications available in the literature (Fletcher & Harris, 2011; Moos et al., 2011; Sáenz et al., 2012; Deligianni et al., 2015; Suseno & Pinnington, 2018) list many types of knowledge, which can be used to analyse the impact of knowledge on innovation and business performance of R&D-intensive companies. However, one should not forget that enterprises differ from one another. Consequently, it can be assumed that their needs regarding different types of knowledge also vary. As outlined earlier, R&D-intensive companies have certain characteristics that make them different from other business entities, for example they need to be innovative (Wang & Li, 2017; Pham et al., 2019), they face challenges related to the commercialisation of innovations (Stevens & Burley, 1997; Hall & Lerner, 2009) or strong competition (Legler et al., 2000; Avsar, 2018). As a result, it can be assumed that two types of knowledge in particular are important for this type of enterprises: market knowledge and technical knowledge. Both are among the most commonly distinguished types of knowledge in the literature (e.g. Fletcher & Harris, 2011; Sáenz et al., 2012).

While technical knowledge has long been recognised in the literature as the basis for innovation in enterprises (e.g. Volberda et al., 2013), many authors emphasise the great importance and underestimation of the role of market knowledge in the development of innovation (e.g. Cillo, 2005; Mina et al., 2014). According to Atuahene-Gima (2005), enterprises need market knowledge when they innovate to identify emerging opportunities. Similarly, Bohlmann et al. (2013) emphasise the importance of information about customer needs, which are part of market knowledge (for more details, see Chapter 2) required in the effective process of new product development. A growing number of authors agree that successful innovation requires both market and technical knowledge (e.g. Shang et al., 2017; Spigel & Harrison, 2018).

Another important issue is the integration of these two types of knowledge, since they are largely useless when existing in separation. Many authors emphasise the importance of knowledge integration and its role for different types of business outcomes, including innovation and business performance (e.g. Malik et al., 2020; Yang et al., 2021; Acharya et al., 2022). Nevertheless, the above-mentioned authors, rather than focusing on the integration of particular specialist types of knowledge, take a more general approach to knowledge integration in an enterprise. However, a diverse resource, such as knowledge, requires a more detailed approach. As a matter of fact, a number of authors, for example Azari et al. (2020), have recognised the existence of a research gap concerning the integration of market and technical knowledge.

The above description is just a preliminary outline of the research gap with a view to justifying why R&D-intensive companies need knowledge, especially market and technical knowledge, and effective ways of integrating them. A more precise description of the research gap is presented in Section 4.3, after reviewing existing research on the characteristics of market and technical knowledge, including sources from which companies acquire them (Chapter 2), methods of measuring companies' effectiveness (Chapter 3) and, above all, existing research on the integration of market and technical knowledge (Sections 4.1 and 4.2).

1.5 Chapter summary

The purpose of this chapter was to select the optimal way of determining R&D-intensive industries, to identify characteristics of enterprises operating in these sectors and demonstrate why they need knowledge, particularly market and technical knowledge, as well as effective ways of integrating these resources. The first part of this chapter presents and compares classifications and typologies of industries in terms of R&D intensity and other related criteria in order to select one that would be best suited to identify R&D-intensive industries for the purpose of analyses conducted in this monograph. It should be emphasised that although many such classifications and typologies exist, they have not been the subject of a comparative analysis so far. On account of its benefits, the author chose the classification created by Galindo-Rueda and Verger (2016), which uses R&D expenditures in relation to gross value added (GVA) to distinguish five groups of industries:

- Low R&D intensity industries
- Medium-low R&D intensity industries
- Medium R&D intensity industries
- Medium-high R&D intensity industries
- High R&D intensity industries

The monograph focuses on the last two groups (medium-high and high), where R&D expenditures divided by gross value added exceed 5%. In the following chapters, these sectors are referred to as R&D-intensive industries, while firms operating in these industries are referred to as R&D-intensive companies.

The next part of this chapter provides an overview of the main characteristics of firms operating in R&D-intensive industries and highlights their importance for the economy. R&D-intensive firms often have high profit margins (Triantis, 2019) and high rates of return (Pham et al., 2019) but frequently have to struggle with challenges, such as a high level of uncertainty and investment risk (Hall &

Lerner, 2009), difficulties with obtaining external funding (Gur & Avşar, 2016; Avsar, 2018), the pressure to innovate (Wang & Li, 2017; Pham et al., 2019) and a very competitive business environment (Avsar, 2018), in which market leaders often change (Honjo et al., 2018). There is no doubt, however, that R&D-intensive firms are extremely important for the economy, given their high private and social rates of return (Fraumeni & Okubo, 2005).

The last section of the chapter explains the role of market and technical knowledge integration in R&D-intensive companies. Knowledge is a particularly important resource for this type of businesses (e.g. Coff, 2003). This is because R&D activities are used to create knowledge that is later expected to generate profits (Hall & Lerner, 2009). Moreover, they operate in a particularly competitive environment characterised by pressure to innovate (Legler et al., 2000; Avsar, 2018; Pham et al., 2019), and knowledge is the basis for innovation (Urbancová, 2013; Ritala et al., 2015; Ode & Ayavoo, 2020). Unfortunately, existing analyses of companies' knowledge-related activities and their impact on innovation and business performance are not detailed enough. In particular, various types of knowledge are often not taken into account (e.g. Mardani et al., 2018; Ferraris et al., 2019; Shujahat et al., 2019). Because of their characteristics, R&D-intensive companies are particularly in need of technical and market knowledge. While technical knowledge is commonly perceived as the basis for innovation (e.g. Volberda et al., 2013), many authors note that the value of market knowledge is underestimated (e.g. Cillo, 2005; Mina et al., 2014). However, the integration of market and technical knowledge is crucially important for R&D-intensive companies. This is because when these types of knowledge exist in separation, they may not produce desired results. The importance of this issue has been recognised by some authors (e.g. Azari et al., 2020). This chapter contains a preliminary outline of the research gap to explain why R&D-intensive companies need market and technical knowledge and their integration. A more detailed description of the research gap is presented in Section 4.3 after a comprehensive analysis of the literature on market and technical knowledge characteristics, methods of measuring enterprises' effectiveness and existing research on the integration of both kinds of knowledge.

Note

1 It should be pointed out that according to some authors, the R&D-intensive category includes some industries that are not listed in Table 1.3. This is because they use definitions based on different classifications/typologies and apply different cut-off points between groups.

Chapter 2

Market and Technical Knowledge: Characteristics and Sources

The purpose of this chapter is threefold. Firstly, it provides a definition of knowledge based on a review of the relevant literature and offers an overview of different knowledge typologies. Secondly, it includes a detailed analysis of the two kinds of knowledge that this monograph focuses on, namely market and technical knowledge, listing their characteristics and explaining the importance of each type of knowledge. Thirdly, it identifies the sources of market and technical knowledge that companies use.

2.1 The concept of knowledge and its typologies

Despite being part of everyday language, the concept of knowledge is not easy to define (Jemielniak, 2012). In fact, many authors of scientific publications use it without giving a precise definition (Schultze, 2004). Those who do, provide very different definitions (Alvesson & Kärreman, 2001; Mertins et al., 2003). It is unlikely that a generally accepted definition will ever be created (Rollett, 2003). Some authors go as far as to say that it is impossible to capture all characteristics of knowledge in a single definition (Jakus et al., 2013). In spite of these difficulties, it is necessary to choose one definition that will be used for the purpose of this monograph. To do so, several definitions found in the literature are shown in Table 2.1.

DOI: 10.1201/9781032642352-2

Table 2.1 Selected definitions of knowledge used in the literature

No.	Definition	Created or applied by	Key words
1.	"Justified true belief"	Nonaka (1994, p. 15); Nonaka and Takeuchi (1995, pp. 58, 86)	justified, belief
2.	"Knowledge is information whose validity has been established through tests of proof"	Liebeskind (1996, p. 94)	information, validity, test
3.	"Knowledge is experience or information that can be communicated and shared"	Allee (1997, p. 27)	experience, information, communicate
4.	"A capacity to act"	Sveiby (1997, p. 37)	capacity, act
5.	"Knowledge is information combined with experience, context, interpretation, and reflection"	Davenport et al. (1998, p. 43)	information, experience, context, interpretation, reflection
6.	"Knowledge is information that is relevant, actionable, and based at least partially on experience. Knowledge is a subset of information; it is subjective; it is linked to meaningful behaviour; and it has tacit elements born of experience."	Leonard and Sensiper (1998, p. 113)	information, relevant, actionable, experience, subset of information, subjective, meaningful behaviour
7.	"Knowledge is actionable information"	O'Dell et al. (1998, p. 8)	actionable information

(Continued)

Table 2.1 (Continued)

No.	*Definition*	*Created or applied by*	*Key words*
8.	"Knowledge is information possessed in the mind of individuals: it is personalized information (which may or may not be new, unique, useful, or accurate) related to facts, procedures, concepts, interpretations, ideas, observations, and judgments"	Alavi and Leidner (2001, p. 109)	personalized information, new, unique, useful, accurate, facts, procedures, concepts, interpretations, ideas, observations, judgements
9.	"Understanding, awareness, or familiarity acquired through study, investigation, observation, or experience over the course of time"	Bollinger and Smith (2001, p. 9)	understanding, awareness, familiarity, study, investigation, observation, experience, time
10.	"Knowledge consists of facts, perspectives and concepts, mental reference models, truths and beliefs, judgments and expectations, methodologies, and know-how."	Wiig (2004, p. 74)	facts, perspectives, concepts, mental reference, truths, beliefs, judgements, expectations, methodologies, know-how, understanding, integrate information, develop new meanings, new insights
11.	"Knowledge is considered to be information that has been processed in some meaningful ways"	Faucher et al. (2008, p. 53)	information, processed, meaningful

Source: Based on publications referenced in the table.

Faucher et al. (2008) note that many definitions of knowledge used in the literature place it above data and information in the DIKW pyramid, which was popularised by Ackoff (1989). According to Ackoff's original model, the hierarchy consists of four components, with data (D) constituting the basis of information (I), which in turn defines knowledge (K), which underlies wisdom (W). The DIKW hierarchy has become popular over the years, and despite certain criticisms (e.g. by Frické (2007)), it has been generally accepted in the literature (Rowley, 2007) and is frequently used (e.g. Davenport & Prusak, 1998; Warier, 2003; Burgin, 2010; Aven, 2013; Kampf, 2013; Algeo, 2014; Kirsch et al., 2015; Spender, 2015; Matthias et al., 2017; Jennex, 2019; Malik et al., 2019). However, many publications ignore the top component of wisdom and focus on the first three (e.g. Tuomi, 1999; Boisot and Canals, 2004; Hicks et al., 2006; Ho, 2012). Moreover, some authors use information and knowledge interchangeably despite numerous reminders in the literature that these two concepts are not equivalent (Kakabadse et al., 2001; Razmerita et al., 2009; Cavaleri & Seivert, 2005). In addition, a number of definitions of knowledge focus on factors such as the following:

- Act, action or actionable (Sveiby, 1997, p. 37; O'Dell et al., 1998, p. 8; Leonard & Sensiper, 1998, p. 113)
- Experience (Davenport et al., 1998, p. 43; Leonard & Sensiper, 1998, p. 113; Allee, 1997, p. 27; Bollinger & Smith, 2001, p. 9)
- Importance or utility (Liebeskind, 1996, p. 94; Leonard & Sensiper, 1998, p. 113)
- Specific kind of information (Leonard & Sensiper, 1998, p. 113; Alavi & Leidner, 2001, p. 109; Faucher et al., 2008, p. 53; Liebeskind, 1996, p. 94; O'Dell et al., 1998, p. 8; Allee, 1997, p. 27)
- Subjectivity (Davenport et al., 1998, p. 43; Leonard & Sensiper, 1998, p. 113; Alavi & Leidner, 2001, p. 109)

Bolisani and Bratianu (2018) point out that for business purposes knowledge should be defined in "operational" not in "abstract" terms. To satisfy this requirement but also keep in line with definitions found in the literature, in this monograph knowledge is defined as "information that is valuable to the company". In other words, information which is valid and relevant (Liebeskind, 1996, p. 94; Leonard & Sensiper, 1998, p. 113), because it is contextualised (Davenport et al., 1998, p. 43) and therefore is actionable (Sveiby, 1997, p. 37; O'Dell et al., 1998, p. 8; Leonard & Sensiper, 1998, p. 113). This definition also assumes that knowledge is above information and data in the DIKW pyramid (Ackoff, 1989).

Just as there are many different definitions of knowledge, there exist multiple typologies or classifications of this resource (Maier, 2004). It should be emphasised that a classification should meet stricter requirements: it must be disjoint and, above all, exhaustive (Bailey, 1994). Nonetheless, both terms are frequently used for the same divisions: for example, the division into tacit and explicit knowledge is referred to as a typology by Paswan and Wittmann (2009) and as a classification by Pathirage et al. (2007). This is probably because for some authors this and other divisions are perceived as disjoint and exhaustive, while others do not treat them as such. It should be noted, however, that the majority of knowledge divisions do not meet the above-mentioned requirements or there is no agreement as to whether they do. For this reason, the author of this monograph uses the term "knowledge typologies". Table 2.2 lists popular typologies of knowledge that can be found in the literature.

One of the most popular divisions of knowledge is the distinction between explicit and tacit knowledge, which was originally proposed by Polanyi (1962) and popularised by Nonaka and Takeuchi (1995). According to another typology, knowledge can be divided into know-what, know-why, know-who and know-how. This is probably the most well-known division because it has been used by the OECD (1996). There are also other versions of this classification, such as the one used by Garud (1997), which does not include "know-who". A less commonly used division was proposed by Nonaka and Takeuchi (1995), who categorised knowledge

Table 2.2 Popular typologies of knowledge used in the literature

No.	*Type of knowledge*	*Created or applied by*
1.	Explicit and tacit knowledge	Polanyi (1962); Nelson and Winter (1982)
2.	Know-what, know-why, know-who (when and where) and know-how	Lundvall and Johnson (1994); OECD (1996)
3.	Individual knowledge of employees, team-level knowledge, company-level knowledge, knowledge stored in the inter-organisational or network system	Nonaka and Takeuchi (1995); Kowalczyk and Nogalski (2007)
4.	Know-how, know-what, know-why	Garud (1997)
5.	Customers, company's own markets, company's own products and services, competitors, employee skills, regulatory environments, methods and processes	KPMG (1998)
6.	Market (or marketing) knowledge, technological (or technical, scientific) knowledge	Dougherty et al. (2000); Sciascia et al. (2009); Takayama (2010); Siegel and Renko (2012); Zhao and Wang (2015)
7.	The company's external and internal knowledge	Argote et al. (2003); Lane et al. (2006); Bigliardi and Galati (2018);
8.	Tacit, explicit, cultural knowledge	Choo (2006)

Source: Based on publications referenced in the table.

depending on the level at which it is stored, which ranges from individual to inter-organisational. In contrast, the typology created by KPMG (1998), rather than being the result of theoretical considerations focuses on business practice and is based on empirical research on the types of knowledge that are of most relevance for an organisation. According to another important typology, knowledge of a company can be divided into external and internal. It is frequently used in the context of absorptive capacity (e.g. Lichtenthaler, 2016).

It can be argued that the use of knowledge typologies is underestimated in the literature. For one thing, they can be the starting point for more effective and more precise analyses of business entities. By exploiting available knowledge typologies, one can adopt perspectives that differ from those applied in the study of knowledge so far, especially the one used in the context of knowledge management, which has dominated the literature on knowledge-related activities of companies (Inkinen, 2016; Gaviria-Marin et al., 2019). This approach distinguishes various processes, such as knowledge acquisition, knowledge creation, knowledge sharing, knowledge application and knowledge implementation (Sun, 2010; Skrzypek, 2013b, 2014; Tan & Wong, 2015; Intezari et al., 2017), which do not sufficiently account for various types of knowledge. For this reason, the use of knowledge typologies in the creation of modern models can lead to more accurate results.

The main purpose of knowledge typologies is to systematise different kinds of this resource, especially in organisations. Each typology has its advantages and disadvantages, so it is important to ensure that whichever one selects meets specific needs and fits the context. This monograph relies on the distinction between market and technical knowledge, which are among the most commonly identified types of knowledge in the literature (e.g. Dougherty et al., 2000; Sciascia et al., 2009; Takayama, 2010; Siegel & Renko, 2012; Zhao & Wang, 2015). Technical knowledge is also described as technology, scientific or scientific-technological knowledge, while market knowledge is sometimes called marketing or even business knowledge (Acs et al., 2013). In the context of various analyses, it may be important to make a distinction between these terms. However, in this monograph, they are used interchangeably, although market and technical knowledge are preferred.

Despite its importance for companies, the division into market and technical knowledge has not been fully investigated in the context of innovation creation and their business performance. For example, Wiklund and Shepherd (2003) argue that market and technical knowledge, when used together, are important resources enabling firms to identify and exploit emerging opportunities (Wiklund & Shepherd, 2003). In this monograph, this division is treated as a typology, since it does not meet the requirements of a classification, which must be disjoint and exhaustive. It should also be pointed out that there are other versions of the division into market and technical (technological) knowledge, which include other types of knowledge, as shown in Table 2.3.

The typology used by Fletcher and Harris (2011) as well as Deligianni et al. (2015) also includes internationalisation knowledge, which can be treated as a

Table 2.3 Selected typologies which include market and technical knowledge

No.	*Type of knowledge*	*Created or applied by*
1.	technological, production, and marketing knowledge	Sapienza et al. (2004)
2.	market, technological, process, product, and organisational knowledge	Moos et al. (2011)
3.	technological knowledge, market knowledge, and internationalization knowledge	Fletcher and Harris (2011); Deligianni et al. (2015)
4.	market knowledge, technology knowledge and financial knowledge	Sáenz et al. (2012)
5.	market, technical, and client specific knowledge	Suseno and Pinnington (2018)

Source: Based on publications referenced in the table.

particular type of market knowledge. The division proposed by Sapienza et al. (2004) includes production knowledge, which can be seen as a component of technology knowledge. Sáenz et al. (2012) take into account financial knowledge, which, from the perspective of the following analyses of innovation creation in companies, is not as relevant nowadays as the other two types. Moos et al. (2011) distinguish as many as five types of knowledge, but product knowledge can be regarded as part of technological knowledge. In conclusion, although there are many different types of knowledge that can be identified in an organisation, the author of this monograph believes it is reasonable to focus on the two types that are recognised by numerous researchers (e.g. Sciascia et al., 2009; Takayama, 2010; Siegel & Renko, 2012; Zhao & Wang, 2015).

2.2 Characteristics and sources of market knowledge

Although the concept of market knowledge has been studied for many years (e.g. Li & Calantone, 1998; Nonaka et al. 1998; Li & Cavusgil, 1999; Eisenstein & Hutchinson, 2006), research on this subject continues (Chollet et al., 2016; Claudy et al., 2016; Scandura, 2019).

Many authors define market knowledge as knowledge about customers and competitors (e.g. Marinova, 2004; De Luca & Atuahene-Gima, 2007). This can be attributed to the impact of popular articles by Narver and Slater (1990) and Kohli and Jaworski (1990, 1993), which focused on the concept of market orientation. Interestingly, in neither case did those authors use the term "market knowledge". Another perspective is offered by Li and Calantone (1998), who define this concept as "organised and structured information about the market" (Li & Calantone, 1998, p. 14). Slater et al. (2012) use the term "market knowledge resources", which include knowledge about customers, competitors and technical knowledge. Following Abernathy and Clark (1985) and Danneels (2002), Burgers et al. (2008, p. 56) define market knowledge in a relatively general manner as knowledge "associated with targeting customer sets, entering markets, distribution channels, marketing approaches, and business models" (Burgers et al., 2008, p. 56). The concept of market knowledge is sometimes used in the context of internationalisation processes to denote knowledge about foreign markets (e.g. Denis & Depelteau, 1985; Erramilli & Rao, 1990). Whatever the case may be, many authors who use this term do not provide its definition, probably because they take it for granted (e.g. Eisenstein & Hutchinson, 2006; Hughes et al., 2008; Sáenz et al., 2012). The crucial component mentioned in most definitions of market knowledge is knowledge about two types of entities, namely customers and competitors. While this kind of knowledge is certainly important, it is not sufficient. The definition proposed by Li and Calantone (1998) is wider. Rather than focusing on customers and competitors, as do definitions proposed by Marinova (2004) and De Luca and Atuahene-Gima (2007), it is better suited to the modern, fast-changing world. Some authors argue that companies striving for a high level of competitiveness have to maintain relationships with many different market participants, for example the seven markets concept described by Fonfara (2014). In spite of being too general, Li and Calantone's definition emphasises the importance of relying on more sources of market information, including insights derived from observing economic trends and macroeconomic indicators, since preferences and needs of customers need not be compatible with what they can actually afford to buy, as demonstrated by the financial crisis of 2007–2009. It should be noted that nowadays expectations regarding market knowledge are even higher. Companies can no longer be satisfied with having knowledge about their own customers, but increasingly need to learn more about customers of their own customers. Consequently, in this monograph market knowledge is defined as market information of relevance to the company, which concerns

- entities associated with the company and having an impact on its activity, especially its current and potential customers, competitors and contractors; and
- phenomena and economic trends that are important for the company.

The above definition is based on the following publications: Li and Calantone (1998), Marinova (2004), De Luca and Atuahene-Gima (2007), Siegel and Renko (2012), and Fonfara (2014).

The fact that the company's business performance largely depends on its market knowledge and its capacity of generating it has been recognised by many authors (e.g. Atuahene-Gima, 2005; Ozkaya et al., 2015; Claudy et al., 2016). This is why, Augusto and Coelho (2009), following Glazer (1991), describe market knowledge as a "strategic resource". According to McKlevie and Wiklund (2004), market knowledge can be used to discover and evaluate emerging opportunities by enabling companies to recognise customers' problems and helping them to determine the market value of new technologies. Slater et al. (2012) identify certain characteristics of market knowledge that make it difficult to imitate. One of them is the fact that market knowledge quickly becomes outdated, especially in dynamic, high-tech markets (Slater et al., 2012, p. 19).

Since sources of organisational knowledge are often analysed together (e.g. Keupp & Gassmann, 2009; Presenza et al., 2017; Bogers et al., 2018), the literature lists relatively few ways by which companies obtain market knowledge, such as talking to customers, observing trends in customer preferences, market research, competitor intelligence, talking to suppliers and collecting big data (Zhou & Li, 2012; Dolnicar & Grün, 2013; Rakthin et al., 2016; Paschen et al., 2019).

Many analyses concerning market knowledge include references to its dimensions or characteristics, for example De Luca and Atuahene-Gima (2007), Bao et al. (2012), Lin et al. (2012). De Luca and Atuahene-Gima (2007), following Galunic and Rodan (1998), introduced four dimensions of market knowledge: breadth, depth, specificity and tacitness. Since then, this perspective has been adopted in many studies (e.g. Slater et al., 2012; Ahmadi et al., 2014; Chen & Lee, 2017). Earlier, these four dimensions were applied to knowledge in general, but not specifically to market knowledge, for example by von Krogh and Roos (1996). Some authors, for example Bao et al. (2012) or Lin et al. (2012), mentioned only two characteristics of market knowledge—breadth and depth.

Breadth of knowledge is defined as "the range of fields over which the firm has knowledge" (Prabhu et al., 2005, p. 115). According to De Luca and Atuahene-Gima (2007, p. 97), market knowledge can be described as broad if it includes a wide range of information about "current and potential customer segments and competitors and also uses a diverse set of parameters related to customers (e.g. needs, behaviors, characteristics) and competitors (e.g. products, markets, strategies) to describe and evaluate them" (De Luca & Atuahene-Gima, 2007, p. 97). Broad market knowledge can help a company to recognise emerging opportunities. However, particular components of market knowledge, for example regarding strategies of competitors, need to be regularly updated. If a company has broad market knowledge, it may not be able to exploit it fully before it becomes obsolete (De Luca & Atuahene-Gima, 2007).

Depth is the second dimension of market knowledge. De Luca and Atuahene-Gima (2007) define it as "the level of sophistication and complexity of a firm's knowledge of its customers and competitors" (p. 98). It is necessary in order to connect relationships that exist among the factors describing key issues about customers and competitors (De Luca & Atuahene-Gima, 2007).

According to the same authors, tacitness, the third dimension of market knowledge, "is the extent to which market knowledge is not explicit but rather is difficult to codify and communicate" (De Luca & Atuahene-Gima, 2007, p. 98). As a result, it is difficult for employees to explain relationships between their actions and their outcomes. Moreover, a high level of tacitness slows down knowledge transfer within the organisation and between its functional units (De Luca & Atuahene-Gima, 2007).

The last dimension of market knowledge is its specificity, which refers to "the extent to which the firm's knowledge is tailored to the requirements of specific contexts in which it is maximally effective but loses its value in other contexts" (De Luca & Atuahene-Gima, 2007, p. 98). Such specific knowledge may be related to a particular product or group of customers but may prove useless when applied to others (Galunic & Rodan, 1998; De Luca & Atuahene-Gima, 2007).

2.3 Characteristics and sources of technical knowledge

In contrast to market knowledge, technical knowledge is much less commonly defined in the literature because many authors use the term "knowledge" to denote either the company's entire store of knowledge or its technical knowledge. The most popular definition was proposed by Burgers et al. (2008), who followed definitions formulated by Abernathy and Clark (1985) and Danneels (2002). According to them, technical knowledge is related to ". . . products, technologies or processes" (Burgers et al., 2008, p. 56). The definition has been used by many others, including Clarysse et al. (2011) and Deligianni et al. (2015). A similar definition was proposed by Yuan Fu et al. (2006), for whom the term includes knowledge about "inventions, publications, trademarks, patents, knowledge recipes, etc." (Yuan Fu et al., 2006, p. 53). Prabhu et al. (2005, p. 115) defined technical knowledge in rather simple terms as "scientific knowledge applied to useful purposes". A different definition worth mentioning is the one proposed by Bohn (1994), who describes technical knowledge as "knowledge about how to produce goods and services" (Bohn, 1994, p. 61). As in the case of market knowledge, many authors write about technical knowledge without defining it (e.g. Di Benedetto & Song, 2003; Fallah & Lechler, 2008; Takayama, 2010; Sáenz et al., 2012).

In this monograph, technical knowledge is defined as the company's knowledge related to the creation of products and services that are or can be offered to customers. This definition is based on definitions formulated by Burgers et al. (2008, p. 56) and Prabhu et al. (2005, p. 115).

Technical knowledge is what enables companies to operate, which is especially true in the case of R&D-intensive firms. While this type of knowledge is recognised as crucial for manufacturing companies (e.g. Fisch & Kertels, 2011), it is equally indispensable for service companies, especially those operating in R&D-intensive industries, such as the IT industry (Fernando, 2015). As already mentioned, many publications on organisational knowledge use the term "knowledge" mainly, and sometimes exclusively, to denote technical knowledge (e.g. Liu & Liu, 2008; Probert et al., 2013; Xu, 2015; Aghasi et al., 2017; Xie et al., 2018). This is probably due to the fact that the importance of technical knowledge has been taken for granted for years. The most frequently mentioned examples of technical knowledge in the literature which highlight its role are patents (e.g. Jaffe, 1986; Hall et al., 2005). It should be noted, however, that technical knowledge is contained in various texts (Bohn, 1994), which do not need to take the form of patents. In fact, most of it resides in the minds of employees, so their departure from the company may have negative consequences (Wong & Radcliffe, 2000). Moreover, in addition to having a number of drawbacks, patents are not an effective way of protecting any kind of technical knowledge. Arguably, the biggest disadvantage of this solution is that in order to patent knowledge, the company has to reveal it (Arundel, 2001), which explains why many firms are reluctant to file for patents and choose to protect their technical knowledge as a trade secret (O'Donnell et al., 2008). As a result, nowadays, for R&D-intensive companies, knowledge in the minds of their employees is probably more important than that stored in the form of patents.

Given that their resources are limited, companies have to continually consider which aspects of technical knowledge are worth developing and to what extent. In contrast to the sources of market knowledge, authors are a bit more likely to specify sources of technical knowledge that companies use. The literature lists various sources of technical knowledge, such as the Internet, conferences, patent databases, technical databases, scientific publications, customers, suppliers, competitors, R&D outcomes, and recruitment or external partners (Caloghirou et al., 2004; Tsai & Wang, 2009; Fletcher & Harris, 2011; Chen & Liu, 2019; Wu et al., 2020).

As in the case of market knowledge, two dimensions are usually mentioned, namely breadth and depth. Authors interested in this resource typically use their own indicators based on the distribution of patents across technological fields (e.g. Bierly & Chakrabarti, 1996; SubbaNarasimha et al., 2003; Moorthy & Polley, 2010). It should be noted that there are relatively few publications devoted to the measurement of technical knowledge, and indicators based on the number of patents have been used to analyse technical knowledge in manufacturing companies, mainly from the pharmaceutical industry (e.g. SubbaNarasimha et al., 2003). In the case of other companies from R&D-intensive industries, they may prove of little use because many companies in these sectors treat their technical knowledge as a trade secret. Moreover, in many cases such knowledge is not even patentable. It should also be pointed out that trade secrets and patents are mutually exclusive (O'Donnell et al., 2008).

Henard and McFadyen (2006) emphasise the importance of the depth and breadth of technical knowledge in R&D activities. The broader this resource is, the more likely company employees are to find novel and complex linkages of information, which can lead to innovation. The depth of technical knowledge has to do with the need to update technological knowledge, which is changing quickly. If a company fails to acquire and integrate new knowledge, "it may find it difficult to 'catch up' to companies that have" (p. 42). Moreover, companies that have been creating and integrating technical knowledge for a longer time have an advantage over those that have just started developing this resource (Henard & McFadyen, 2006).

2.4 Chapter summary

The purpose of this chapter was to present and define knowledge, the monograph's central concept, include a review of various knowledge typologies, provide a detailed analysis of its two types (market and technical knowledge), and identify ways in which companies acquire these resources. Based on the many definitions available in the literature, the author has defined knowledge as "information that is valuable to the company". In other words, information that is valid and relevant (Liebeskind, 1996, p. 94; Leonard & Sensiper, 1998, p. 113), because it is contextualised (Davenport et al., 1998, p. 43) and therefore is actionable (Sveiby, 1997, p. 37; O'Dell et al., 1998, p. 8; Leonard & Sensiper, 1998, p. 113). This definition also assumes that knowledge is above information and data in the DIKW pyramid (Ackoff, 1989).

In addition, a number of knowledge typologies have been presented, including the division into market and technical knowledge, which is crucial for the following analyses.

Market knowledge is defined as market information of relevance to the company, which concerns

- entities associated with the company and having an impact on its activity, especially its current and potential customers, competitors and contractors; and
- phenomena and economic trends that are important for the company.

The above definition is based on the following publications: Li and Calantone (1998), Marinova (2004), De Luca and Atuahene-Gima (2007), Siegel and Renko (2012), and Fonfara (2014).

Technical knowledge is defined as knowledge related to the creation of products and services that are or can be offered to customers. This definition is based on definitions formulated by Burgers et al. (2008, p. 56) and Prabhu et al. (2005, p. 115).

Various sources of market and technical knowledge have been identified in the course of the literature review. In the case of market knowledge, these include talking to customers and suppliers, market research or competitor intelligence (Zhou & Li, 2012; Dolnicar & Grün, 2013; Rakthin et al., 2016). In the case of technical knowledge, these include suppliers, recruitment, external partners, R&D outcomes, Internet, patent databases, technical databases or conferences (Caloghirou et al., 2004; Fletcher & Harris, 2011; Wu et al., 2020). Nevertheless, a limited number of market and technical knowledge sources have been identified in the literature. This is because authors (e.g. Keupp & Gassmann, 2009; Presenza et al., 2017; Bogers et al., 2018) often present only a general analysis of knowledge sources that companies use without specifying what type of knowledge companies acquire from them, for example market knowledge. Moreover, the literature lacks a distinction between sources of specific knowledge used by R&D-intensive companies. As a result, there exists a research gap concerning sources of market and technical knowledge used by R&D-intensive companies and their relative usefulness.

Chapter 3

Organisational Innovativeness and Business Performance as Measures of R&D-Intensive Companies' Effectiveness

This chapter focuses on two concepts that are later used to measure organisational effectiveness. The first part contains a discussion of the concepts of innovation and organisational innovativeness, including their relationship with knowledge. The second part deals with the concept of business performance.

3.1 Innovation and its types

The term "innovation" was popularised through the works of Schumpeter published in 1930s and 1940s, though some authors, for example Baregheh et al. (2009, p. 1323) trace the origin of the concept back to the end of the 18th century, while Edler and Fagerberg (2017) emphasise that the phenomenon is "as old as mankind itself" (p. 3). Nowadays, the term is commonly used in various contexts. Companies mention it in their mission statements and politicians use it in their speeches (Kahn,

DOI: 10.1201/9781032642352-3

2018, p. 453). Damanpour and Schneider (2006, p. 216) note that innovation is analysed and, consequently, defined from different perspectives depending on the field of study. The perspective adopted in this monograph is that of an organisation and business activity.

According to Berkun (2010), the term "innovation" is overused nowadays and, as a result, it loses its meaning. To make matters worse, there is no single, commonly accepted definition of innovation (Kerzner, 2019). Table 3.1 shows some examples of existing definitions.

As noted by Johannessen et al. (2001), Gupta et al. (2007) and Pohulak-Żołędowska (2016), almost every definition of innovation includes the aspect of novelty. This conclusion is confirmed by the list of keywords in Table 3.1. Of the 17 definitions, 12 contain the word "new". Among other frequently used words

Table 3.1 Selected definitions of innovation

No.	Definition	Author(s)	Keywords
1.	"By innovation is meant the generation, acceptance, and implementation of new ideas, processes, products or services"	Thompson (1965, p. 2)	new; generation; acceptance; implementation; ideas; processes; products; services
2.	"Commercial or industrial application of something new—a new product, process, or method of production; a new market or source of supply; a new form of commercial, business, or financial organization"	Schumpeter (1983, p. 10)	application; new; market; product; process; method of production; source of supply; commercial; business; financial; organization
3.	"Innovation is taken as being a synonym for the successful production, assimilation and exploitation of novelty"	European Commission (1995, p. 1)	successful; novelty; production; assimilation; exploitation
4.	"An innovation is an idea, practice, or object that is perceived as new by an individual or other unit of adoption"	Rogers (1995, p. 11)	idea; practice; object; new
5.	"The successful implementation of creative ideas within an organization"	Amabile et al. (1996, p. 1155)	successful; implementation; creative; idea; organization

(Continued)

Table 3.1 (Continued)

No.	*Definition*	*Author(s)*	*Keywords*
6.	"Any policy, structure, method or process, product or market opportunity that the manager of the innovating unit perceived to be new"	Nohria and Gulati (1996, p. 1251)	new; structure; method; process; product; market opportunity; perception
7.	"Implementing new ideas that create value"	Linder et al. (2003, p. 44)	new; ideas; create; value
8.	"Generation of novel combinations from existing knowledge"	Leiponen (2006, p. 239)	generation; novel; combinations; knowledge
9.	"Creation of new knowledge and ideas to facilitate new business outcomes, aimed at improving internal business processes and structures and to create market driven products and services"	Du Plessis (2007, p. 21)	creation; new; knowledge; ideas; business outcomes; improving; market driven; products; services
10.	"Innovation = Invention + Exploitation"	Roberts (2007, p. 36)	invention; exploitation
11.	"Multi-stage process whereby organizations transform ideas into new/improved products, service or processes, in order to advance, compete and differentiate themselves successfully in their marketplace"	Baregheh et al. (2009, p. 1334)	new, improved; organization; transform; ideas; product; service; advance; compete; differentiate; successful; marketplace
12.	"Innovation means something 1) new with high-level of originality, 2) in whatever area 3) that also breaks in to (or obtains a foothold in) society, often via the market, and 4) mean something revolutionary for people."	Frankelius (2009, p. 49)	new; originality; revolutionary; market; whatever area

(Continued)

Table 3.1 (Continued)

No.	Definition	Author(s)	Keywords
13.	"New ways of doing things, in science and technology but also associated institutions and social practices"	Leach et al. (2012, p. 12)	new; science; technology; institutions; social practices
14.	"Innovation is the specific tool of entrepreneurs, the means by which they exploit change as an opportunity for a different business or a different service. It is capable of being presented as a discipline, capable of being learned, capable of being practiced"	Drucker (2014, p. 23)	tool of entrepreneurs; exploitation of change; opportunity
15.	"Innovation is something new and stable"	Chechurin (2016, p. 21)	new; stable
16.	"Innovation is the initial commercialisation of invention by producing and marketing new good or service or by using a new method of production"	Grant (2016, p. 243)	commercialisation; invention; new; producing; marketing; new good; new service; new method of production
17.	"An innovation is a new or improved product or process (or combination thereof) that differs significantly from the unit's previous products or processes and that has been made available to potential users (product) or brought into use by the unit (process)."	OECD (2018, p. 32)	new; improved; product; process; differs significantly; available to potential users; brought into use
18.	"A new thing different from what already exists that has been developed using existing knowledge and that responds to the needs of the market"	Distanont and Khongmalai (2020, p. 17)	new; different; knowledge; market needs

Source: Based on publications referenced in the table.

are "idea(s)", "product" and "market". Fagerberg (2004) points out that many of the existing definitions make a distinction between "invention" and "innovation". Invention refers to the creation of a new product, idea or process, while innovation signifies its implementation (Fagerberg, 2004; Roberts, 2007; Grant, 2016; Marques, 2014; Gault, 2018). This view is shared by Damanpour (1987), who notes that companies innovate in the hope of some rewards, which can only appear when an idea is implemented. This aspect is also recognised in some definitions, which contain words like "implementation', "application" or "exploitation". It is expressed most succinctly by Roberts (2007, p. 36): "Innovation = Invention + Exploitation". A similar view can be found in the definition proposed by Linder, Jarvenpaa and Davenport (2003, p. 44), which adds the element of "value". Chechurin (2016, p. 21) emphasises the aspect of stability, which means that in order to be called an innovation, a product needs to have a following or be bought, otherwise it is nothing more than a gadget (Chechurin, 2016, p. 21). This opinion is shared by Pohulak-Żołędowska (2016), who thinks that an innovation without market success can be considered an invention. The definition proposed by Leiponen (2006, p. 239) is worth noting because it emphasises the relationship between knowledge and innovation. A very interesting definition of innovation was proposed by the OECD in the Oslo Manual (OECD, 2018, p. 32). It is frequently quoted in the literature, probably because of its precision, clarity and practical approach.

There are also a number of ways to categorise innovation. Probably the most common ones are those where innovation is classified by the object of innovation or the degree of novelty (Massa & Testa, 2008) or "radicalness" (Varis & Littunen, 2010, p. 130). Less popular divisions are based on the criterion of risk (Kaluzny et al., 1974). Several examples are presented in Table 3.2.

As can be seen in Table 3.2, the most common types of innovation, taking into account the area of application, are product and process innovation. Other popular

Table 3.2 Selected classifications of innovation

No.	*Types of innovation*	*Created or applied by*
1.	Technical; administrative	Evan (1966, p. 51)
2.	Product or service; production process; organisational structure; people	Knight (1967, p. 482)
3.	Radical; incremental	Dewar and Dutton (1986, p. 1422)
4.	Technological; administrative; ancillary	Damanpour (1987, p. 684)
5.	Radical; incremental; architectural; modular	Henderson and Clark (1990, p. 12)
6.	Product and process	Archibugi et al. (1994, p. 8)

(Continued)

Table 3.2 (Continued)

No.	Types of innovation	Created or applied by
7.	New products; new services; new ways of organizing; new methods of production; new sources of supply; opening new markets	Johannessen et al. (2001, p. 21)
8.	Product; process; business system	Hovgaard and Hansen (2004, p. 27)
9.	Product (including service) innovations, process innovations, marketing innovations and organisational innovations	OECD (2005, p. 47)
10.	Innovative products: type 1—new to market, technology as currently used by firm; type 2—new to market, new technology to the firm, but not to the world; type 3—new to market, new technology to the world.	Mosey (2005, p. 116)
11.	Product; service; process	Oke et al. (2007, p. 738)
12.	Product, process, managerial, marketing, institutional	Hjalager (2010, pp. 2–3)
13.	Product innovation—new to the firm; product innovation—new to the market; process innovation; new/significantly changed strategy; new/significantly changed organisational structures; new/significantly changed market concept	Tödtling et al. (2012, p. 334)
14.	Radical; evolutionary; incremental	Dumay et al. (2013, p. 609)
15.	Radical-autonomous; radical-systemic; incremental-autonomous; incremental-systemic	Partanen et al. (2014, pp. 1045–1049)
16.	Product (service); process; paradigm (mental model); position—each type can be either incremental or radical	Bessant and Tidd (2015, pp. 30–31)
17.	Improved product launching to existing market; improved product launching to new market; new product launching to existing market; new product launching to new market	Oh et al. (2015, p. 42)
18.	Product; process; management	Ali et al. (2016, p. 5317)
19.	Disruptive incremental; disruptive radical; sustaining incremental; sustaining radical	Pohulak-Żołędowska (2016, p. 458)
20.	Disruptive; sustaining; efficiency	Flavin and Quintero (2018, p. 2)

(Continued)

Table 3.2 (Continued)

No.	*Types of innovation*	*Created or applied by*
21.	Product innovation; process innovation; marketing innovation; business model innovation; supply chain innovation; organisational innovation	Kahn (2018, p. 454)
22.	Product; process; organisational; management; production; commercial/marketing; service	Trott (2021, p. 17)

Source: Based on publications referenced in the table.

types include marketing, organisational or supply chain innovation. Older publications contain a division into technological and administrative innovation.

Many of the divisions listed in Table 3.2 are based on the criterion of novelty or "radicalness". A popular example of this classification is the division into incremental and radical innovation (e.g. Dewar & Dutton, 1986; Koberg et al., 2003; Ritala & Hurmelinna-Laukkanen, 2013; Sheng & Chien, 2016). Differences between these two categories are clearly defined and exemplified by Norman and Verganti (2014, p. 82)—"incremental innovation: improvements within a given frame of solutions (i.e., 'doing better what we already do'); and radical innovation: a change of frame (i.e., 'doing what we did not do before')", or, in other words, "incremental innovation tries to reach the highest point on the current hill. Radical innovation seeks the highest hill" (Norman & Verganti, 2014, p. 79). Both types of innovation are important for the economy and companies. As noted by Silverberg (2002), according to Schumpter's simplified approach, radical innovation is what drives the economy. Innovation research indicates that many changes, for example technical ones, are the result of learning, that is marginal gains in skills or incremental organisational improvements (Silverberg, 2002).

The division into radical and incremental innovation has been very popular for many years, though Henderson and Clark (1990) consider it to be incomplete. This is why they suggested adding two more types: architectural and modular innovation (p. 12). Another aspect associated with the novelty of innovation is the scope of novelty, which was classified by the OECD into three categories (2005, p. 57):

- New to the firm
- New to the market
- New to the world

As noted by numerous authors, for example Johannessen et al. (2001) or Garcia and Calantone (2002), because of the multiplicity of definitions and the lack of consistent measures, it is difficult to analyse and compare studies of innovation. For example, an innovation that one author calls "really new" is described as "discontinuous" or "radical" by someone else (Garcia & Calantone, 2002, p. 110).

The definition of innovation used in the monograph is based on the popular and clear definition proposed by the OECD (2018) and follows its recommendations in this regard. Innovation is therefore defined here as the implementation of new or improved products, processes and organisational or marketing methods which have been developed by a given company or adopted from other firms or organisations.

3.2 Organisational innovativeness

The importance of innovation for an organisation is viewed from various perspectives. It is regarded as essential for business survival (e.g. Dodgson et al., 2014) and the driver of "the core renewal process" (Bessant et al., 2005, p. 1366). Companies have to innovate in order to adapt to changing needs and lifestyles of their customers and to exploit opportunities associated with technological developments or changing markets (Rowley et al., 2011). Innovation is often discussed in the context of its impact on the competitiveness of companies. It can be the key element (Nonaka & Takeuchi, 1995; Johannessen et al., 2001) or even the main source of competitive advantage (Thames & Webster, 2009). Many authors point out that in order to remain competitive nowadays (Johannessen et al., 2001; Rud, 2009; Keiningham et al., 2019), or just to survive (Varis & Littunen, 2010) companies have to keep innovating.

In addition to affecting competitiveness, innovation can improve other aspects of business operations, for example it can help to increase productivity or reduce costs (Thames & Webster, 2009). According to Rud (2009), firms that do not offer innovative products or services are obliged to compete on price, which results in lower profit margins. Drucker (1994) notes that in a knowledge-based economy organisations that have not implemented a systematic innovation process will not be able to maintain or attract new specialists with expertise that these organisations depend on for survival (Drucker, 1994).

It is often emphasised that knowledge is an important element of innovation, for example Nonaka and Takeuchi (1995), Armbrecht Jr. et al. (2001), Johannessen et al. (2001), Gloet and Terziovski (2004), Subramaniam and Youndt (2005), Popadiuk and Choo (2006), Du Plessis (2007), Kamaşak and Bulutlar (2010), Delgado-Verde et al. (2011), López-Nicolás and Meroño-Cerdán (2011), Zheng et al. (2011) or Urbancová (2013). According to Schiuma and Lerro (2008), research on knowledge and innovation has been so interconnected that borders between particular research strands have often been blurred. Nonaka and Takeuchi (1995) were among the first authors to recognise this interdependence. They viewed knowledge and its role in Japanese companies as the source of their market success, arguing that knowledge creation leads to continuous innovation, and consequently, to competitive advantage (Nonaka & Takeuchi, 1995). The relationship between the two factors was also noticed by Drucker, who defined innovation as "the application of knowledge to produce new knowledge" (1994, p. 173).

According to Carneiro (2000), innovation should be seen as a process which requires investment where knowledge is the capital. A similar view was expressed by Tödtling et al. (2009), who believed that innovation is the result of an interactive process where knowledge is generated and implemented. While the process of innovation is crucially dependent on the development of internal knowledge, the acquisition of external knowledge is also important (DeCarolis & Deeds, 1999). This view is shared by Darroch (2005), who also believes that in order to innovate, companies need both internal and external knowledge resources. The more knowledge there is and the more diversified it is, the better.

Many authors emphasise the particular significance of tacit knowledge in the creation of innovation, for example Leonard and Sensiper (1998), Perraton and Tarrant (2007), Erden et al. (2008) and Senker (2008). While explicit knowledge, that is knowledge that can be articulated or codified, is valuable, tacit knowledge, which cannot be easily expressed or extracted, is especially useful as a source of many opportunities for companies. For one thing, owing to its nature, it cannot easily be copied by competitors (Seidler-de Alwis & Hartmann, 2008). A qualitative study conducted by Blümm (2002) suggests that by exploiting tacit knowledge companies can shorten different stages of the innovation process. In fact, in some cases, tacit knowledge enabled firms to overcome crises and avert the risk of failure in the innovation process (Blümm, 2002).

Along with the recognition of the role of knowledge in the creation of innovation, many authors started to focus on the importance of knowledge management in this process, for example Gloet and Terziovski (2004), Kianto (2011), López-Nicolás and Meroño-Cerdán (2011). An empirical study conducted by Palacios et al. (2009) indicates that knowledge management can improve a company's capacity to innovate by developing capabilities relating to knowledge transfer and implementation and diversifying organisational memory. Some authors focus their attention on specific knowledge management processes, such as knowledge dissemination in the organisation (Darroch, 2005; Lambooy, 2005) or knowledge acquisition (Papa et al., 2020). In short, knowledge is certainly an element that is inextricably linked to innovativeness. Companies that want to be more innovative must focus on activities related to this resource.

Another important task is to accurately define organisational innovativeness. Therefore, the following part of the chapter provides a review of different definitions of "organisational innovativeness". As this monograph concentrates on organisations, the term "innovativeness" is assumed to apply to organisations.

Five dimensions of organisational innovativeness can be found in the literature, which relate to products, markets, processes, behaviours and strategies (Gatautis et al., 2019). However, Wang and Ahmed (2004) demonstrate that there are few studies that take into account all five dimensions, and some authors adopt a unidimensional approach. Following the suggestion of Salavou (2004), this monograph focuses on the product dimension, which includes services.

Another point worth noting in this context and made by Damanpour (1991) is the fact that it makes more sense to analyse innovativeness when dealing not with one but many innovations. Table 3.3 contains a selection of definitions of the terms "innovativeness" or "innovative" applied to an organisation or a firm.

Table 3.3 Definitions of "organisational innovation", "organisational innovativeness" and "innovative organisation"

No.	Definition	Created or applied by	Keywords
1.	"An innovative company improves or innovates more than 50 per cent of its products in half the average life cycle, while staying in profit"	Vrakking (1990, p. 95)	improve; products; profit
2.	"a firm's tendency to engage in and support new ideas, novelty, experimentation, and creative processes that may result in new products, services, or technological processes"	Lumpkin and Dess (1996, p. 142)	tendency to engage; new; ideas; novelty; experimentation; creative process; products; service; technological processes
3.	"An enduring trait that is consistently exhibited by truly innovative firms over a period of time"	Subramanian (1996, p. 236)	enduring trait; consistently exhibited; period of time
4.	"The notion of openness to new ideas as an aspect of a firm's culture"	Hurley and Hult (1998, p. 44)	openness; ideas; culture
5.	"Capacity to introduce of some new process, product, or idea in the organization"	Hult et al. (2004, p. 430)	capacity; introduce; new; process; product; idea
6.	"Capability of organisations to master and maintain holistic value-creating dynamics in which the opportunities of change are exploited and new ideas are generated, translated and implemented into practice"	Jin et al. (2004, p. 257)	capability; master and maintain; value-creating; dynamics; opportunities; change; exploit; new; ideas; implement; practice
7.	"An organisation's overall innovative capability of introducing new products to the market, or opening up new markets, through combining strategic orientation with innovative behaviour and process"	Wang and Ahmed (2004, p. 304)	capability; introduction to the market; new; products; opening up new markets; strategic orientation; innovative behaviour and process

(Continued)

Table 3.3 (Continued)

No.	*Definition*	*Created or applied by*	*Keywords*
8.	"The development or adoption of an idea or behaviour into business operations that is new to the whole organization"	Wong and Chin (2007, p. 1291)	development; adoption; behaviour; business operations; new
9.	"Tendency of the organization to develop new or improved products/services and its success in bringing those products/services to the market"	Gumusluoglu and Ilsev (2009, p. 467)	tendency; development; new; improved; products; services; success; market
10.	"An innovative firm reports one or more innovations within the observation period"	OECD (2018, p. 34)	report innovation; one or more innovations; observation period

Source: Based on publications referenced in the table.

As noted by Cho and Pucik (2005), the existence of many different definitions causes problems for researchers and leads to disparate results. Some of those listed in Table 3.3 are very general, for example Hurley and Hult (1998, p. 44), while others contain more details, for example Jin et al. (2004, p. 257) or Wang and Ahmed (2004, p. 304).

Taking into account keywords, the above definitions can be divided into three groups, which emphasise the following aspects:

- Objective (measurable) effects of innovation, for example Vrakking (1990, p. 95); Wong and Chin (2007, p. 1291); Gumusluoglu and Ilsev (2009, p. 467) and OECD (2018, p. 34)
- Capability to innovate, for example Jin et al. (2004, p. 257); Hult et al. (2004, p. 430) and Wang and Ahmed (2004, p. 304)
- Continued desire to innovate, for example Hurley and Hult (1998, p. 44), Lumpkin and Dess (1996, p. 142), Gumusluoglu and Ilsev (2009, p. 467) and Subramanian (1996, p. 236)

These three groups are not mutually exclusive, as is the case with the definition proposed by Gumusluoglu and Ilsev (2009, p. 467), which can be classified into two groups. The monograph focuses on the first aspect, namely the existence of measurable effects of innovation which can be quantified empirically.

It should be pointed out that many authors do not provide an explicit definition of organisational innovation but limit themselves to explaining how it was measured, for example Kivimäki et al. (2000, p. 35). However, it is important to give an actual definition that should be consistent with the measure used in the study. One of the latent variables used in the quantitative study conducted by the author is based on the following definition of innovativeness proposed by the OECD (2018, p. 34): "An innovative firm reports one or more innovations within the observation period", which is brief and can easily be operationalised.

The level of innovativeness is an important measure of companies' effectiveness, especially for those operating in R&D-intensive industries. It should be remembered, however, that innovation is just a means which companies use to achieve more important goals. Another key measure of a firm's activity is its business performance.

3.3 Business performance

For many years business performance has been regarded as important for strategic management and has been frequently used as a dependent variable in empirical studies (Venkatraman & Ramanujam, 1986; Taouab & Issor, 2019). Its significance is best expressed by Venkatraman and Ramanujam (1986) who maintained that "for the strategy researcher, the option to move away from defining (and measuring) performance or effectiveness is not a viable one. This is because performance improvement is at the heart of strategic management" (p. 801). A number of terms are used in the literature to refer to this concept, including "organizational performance", "company performance", "firm performance" or just "performance". The preferred term in this monograph is "business performance", which is widespread in the literature. It is worth noting, however, that this term is often used without being analysed in detail, with certain exceptions (e.g. Morgan & Strong, 2003). Selected definitions of business performance are listed in Table 3.4.

The above definitions can be divided into two broad groups: the first one includes those phrased in highly abstract terms, which first need to be operationalised in order to be suitable for measuring business performance of companies (e.g. Smith & Reece, 1999; Neely et al., 2002; Peterson et al., 2003; Prakash et al., 2017; Cho & Lee, 2018). The second group includes more commonly used definitions, which are operationalised and are based on measures used by their authors (e.g. Lau & May, 1998; Calantone et al., 2002; Najib & Kiminami, 2011; Bresciani & Ferraris, 2016; Choi & Williams, 2016; Adel et al., 2020; Sarwoko & Nurfarida, 2021; Zhang et al., 2022).

In addition to the above division, one can distinguish between definitions that are relatively succinct (e.g. Raymond et al., 2013; Prakash et al., 2017, p. 80; Ratajczak-Mrozek, 2017) and those that are more complex (e.g. Neely et al., 2002; Peterson et al., 2003; Hult et al., 2004). There is also the case of Cho and Lee (2018),

Table 3.4 Selected definitions of "business performance", "organisational performance", "company performance", "firm performance" and "performance"

No.	*Definition*	*Created or applied by*	*Keywords*
1.	"This study defined business performance by four measures: five-year trends of sales growth, asset growth, return on assets, and return on equity"	Lau and May (1998, p. 212)	measures; five-year-trends; sales growth; asset growth; return on assets; return on equity
2.	"Business performance is defined as the ability of the operations to satisfy the desires of the company's major stakeholders"	Smith and Reece (1999, p. 153).	operations; ability; operations; major stakeholders
3.	"Sales growth and return on equity (ROE)"	Zahra et al. (2000, p. 936)	sales; growth; return on equity
4.	"Business performance is defined as the measures of growth and profitability of the firm through its business endeavors and deployment of organizational and technology resources"	Croteau et al. (2001, p. 4)	measures; growth; profitability; business endeavours; organizational resources; technology resources
5.	"Three were objective measures (ROI [return on investment], ROA [return on assets, and ROS [return on sales]), and one was subjective (overall profitability)"	Calantone et al. (2002, p. 519)	return on investment; return on assets; return on sales; profitability
6.	"Function of the efficiency and effectiveness of the actions it has undertaken"	Neely et al. (2002, p. xiii)	function; efficiency; effectiveness; actions; efficiency; effectiveness
7.	"Organizational performance may be defined as the ability of an organization to use its resources efficiently and to produce outputs that are consistent with its objectives and relevant for its users"	Peterson et al. (2003, p. xiii)	ability; use resources efficiently; produce outputs; consistent; objectives; relevant for users

(Continued)

Table 3.4 (Continued)

No.	*Definition*	*Created or applied by*	*Keywords*
8.	"Business performance is defined here as the achievement of organizational goals related to profitability and growth in sales and markets share, as well as the accomplishment of general firm strategic objectives"	Hult et al. (2004, pp. 430–431)	organizational goals; profitability; growth; sales; market sales; market share; strategic objectives
9.	"A composite of three measures: sales volume, profitability, and market share."	Najib and Kiminami (2011, p. 81)	sales volume; profitability; market share
10.	"Growth and profitability"	Raymond et al. (2013, p. 478)	growth; profitability
11.	"Business performance is an indicator which measures how well an organization accomplishes its objectives."	Prakash et al. (2017, p. 80)	indicator; measures; objectives
12.	"Financial and non-financial performance"	Ratajczak-Mrozek (2017, p. 250)	financial; non-financial
13.	"An organization has a set of goals. Business performance can be defined as how much an organization achieves these goals."	Cho and Lee (2018, p. 128)	goals; achievement
14.	". . . business performance can be defined as how much an organization can cope with fluctuating environmental factors such as profits, productivity, employee satisfaction, social responsibility and business survival"		fluctuating environmental factors; profits; productivity; employee satisfaction; social responsibility; business survival
15.	". . . business performance (. . .) is measured in four different ways: changes in operating revenue, disruption of supply chain, business closures, and cash flows"	Zhang et al. (2022, p. 615)	changes; operating revenue; disruption; supply chain; business closures; cash flow

Source: Based on publications referenced in the table.

who proposed two alternative definitions, admitting that "business performance can be defined as many different ways depending on purposes" (p. 128).

Taking into account the keywords, it can be noticed that the definitions involving specific measures are relatively similar, while those expressed in more abstract terms are rather different. The most frequent keywords in the first group include

- sales (e.g. Lau & May, 1998; Zahra et al., 2000; Calantone et al., 2002; Hult et al., 2004; Najib & Kiminami, 2011),
- growth (e.g. Lau & May, 1998; Zahra et al., 2000; Croteau et al., 2001; Hult et al., 2004; Raymond et al., 2013),
- profitability (e.g. Croteau et al., 2001; Calantone et al., 2002; Hult et al., 2004; Najib & Kiminami, 2011; Raymond et al., 2013),
- market share (e.g. Hult et al., 2004; Najib & Kiminami, 2011), and
- return on (e.g. Lau & May, 1998; Zahra et al., 2000; Calantone et al., 2002).

The most popular keywords used in the more abstract definitions include

- efficiently (e.g. Neely et al., 2002; Peterson et al., 2003),
- ability (e.g. Smith & Reece, 1999; Peterson et al., 2003), and
- objectives (e.g. Peterson et al., 2003; Prakash et al., 2017).

The problem with defining business performance is to select appropriate measures. It was recognised a long time ago by Seashore and Yuchtman (1967), who noted that given the complexity of the concept its measurement should not be based on a single criterion but should account for a number of variables. Since then this view has been widely accepted and it is now generally agreed that business performance can be measured using either financial or operational indicators, or both (Venkatraman & Ramanujam, 1986). The most common indicators employed for this purpose include

- sales growth (e.g. Lau & May, 1998; Smith & Reece, 1999; Zahra et al., 2000; Hult et al., 2004; Rhee et al., 2010; Raymond et al., 2013; Ratajczak-Mrozek, 2017),
- return on assets (e.g. Lau & May, 1998; Calantone et al., 2002; Tzelepis & Skuras, 2004; Ratajczak-Mrozek, 2017),
- return on equity (e.g. Lau & May, 1998; Smith & Reece, 1999; Zahra et al., 2000),
- return on investment (e.g. Calantone et al., 2002; Fonfara, 2009, 2012),
- market share (e.g. Hult et al., 2004; Fonfara, 2009, 2012; Rhee et al., 2010; Najib & Kiminami, 2011; Ratajczak-Mrozek, 2017),
- sales volume (e.g. Fonfara, 2009, 2012; Najib & Kiminami, 2011),
- profitability (e.g. Croteau et al., 2001; Rhee et al., 2010; Najib & Kiminami, 2011), and
- company growth (e.g. Tzelepis & Skuras, 2004; Ayatse et al., 2017; Bocquet et al., 2017).

According to Barney (2014), while financial indicators are very popular (e.g. return on assets, return on equity, return on investment or profitability), relying exclusively on such data is associated with serious drawbacks. For one thing, managers are in a position to influence this kind of information, for example by selecting the method of inventory valuation or depreciation. Another important fact is that financial indicators almost completely ignore intangible assets, including intangible capabilities and resources (Barney, 2014), which are a very important factor determining the performance of R&D-intensive companies. Another general problem connected with any performance indicators is comparability of underlying data, for example, in studies involving companies of different sizes. One commonly used approach to this problem is to analyse indicators in relation to nearest competitors, for example Fonfara (2009, 2012), Rhee et al. (2010), Oehmichen and Puck (2016) and Ratajczak-Mrozek (2017).

For the purpose of the study described later in this monograph, the author has selected the definition proposed by Neely et al. (2002), who define business performance as ". . . function of the efficiency and effectiveness of the actions it [company] has undertaken" (p. xiii). Following the approach recommended by Barney (2014), the concept is measured by means of financial and non-financial indicators.

3.4 Chapter summary

The purpose of this chapter was to present various ways of measuring the effectiveness of companies, namely their innovativeness and business performance. In the first part of the chapter, several definitions of innovation have been analysed, taking into account their keywords. Different types of innovation and their importance in companies have been discussed. The theoretical relationship between innovation and knowledge has also been highlighted.

The second part has focused on the concept of "innovativeness" and definitions of "innovative" companies. After a thorough analysis, the author has selected the definition provided by the OECD (2018, p. 34): "an innovative firm reports one or more innovations within the observation period".

The last part of the chapter deals with ways of measuring business performance, which is the key aspect reflecting the effectiveness of companies. Innovativeness, while being important, especially for R&D-intensive firms, is just a means to achieving a higher level of business performance. After analysing a number of definitions in terms of their keywords, the author has selected the definition proposed by Neely et al. (2002), who define business performance as a ". . . function of the efficiency and effectiveness of the actions it [company] has undertaken" (p. xiii), and following the approach of Barney (2014) it has been decided to measure business performance by employing both financial and non-financial indicators.

Chapter 4

Integration of Market and Technical Knowledge in R&D-Intensive Companies

Given the considerable amount of research concerning knowledge integration, the purpose of this chapter is to review the existing literature on the subject, with emphasis on the integration of market and technical knowledge. The presentation covers four theoretical perspectives, namely the RBV and the KBV along with the concepts of dynamic capabilities and R&D-marketing integration. The chapter ends with a reiteration of the research gap and a detailed description of the conceptual framework of the study, which seeks to determine how innovativeness and business performance of companies are affected by the processes analysed in the study.

4.1 RBV, KBV and the concept of dynamic capabilities

The RBV is a popular or, arguably, the most popular theory used for analysing competitive advantage and planning a company's activities in the long term (Foss & Foss, 2004; Foss & Ishikawa, 2007; Mitręga, 2016). Its origin can be traced back to Penrose (1959), though the term itself was first used by Wernerfelt (1984). The theory was later developed by Barney (1986, 1991), Dierickx and Cool (1989), Conner (1991) and Peteraf (1993). According to Foss and Ishikawa (2007), the RBV appeared in response to criticisms of Porter's treatment of a firm as a black box and his belief that competitive imperfections are the source of profit for some companies. In contrast to his approach, the proponents of the RBV focused on

DOI: 10.1201/9781032642352-4

specific resources that companies possess. The underlying element of RBV was not an oligopoly or a monopoly but a model of competitive equilibrium with factor market imperfections (Foss & Ishikawa, 2007). The main premise of the RBV is associated with the question about why firms differ from one another and how they achieve and maintain competitive advantage (Hoskisson et al., 1999). Czerniachowicz (2012) underlines that the RBV in the first place focuses on the company's resources and then on its business environment. In order to achieve competitive advantage, an organisation needs to identify its resources and develop them appropriately. Other important considerations in the RBV include resource allocation and creation with a view to gaining key capabilities.

The underlying assumption of the RBV is that firms differ from one another in terms of their resources and capabilities. The focus is on resources, which enable the company to gain competitive advantage and on capabilities that it needs to have in order to exploit its resources. Because resources may not be transferrable between organisations, disparities between them can be long-lasting (Barney, 1991; Peteraf, 1993; Matwiejczuk, 2011). The fact that resources are not entirely transferrable can also mean that effects achieved by companies with a certain type of resource can also differ, for example, when a company does not have information about the way a given resource is used by its competitor (Marcinkowska, 2017).

The term "resources" refers to the stock of factors owned or controlled by a company (Amit & Schoemaker, 1993, p. 35). Capabilities are a special category of resources, which are embedded in the organisation and are not transferrable; their purpose is to improve the productivity of other resources (Makadok, 2001, p. 389). Amit and Schoemaker (1993) define capabilities as "the firm's capacity to deploy resources" (p. 35). Barney and Hesterly (2012) note that capabilities themselves are not sufficient to implement a business strategy but enable a company to use other resources in the implementation process.

According to the RBV, in order to be useful in achieving competitive advantage, resources owned or controlled by a company need to be valuable, rare, imperfectly imitable and non-substitutable (Barney, 1991). These criteria, represented by the acronym VRIN, are commonly used in the literature to assess resources. Barney (1995) modified his assessment framework by adding the element of "organisation", explaining that ". . . competitive advantage potential depends on the value, rareness, and imitability of its resources and capabilities. However, to fully realize this potential, a firm must also be organized to exploit its resources and capabilities" (Barney, 1995, p. 56). Resources or capabilities can thus be assessed by asking questions about the four key components represented by each letter of the VRIO acronym (Knott, 2015):

- Value—does a resource enable a firm to exploit an environmental opportunity and/or neutralise an environmental threat?
- Rarity—is a resource currently controlled by only a small number of competing firms?

- Imitability—do firms without a resource face a cost disadvantage in obtaining or developing it?
- Organisation—are a firm's other procedures and policies organised to support the exploitation of its valuable, rare, and costly to imitate resources?

As noted by Obłój (2007), according to the RBV, there are two aspects of resources that make it difficult to imitate or substitute them. The first one is the process of creating or acquiring resources, the so-called path dependence. It usually depends on the way and time when a given resource was created. The second limiting factor is the ambiguous or complex configuration of resources, known as causal ambiguity. Both factors provide mechanisms of protection against competition—the so-called isolating mechanisms (Obłój, 2007).

Czakon (2010) points out that from the perspective of the RBV, differences between resources can be analysed at two levels. The first one is the diversity of resources in terms of quantity and quality as well as ways of exploiting them. The second level of analysis refers to the configuration of resources, since different configurations enable different companies to achieve the same or similar goals (Czakon, 2010).

The RBV gave rise to a number of important concepts, which are sometimes known as variants or extensions of the original theory, such as the KBV, the dynamic capabilities approach, the relational view or the natural-RBV (Hart, 1995; Carter et al., 2017; Nieves & Haller, 2014). The first two are particularly relevant in the context of this monograph.

Interest in knowledge-related problems in the context of organisations grew in response to changes that took place in the economy during the last decades of the 20th century. It was the beginning of a knowledge-based post-industrial economy, often described as the "new economy" (Grant, 2002). It is therefore not surprising that the proponents of the RBV also started to pay more attention to or recommend a greater focus on intangible resources, particularly knowledge (e.g. Grant, 1996b; Rouse & Daellenbach, 2002). This re-orientation led to the emergence of the knowledge based-view (KBV), which was the result of various ideas and studies conducted at the start of the 1990s (Grant, 2002).

The KBV is usually described as an extension of the RBV (e.g. Hoskisson et al., 1999; Gassmann & Keupp, 2007). According to numerous authors (e.g. Hill & Deeds, 1996; Grant, 1996a, 2002), the KBV lacks some important elements to merit the status of a theory of the firm. Rather, it is a collection of ideas concerning key aspects of business operation, where the role of knowledge is emphasised (Grant, 2002).

According to the KBV, value in an organisation is mainly created owing to intangible knowledge-based resources and capabilities rather than by exploiting financial or physical resources (Grant, 1997; DeCarolis & Deeds, 1999; Theriou et al., 2009; Kim et al., 2014). Although the RBV recognises the role of knowledge in gaining competitive advantage, the proponents of the KBV maintain that the RBV underestimates its importance by treating it as a generic resource, without specific properties. As a result, the RBV does not distinguish between different knowledge-based capabilities. Another problem is the lack of a clear distinction between capabilities and resources (Hill & Deeds, 1996; Kaplan et al., 2001).

In contrast to the RBV, the KBV emphasises the role of an organisation, especially the hierarchy, which is different from market relationships (Macher, 2006). Knowledge is treated as a valuable and rare resource and companies should strive to create new knowledge and develop new capabilities (Światowiec-Szczepańska, 2012). Organisational knowledge includes various kinds of information, for example about who knows what. In addition to being distributed among the company's employees, this knowledge is also embedded in the form of cooperation between them. Organisations differ from the market in that they facilitate coordination and communication, and consequently, the exchange of knowledge by implementing procedures, routines or a company-specific code of communication (Monteverde, 1995; Kogut & Zander, 1992, 1996).

According to Grant (1997), the KBV is based on a few assumptions regarding knowledge, its characteristics, its creation and its applications:

- Knowledge is strategically important for a company because it is a very productive resource which greatly contributes to value added.
- Different types of knowledge differ with respect to their transferability; this difference is particularly evident when one compares explicit knowledge, which is easily transferrable, with tacit knowledge, which is best demonstrated once it has been implemented; transferability of knowledge also depends on the recipient's ability to integrate different units of knowledge.
- Employees are the main creators of knowledge and in the case of tacit knowledge, they are also its main carriers; if learning capabilities are limited, the creation of new knowledge requires specialisation; in other words, to achieve a greater depth of knowledge, it is necessary to limit its breadth; nonetheless, the creation of new products usually requires different kinds of knowledge.
- Knowledge, above all, explicit knowledge, once created, can be implemented at minimal marginal cost.

The most important element, according to Grant (1997), is the fact that the creation of new products usually requires different kinds of specialised knowledge. For this reason, Grant believes that a company exists so that its employees can specialise in developing a certain kind of narrow, in-depth knowledge, while the company as a whole coordinates the integration of knowledge resources to enable the conversion of inputs into outputs. Thus, the company's main role is to integrate organisational knowledge (Grant, 1996b, 1997).

Acedo et al. (2006) distinguish two major groups among the proponents of the KBV. Those in the first group maintain that knowledge is a strategic resource (e.g. Conner & Prahalad, 1996; Grant, 1996a), which exists at the level of individual employees; consequently, it needs to be integrated (Kogut & Zander, 1992; Grant, 1996a, 1996b). The second group, represented by Tsoukas (1996) and Spender (1996), emphasises the role of social and tacit knowledge residing within groups (Spender, 1996).

Referring to Prahalad and Hamel (1990), Leiponen (2006) emphasises the importance of integration of complementary intellectual resources, which can reside in different parts of the organisation. When different employees or organisational units have complementary expertise, its value is the highest once it is integrated. Without integration, each firm loses an opportunity for synergy gains. According to the author of this monograph, synergy effects in an organisation can definitely be expected as a result of integrating market and technical knowledge.

Another concept developed on the basis of the RBV and promoted by a number of authors (e.g. Cyfert & Krzakiewicz, 2019) is that of dynamic capabilities. It was first introduced by Teece and Pisano (1994) and elaborated by Teece et al. (1997); since then it has been widely adopted and is now frequently used to explain the company's long-term competitive advantage. Although its origins can be traced back to the RBV, Ambrosini et al. (2009) point out that the concept of dynamic capabilities focuses on sources of competitive advantage in a different setting. While the RBV assumes a stable environment, dynamic capabilities, as the name indicates, focus on a changing environment (Ambrosini et al., 2009). Nonetheless, despite its popularity, there is no generally accepted definition of dynamic capabilities. Table 4.1 presents selected definitions of this concept.

The majority of the definitions listed above focus on activities undertaken by companies, represented by various action verbs, such as *create, acquire, integrate, modify, configure, reconfigure, deploy, redeploy* and *renew*, used mainly in relation to resources and on various kinds of *capabilities—operational, ordinary* and *lower order*—as well as with respect to *business assets, routines, skills* and *functional competences* (Teece et al., 1997, p. 515; Zahra & George, 2002, p. 148; Zollo & Winter, 2002, p. 340; Winter, 2003, p. 991; López, 2005, p. 664; Zahra et al., 2006, p. 924; Helfat et al., 2007, p. 4; Hou, 2008, p. 1257; Wang & Ahmed, 2007, p. 35; Lee & Kelley, 2008, p. 156; Protogerou et al., 2012, p. 621; Piening, 2013, p. 216; Simon et al., 2015, p. 916).

Among the most common keywords or phrases used in the definitions are "resources" and "resource base", which are usually combined with the verb "reconfigure" (e.g. Teece et al., 1997, p. 515; Zahra & George, 2002, p. 148; Zahra et al., 2006, p. 924; Wang & Ahmed, 2007, p. 35; Simon et al., 2015, p. 916) and "integrate" (e.g. Teece et al., 1997, p. 515; Wang & Ahmed, 2007, p. 35; Lee & Kelley, 2008, p. 156). A few definitions contain the word "routine", although its meaning is not always the same. For Eisenhardt and Martin (2000, p. 1107) dynamic capabilities are "organizational and strategic routines". Likewise, Piening (2013, p. 216) defines them as "bundles of interrelated routines". For Zollo and Winter (2002, p. 340), dynamic capabilities represent a "stable pattern of collective activity", which is used to generate and change "operating routines". A similar perspective is offered

Table 4.1 Selected definitions of dynamic capabilities

No.	*Definition*	*Author(s)*	*Keywords or key phrases*
1.	"Appropriately adapting, integrating, and reconfiguring internal and external organizational skills, resources, and functional competences to match the requirements of a changing environment."	Teece et al. (1997, p. 515)	adapting; integrating; reconfiguring; organizational skills; resources; functional competences; environment
2.	"Dynamic capabilities thus are the organizational and strategic routines by which firms achieve new resource configurations as markets emerge, collide, split, evolve, and die."	Eisenhardt and Martin (2000, p. 1107)	strategic routines; new resource configurations
3.	"Broadly defined, dynamic capabilities are the organizational and strategic processes by which managers manipulate resources into new productive assets in the context of changing markets."	Galunic and Eisenhardt (2001, p. 1229)	strategic processes; managers manipulate resources; new productive assets; changing markets
4.	". . . dynamic capabilities are essentially change-oriented capabilities that help firms redeploy and reconfigure their resource base to meet evolving customer demands and competitor strategies"	Zahra and George (2002, p. 148)	change-oriented capabilities; redeploy; reconfigure; resource base; evolving customer demands; competitor strategies
5.	"A dynamic capability is a learned and stable pattern of collective activity through which the organization systematically generates and modifies its operating routines in pursuit of improved effectiveness"	Zollo and Winter (2002, p. 340)	learned pattern; stable pattern; collective activity; systematically; generate; modify; operating routines; improved effectiveness
6.	". . . one can define dynamic capabilities as those that operate to extend, modify or create ordinary capabilities."	Winter (2003, p. 991)	extend; operate; modify; ordinary capabilities

7.	"Dynamic capabilities are complex, higher order organizational processes which provide adequate conditions for the modification and renewal of the firm's stock of business assets."	López (2005, p. 664)	complex; higher order; organizational processes; adequate conditions; modification; renewal; business assets
8.	"We view dynamic capabilities as the abilities to reconfigure a firm's resources and routines in the manner envisioned and deemed appropriate by the firm's principal decision-maker(s)."	Zahra et al. (2006, p. 924)	abilities; reconfigure; resources; routines; decision-maker
9.	"A dynamic capability is the capacity of an organization to purposefully create, extend, or modify its resource base."	Helfat et al. (2007, p. 4)	capacity; create; extend; modify; resource base
10.	"Dynamic capabilities are the ability of a firm to deploy new configurations of operational competencies relative to the competition by effectively sensing the environment, as well as absorptive, integrating, innovative activities."	Hou (2008, p. 1257)	ability; new configurations; operational competencies; competition; effectively; sensing; environment; absorptive; integrating; innovative; activities
11.	"We define dynamic capabilities as a firm's behavioural orientation constantly to integrate, reconfigure, renew and recreate its resources and capabilities and, most importantly, upgrade and reconstruct its core capabilities in response to the changing environment to attain and sustain competitive advantage."	Wang and Ahmed (2007, p. 35)	behavioural orientation; integrate; reconfigure; renew; recreate; resources; capabilities; upgrade; reconstruct; core capabilities; changing environment; competitive advantage
12.	". . . set of practices aimed at enabling novel approaches for assembling and integrating resources to achieve innovative outcomes."	Lee and Kelley (2008, p. 156)	practices; enabling; novel approaches; assembling; integrating; resources; innovative outcomes

(Continued)

Table 4.1 (Continued)

No.	*Definition*	*Author(s)*	*Keywords or key phrases*
13	"A dynamic capability is the firm's potential to systematically solve problems, formed by its propensity to sense opportunities and threats, to make timely and market-oriented decisions, and to change its resource base."	Barreto (2010, p. 271)	systematically; solve problems; opportunities; threats; market-oriented decisions; change resources base
14.	"We define dynamic capabilities as higher order capabilities that allow firms to exploit existing lower order capabilities and more importantly to identify and acquire new technological and/or marketing capabilities."	Protogerou et al. (2012, p. 621)	higher order capabilities; exploit; lower order capabilities; identify; acquire; technological capabilities; marketing capabilities
15.	"Dynamic capabilities can be described as bundles of interrelated routines which, shaped by path dependency, enable an organization to renew its operational capabilities in pursuit of improved performance."	Piening (2013, p. 216)	interrelated routines; path dependency; renew; operational capabilities; improved performance
16.	"A dynamic capability is the firms' potential to systematically solve problems, formed by its propensity to sense opportunities and threats, to make timely decisions, and to implement strategic decisions and changes efficiently to ensure the right direction."	Li and Liu (2014, p. 2794)	potential; systematically; solve problems; propensity to sense; opportunities; threats; timely decisions; decisions; implement; strategic decisions; changes; efficiently; right direction
17.	"Dynamic capabilities: the ability and processes of the firm to reconfigure its resources and thus allow the organisation to adapt and evolve."	Simon et al. (2015, p. 916)	ability; processes; reconfigure; resources; adapt; evolve
18.	"We define dynamic capabilities as a meta-routine designed to improve a company's operating routines."	Wilhelm et al. (2015, p. 328)	meta-routine; improve; operating routines

Source: Based on publications referenced in the table.

by Zahra et al. (2006, p. 924), who define dynamic capabilities as "abilities to reconfigure a firm's resources and routines". A number of definitions contain another keyword, namely "modify", which is used in relation to "operating routines" (Zollo & Winter, 2002, p. 340), "ordinary capabilities" (Winter, 2003, p. 991), "business assets" (López, 2005, p. 664) or "resource base" (Helfat et al., 2007, p. 4). Dynamic capabilities refer to strategic activities, as evidenced by the use of the adjective "strategic", for example strategic routines (Eisenhardt & Martin, 2000, p. 1107), strategic processes (e.g. Galunic & Eisenhardt, 2001, p. 1229) or strategic decisions (Li & Liu, 2014, p. 2794). Another common keyword is "change", which refers to either the environment (Teece et al., 1997, p. 515; Wang & Ahmed, 2007, p. 35) or the market (Galunic & Eisenhardt, 2001, p. 1229). Zahra and George (2002, p. 148) emphasise the role of "evolving customer demands" (p. 148), which is indirectly connected with market changes. The word "change" also appears in some other contexts. Zahra and George (2002) use the adjectival phrase "change-oriented" (p. 148) to describe dynamic capabilities; for Barreto (2010) "a dynamic capability is the firm's potential (. . .) to change its resource base" (p. 271), while Li and Liu (2014) maintain that "a dynamic capability is the firms' potential to (. . .) implement strategic decisions and changes efficiently . . ." (p. 2794). A number of authors emphasise the deliberate and regular application of dynamic capabilities. In this way, the company systematically "generates and modifies its operating routines" (Zollo & Winter, 2002, p. 340) or solves problems (Barreto, 2010, p. 271; Li & Liu, 2014, p. 2794). This means that activities associated with dynamic capabilities cannot be conducted in an ad-hoc manner.

After careful consideration, the author of this monograph has decided to select the definition proposed by Winter (2003, p. 991), who describes dynamic capabilities "as those that operate to extend, modify or create ordinary capabilities". The definition was selected for the sake of its clarity.

It includes the term "ordinary capabilities", which Winter (2003) also calls "zero-level" capabilities and other authors (e.g. Helfat & Winter, 2011) refer to them as operational capabilities. According to Winter (2003, p. 991), ordinary capabilities "permit a firm to 'make a living' in the short term". Interestingly, Helfat and Winter (2011) argue that there are three reasons why capabilities cannot easily be divided into operational and dynamic. Firstly, change will always be present, to a greater or lesser extent. Secondly, it is impossible to distinguish capabilities which support non-radical change from those that support radical change; nor is it possible to determine whether they support the existing or new business operations. Thirdly, some capabilities can be used for both operational and dynamic purposes.

The idea of resource integration is mentioned in a few definitions of dynamic capabilities (e.g. Teece et al., 1997, p. 515; Wang & Ahmed, 2007, p. 35; Lee & Kelley, 2008, p. 156). Knowledge integration is also regarded as a dynamic capability (e.g. Makkonen et al., 2014) but has received relatively little research attention. It is also differently defined. Sometimes, it is treated in a very general manner (e.g. Verona & Ravasi, 2003; Martinelli et al., 2018); in other cases, it is analysed in rather specific contexts, for example knowledge integration in family-owned enterprises (Chirico & Salvato, 2008) or integration of external knowledge (Villar et al., 2014). Verona and Ravasi (2003) perceive the company's ability to integrate knowledge as a dynamic capability and define it as "the capacity to shape and manage a context that stimulates latent and dispersed knowledge-resources, so that they can jointly contribute to developing and launching new products" (Verona & Ravasi, 2003, p. 579). Although this definition is very general, the empirical example provided by the authors gives an indication of how important it is to integrate market and technical knowledge. Unfortunately, Verona and Ravasi do not develop this aspect any further and their case study concerns just one firm.

The author of this monograph believes that the problem of market and technical knowledge integration should be analysed from the perspective of dynamic capabilities to fill an evident research gap resulting from the lack of studies on this topic. This goal can be achieved by postulating a new, more detailed dynamic capability, namely the market and technical knowledge integration capability.

In addition to the KBV and the concept of dynamic capabilities, the problem of market and technical knowledge integration is closely connected with R&D-marketing integration, which refers to the integration between employees involved in research and development (equipped with technical knowledge) and those dealing with marketing activities (equipped with market knowledge). Given its popularity and a large number of studies it has generated, the concept is highly relevant for the research problem analysed in this monograph.

4.2 The concept of R&D-marketing integration

Although there are many studies on the topic of R&D-marketing integration, no comprehensive analysis of this problem has been undertaken since the review article published by Griffin and Hauser (1996). Since then, many authors have developed the concept with their valuable contributions. To make a systematic review of publications on R&D-marketing integration, the author of this monograph has divided them into three periods to highlight differences between the number and character of studies published in each period.

The development of the concept of R&D-marketing integration can be divided into three periods:

1 Up to 1986—relatively little interest in R&D-marketing integration.
2 From 1987 to 2000—growing interest in R&D-marketing integration.
3 Since 2001—the stable interest in R&D-marketing integration.

4.2.1 *Up to 1986: relatively little interest in R&D-marketing integration*

Interest in R&D-marketing integration started in the 1970s, though first attempts to analyse this problem appeared in earlier publications (e.g. Gerstenfeld et al., 1969).

R&D-marketing integration was first recognised as important mainly in relation to companies' success regarding innovation (e.g. Souder & Chakrabart, 1978; Bonnet, 1986; Gupta et al., 1986a, 1986b). According to Mansfield (1982), in companies where there is no close cooperation between employees of R&D and marketing departments, alignment between R&D activities and market requirements is achieved either with a delay or coincidentally, or both. Some authors, recognising that R&D-marketing integration was particularly important for high-tech or advanced tech companies, focused their research in this area on this group of companies (e.g. Gupta et al., 1985; Bonnet, 1986).

Although the topic was recognised as important, research on R&D-marketing integration had a number of practical challenges. Arguably, one of the more interesting problems noticed by authors in this regard was the fact that people employed in R&D departments focus on long-term outcomes of their work (Carroad & Carroad, 1982), while employees of marketing departments, obliged to deal with current problems, are much more concerned about the short-term perspective (Monteleone, 1976). These observations were empirically confirmed by Gupta et al. (1986a), who analysed differences between R&D and marketing managers.

Souder (1980) was aware of the complexity associated with managing what he called the "interface" between R&D and marketing activities. He identified four types of problems in this area (Souder, 1980, pp. 10–12):

- Lack of communications—manifested by attitudinal, physical and verbal distances between the R&D and marketing departments.
- Too-good friends—as a result of excessive regard and respect shown by members of one department towards colleagues from another department and vice versa, they are more likely to overlook certain observations and information and less likely to challenge judgements of the other party.
- Lack of appreciation—negative emotional feelings harboured by members of each department towards the other impede collaboration and cause employees to intentionally avoid one another.
- Distrust—manifested in the form of extremely negative feelings towards members of the other department, such as hostile behaviours, negative attitudes, fears or deep-seated jealousies.

Souder divided these problems into relatively mild—lack of communications and too-good friends, and severe—lack of appreciation and distrust. He found that over half of R&D projects at firms participating in his study were affected by these problems. Interestingly, two thirds of projects where these problems had not occurred ended in a commercial success. In contrast, only a third of R&D projects where mild problems had been reported were successful. In the case of projects affected by severe problems, the success rate was only 14.8% (Souder, 1980).

Results of Souder's studies indicate that certain differences in orientation and perspectives exhibited by employees of R&D and marketing departments are actually expected and desirable (Souder, 1980, 1981), but should not be excessive. Moreover, it can also be concluded that even small problems in relationships between the two departments can decrease the effectiveness of the company's operations and, consequently, its business performance. Finally, the above results are a good illustration of the research problem analysed in this monograph and challenges associated with it, as well as its importance in companies, especially those operating in R&D-intensive industries.

Until 1986, research focused on highlighting the role of R&D-marketing integration and identifying problems that could be encountered (e.g. Monteleone, 1976; Carroad & Carroad, 1982; Millman, 1982); some solutions were also proposed (e.g. Souder, 1977, 1980), but their number was limited. The period of relatively little interest in R&D-marketing integration ended with the publication of a seminal article by Gupta et al. (1986b), which probably encouraged other authors to conduct more in-depth studies on R&D-marketing integration, as it remains one of the most frequently cited articles on this topic. The same three authors created the theoretical framework for R&D and marketing integration, which later became very popular.

4.2.2 1987–2000: growing interest in R&D-marketing integration

In the second period, the number of publications devoted to R&D-marketing integration considerably increased. Some authors narrowed down their research attention to one sector, for example the chemical industry (Norton et al., 1994), pharmaceuticals (e.g. Pearson & Ball, 1993; Wang, 1996, 1997; Rafiq & Saxon, 2000), telecommunications (Saghafi et al., 1990; Lapierre & Hénault, 1996) or even the food industry (Viaene & Januszewska, 1999). In comparison with the previous period, many more studies focused on high-tech companies (e.g. Gupta & Wilemon, 1988, 1990; Song & Parry, 1992, 1997; Parry & Song, 1993; Norton et al., 1994; Song et al., 1997; Wang, 1996, 1997; Rafiq & Saxon, 2000).

R&D-marketing integration was also investigated in more countries, including the Federal Republic of Germany (Brockhoff & Chakrabarti, 1988), Belgium (Moenaert & Souder, 1990, 1996; Moenaert et al., 1992, 1994, 1995), Great Britain (Shaw & Shaw, 1998), and Canada (Lapierre & Hénault, 1996), but by far the most studies concerned Japan (Jacobs & Herbig, 1998; Norton et al., 1994; Parry & Song, 1993; Song & Parry, 1992, 1993a, 1993b, 1997; Song & Dyer, 1995). There were also articles dealing with a wider scope of integration, namely between R&D,

marketing and manufacturing (e.g. Kahn & McDonough III, 1997a, 1997b; Song et al., 1997).

The research output in this period included, above all, a number of articles containing proposals concerning ways of improving the effectiveness of R&D-marketing integration or solutions to problems associated with such efforts. One of them is another article by Gupta and Wilemon (1988), which reports results of a study of R&D directors of technology-intensive companies. The authors found that R&D managers from companies characterised by a high level of R&D-marketing integration perceived marketing information as realistic and valid, objective, consistent and complete, useful and appealing. Marketing managers were perceived by R&D managers as social and friendly, helpful and competent, trustworthy, cooperative, knowledgeable and open, easy to work with and fair. These positive perceptions of marketing managers and R&D managers' satisfaction with marketing information were found to be positively correlated. Moreover, employees of both departments were involved in early stages of product development. Gupta and Wilemon concluded that organisational practices with the greatest influence on R&D-marketing cooperation included the operating characteristics of both groups, organisational innovativeness and risk taking capacity as well as the amount of organisational support for R&D-marketing integration. It was also found that positive relationships between the two departments could be fostered by raising and clarifying important issues, asking questions, resolving conflicts at early stages and at low levels of the organisational structure. According to the authors, senior management had an important role to play in this regard by creating an environment that was conducive to the integration of both groups of employees, especially in the case of some technological companies, where marketing activities may be underestimated, which in turn might have a negative impact on the credibility of marketing staff (Gupta & Wilemon, 1988).

Gupta and Wilemon published two other articles which addressed the question of how to improve R&D-marketing relations. The first focused on R&D's perspective (Gupta & Wilemon, 1990) and the second on marketing's perspective (Gupta & Wilemon, 1991). The authors analysed mutual expectations of each group and the role played by senior management in creating greater cooperation between them.

According to R&D directors, their activities should focus on promoting mutual understanding, encouraging teamwork, being responsive to market needs, promoting quality information exchanges with members of the marketing team, increasing involvement in business and marketing programs. Regarding the expectations towards colleagues from the marketing department, the most popular answers included encourage teamwork, promote mutual understanding, improve marketing research, hire more qualified personnel, balance short- and long-term needs and develop clear product specifications. Asked about what senior management should do to improve relations between the two departments, R&D managers said: encourage teamwork, show personal interest in product development activities, perceive R&D as business partner, reward R&D/marketing jointly, balance long- and short- term requirements, understand marketing's importance, encourage greater communication, change organisational structure, support training programs and seminars that emphasise integration, increase resources and change hiring policies (Gupta & Wilemon, 1990).

In the next study Gupta and Wilemon (1991) put the same questions to marketing directors of seven technological industries. According to the respondents, relationships with R&D staff could be improved if they tried to encourage teamwork, improve the quality and timeliness of market information delivered to R&D, take R&D people out of the lab, develop informal relationships with R&D, learn about technology and formalise the product development process. Marketing directors thought that colleagues from the R&D department should become market oriented, increase the quality of information exchange (e.g. by communicating in a more understandable, jargon-free manner), change their attitude and be more flexible, respond quickly, promote the spirit of co-operation and participate in marketing activities. Expectations towards senior management included making organisational design changes, showing personal interest in new product development (NPD), providing strategic direction to NPD efforts, encouraging teamwork, increasing resources, supporting training programs and seminars, understanding marketing's importance, rewarding R&D/marketing jointly and changing hiring policies (Gupta & Wilemon, 1991).

While mutual expectations of R&D and marketing managers were largely different, they included expressions of willingness to cooperate with the other group. One important expectation mentioned by R&D managers was that the quality of marketing research should be improved. Nonetheless, as Gupta and Wilemon note, according to marketing directors, R&D employees did not understand the challenges associated with obtaining objective market data (Gupta & Wilemon, 1990, 1991). This example can be regarded as a good illustration of difficulties that can be encountered in the process of integrating R&D and marketing employees, especially the lack of mutual understanding of the nature of work that each department is tasked with.

The longest list of suggestions from both groups of respondents concerned things senior management should do to improve R&D-marketing relations, which were quite consistent and included introducing organisational changes, encouraging teamwork and showing personal interest in new product development (Gupta & Wilemon, 1990, 1991).

Another insightful article was written by Shaw and Shaw (1998), who examined the conflict between engineers and marketers from the perspective of engineers. Their study confirmed many findings reported by Gupta and Wilemon (1988, 1990, 1991) and provided some additional ones. Shaw and Shaw found that relationships between the two groups were also affected by the physical location of their workplaces. Companies where these two departments were separated, distrust and lack of mutual understanding were more common. The study revealed that both departments should be as close as possible to one another, ideally in the same building, to ensure the most positive effects. Another factor identified by the authors was the role of marketing training for engineers. After participating in such trainings, engineers perceived meetings with marketers as more useful. Nonetheless, such inter-departmental meetings could be quite tense. Consequently, the authors recommended caution, noting that marketing knowledge acquired by engineers could be also be a source of conflict (Shaw & Shaw, 1998).

A study conducted by Hise et al. (1990) investigated the cooperation between marketing and R&D and its effect on the success level of new products developed by manufacturing companies. They found that collaboration between the two departments was a key factor in explaining the success rates of new products and should be the focus of management efforts at the design stage of new product development.

After reviewing prior research, Griffin and Hauser (1996) identified six main approaches that companies employ to integrate R&D and marketing and developed a causal map for analysing this integration. They found that integrating mechanisms were linked to success in new product development. The key aspects identified by the authors included structural/process dimensions, such as informal social systems, incentives and rewards, relocation and physical facilities design, organisational structures, personnel movement, and formal integrative management processes (Griffin & Hauser, 1996). These dimensions were later used by other authors to create models for studies of R&D-marketing integration, for example Leenders and Wierenga (2002) or Lu and Yang (2005).

A different research perspective was adopted by Lucas and Bush (1988), who measured personality traits of R&D managers and marketers and how they were correlated with new product success rates as well as the number of products introduced. They identified personality factors that were particularly relevant in this context. In companies with higher success rates of new products, marketers were described as "realistic" and "tough minded". In companies introducing more new products, R&D managers were characterised by "conformity" and "greater humility". Traits such as "happy-go-lucky" and "enthusiastic" were positively correlated with the number of new products in the case of R&D managers and to new product success rates, in the case of marketers (Lucas & Bush, 1988).

4.2.3 Since 2001: the stable interest in R&D-marketing integration

The last period was associated with economic changes resulting from the growing use of computers and, later on, with the spread of broadband Internet services. These technological advances brought about changes in the way companies operated, especially in R&D-intensive industries. In February 2001, a group of software engineers published the Manifesto for Agile Software Development, which laid out core values and principles that, according to its authors, should be followed in software development and in cooperation with customers (Beck et al., 2001).

In the 21st century, research on R&D-marketing integration has concentrated on China (e.g. Li & Atuahene-Gima, 2001; Perks et al., 2009, 2010; Eng & Ozdemir,

2014; Yao et al., 2014; Yongsheng & Jinjie, 2019) and South Korea (Cho & Hahn, 2004; Shin & Roh, 2015; Shim et al., 2016). There have also been more studies and analyses comparing R&D-marketing integration in different countries, for example the United Kingdom and Slovenia (Fain & Wagner, 2014), the United States, China and Japan (Song & Thieme, 2006), Singapore and New Zealand (Garrett et al., 2006), Great Britain and Germany (Shaw et al., 2004) or selected EU countries (Boles & Link, 2017). It should be noted, however, that comparative studies of R&D-marketing integration were also conducted earlier, for example between the United States and Japan by Norton et al. (1994).

The majority of studies dealt with high-tech companies (e.g. Jin, 2001; Li & Atuahene-Gima, 2001; Maltz et al., 2001; Cho & Hahn, 2004; Lu & Yang, 2004, 2005; Becker & Lillemark, 2006; Perks et al., 2009, 2010; Eng & Ozdemir, 2014; Li & Chen, 2016; Shim et al., 2016; Boles & Link, 2017). As in the previous period, some authors examined a broader scope of integration, for example involving R&D, marketing and manufacturing (e.g. Brettel et al., 2011; Eng & Ozdemir, 2014) or R&D, marketing and finance (e.g. Hempelmann & Engelen, 2015).

One important characteristic of this period is the appearance of a greater number of conceptual frameworks or models of various complexity, which were used to study the collaboration between R&D and marketing (e.g. Jin, 2001; Wang & Montaguti, 2002; Lu & Yang, 2004; Song & Thieme, 2006; Kang et al., 2007; Massey & Kyriazis, 2007; Song & Song, 2010; Li & Chen, 2012; Wang & Lee, 2014; Wang et al., 2014; Li & Chen, 2016; Homburg et al., 2017; Ali & Matsuno, 2018). These frameworks and models included a number of factors, solutions or tools that could be used to foster R&D-marketing integration, for example communication intensity or information credibility (Wang & Montaguti, 2002), formalisation, harmony, centralisation, perceived environmental uncertainty, participation in decision making (Song & Thieme, 2006), environmental context, marketing and technical capability, firm resources (Ali & Matsuno, 2018), physical separation, cultural difference, goal incongruity, tools such as communication and decision-aiding IT (Song & Song, 2010), communication frequency and quality, bidirectional communication, affect-based and cognition-based trust (Massey & Kyriazis, 2007), professional orientation, firm size, social and organisational context, time orientation (Jin, 2001), perceived importance of cooperation or innovation strategy (Lu & Yang, 2004), organisational citizenship behaviour, social orientation (Li & Chen, 2012), R&D culture and power, company strategy, market environment (Homburg et al., 2017), senior management attitude, quality of R&D-marketing relations, organisational structure or methods used to organise new product activities (Wang & Lee, 2014), communication effect, communication procedure, resource sharing, technical process proficiency and marketing process proficiency (Wang et al., 2014), senior management emphasis, cross-functional training, helping behaviour and task interplay (Li & Chen, 2016). Nonetheless, many studies conducted in this period still relied on the framework proposed by Gupta et al. (1986b), Fain et al. (2011) or Fain and Wagner (2014).

Some frameworks were based on selected factors identified in the previous period by Griffin and Hauser (1996) and included additional elements, such as information and communication technology (Leenders & Wierenga, 2002) or perceived importance of integration (Lu & Yang, 2005).

Not surprisingly, another area investigated in this period is the possibility of using IT tools to support R&D-marketing integration. Song and Song (2010) focused on two groups of IT tools: communication technologies and decision-aiding technologies. Communication technologies were found to be most useful for mitigating the negative effects of physical separation. Decision-aiding technologies turned out to be more useful for counteracting negative effects of cultural differences or goal incongruity (Song & Song, 2010). Similar results were obtained by Leenders and Wierenga (2002), who concluded that the use of information and communication technologies was conducive to R&D-marketing integration and facilitated daily communication between both groups, which had a positive effects on knowledge creation (Leenders & Wierenga, 2002). Another idea for improving the interface and cooperation between the marketing and R&D departments was to use social media (blogs, microblogs, and wikis). Using insights from a qualitative study, Chirumalla et al. (2018) proposed a process of social media engagement consisting of three stages: coordinative, cooperative, and coproductive engagement. They found that to be useful, social media activities required systematic organisation and careful planning. In other words, they might not bring expected results if used inappropriately or not in the right context (Chirumalla et al., 2018). This result was consistent with the findings of Nijssen and Ordanini (2020), who concluded that the existence of a social media strategy was positively correlated with the level of social media use in NPD and the level of cooperation between R&D and marketing.

Research conducted since 2001 has contributed many valuable insights about characteristics of R&D-marketing integration and provided useful guidance on how to make it more effective. For example, Lu and Yang (2004) found that in order to achieve better results in new product development, companies have to take steps to improve the effectiveness of R&D-marketing cooperation by paying more attention to education, which is an important task for managers.

The study carried out by Maltz et al. (2001) showed that inter-functional rivalry "reduces R&D's use of information supplied by marketing personnel" (p. 69) and "lowers the perceived quality of information transferred" (p. 69). On the other hand, measures to improve inter-functional cooperation, such as the creation of cross-functional teams, were found to improve the use of information and decrease rivalry between departments.

Many authors continued to emphasise the importance of physical proximity between R&D and marketing departments to enable the most effective cooperation (Leenders & Wierenga, 2002; Lu & Yang, 2005). If such an arrangement was not possible, information and communication technology (ICT) tools should be used to minimise the negative effects of physical distance (Lu & Yang, 2005).

Li and Chen (2012) concluded that "the relationship between social orientation and R&D-marketing collaboration is found to be mediated by organisational citizenship behaviour (i.e., helping behaviour and civic virtue), and social orientation has no direct effect on the collaboration" (p. 151). The authors also confirmed the conclusion made by Maltz et al. (2001), who found that more socially orientated R&D managers tend to find information they receive as being better quality. Consequently, Li and Chen (2012) argued that companies wishing to foster R&D-marketing integration should encourage employees from both departments to participate in informal meetings, such as joint day trips or picnics.

A study by Wang et al. (2014) revealed the importance of effective communication protocols between both departments. The authors concluded that top level management should organise frequent meetings between R&D and marketing staff where open communication is encouraged in order to defuse existing conflicts and disputes and prevent their escalation. According to Sanzo et al. (2012), such conflicts could be mitigated by clearly defining goals, organisational procedures and tasks of both departments.

The beginning of the 21st century was also the time when some authors started to argue that measures designed to achieve the highest possible integration between R&D and marketing activities did not always bring desired effects. For example, Brettel et al. (2011) found that the impact of R&D and marketing integration on efficiency "depends on the process stage and the degree of innovativeness" (p. 262). Jin (2001) analysed the relationship between product newness and role flexibility of R&D/marketing and found that three levels of product newness—newness to the market, newness to the company and newness to the technology—require different levels of R&D-marketing integration. A study by Leenders and Wierenga (2008), which relied on data from the pharmaceutical industry, revealed that benefits from more integration between marketing and R&D were positively correlated with the level of new product development resources; when these resources were low, integration efforts might not bring the expected results. Another key factor identified in the study was the strategic scope. The impact of integration on NPD was found to be stronger for companies that focused on fewer groups of products or market segments.

Li and Atuahene-Gima (2001) examined the impact of R&D-marketing interaction on NPD in Chinese technology companies and found that the influence of marketing during the NPD process could be dysfunctional when a new product is more innovative. It is important, however, to keep in mind that this finding is associated with a specific cultural context—China is an example of a country with a culture of high uncertainty avoidance (Tung et al., 2014). Rubera et al. (2012) carried out a qualitative study of 11 NPD projects implemented by five firms, and concluded that the level of integration R&D-marketing integration should depend on the type of new product under development. One of the key findings from a study by Shim et al. (2016) is that the level R&D-marketing integration should be determined by "the quality and quantity of the resources devoted to the NPD process" (pp. 310–311). The authors emphasise that integration efforts should be guided by different performance criteria: in addition to supporting integration in pursuit of technological innovation, managers should also limit excessive collaboration if it has a negative effect on time to market and product sales. This conclusion was similar to the one reached by Rubera et al. (2012).

In summary, despite multiple opinions as to what levels of integration are optimal, it can be concluded that the majority of studies and authors support the view that a high level of R&D-marketing integration is desirable (e.g. Li & Calantone, 1998; Rafiq & Saxon, 2000; Lu & Yang, 2004; Garrett et al., 2006; Song & Thieme, 2006; Song & Song, 2010; Yao et al., 2014).

As can be seen from the above analysis, research on R&D-marketing integration has greatly contributed to the integration between market and technical knowledge in companies. Nonetheless, some research gaps still remain and are described in more detail in the following section.

4.3 Conceptual framework of the study

In this monograph, the integration between market and technical knowledge is analysed from a theoretical perspective, informed by the KBV, dynamic capabilities and R&D-marketing integration. As already mentioned, the majority of useful insights on this topic have come from studies of R&D-marketing integration. It should be noted, however, in contrast to the other two approaches, it focuses on a slightly different problem and employs different terminology. Authors investigating R&D-marketing integration concentrate on practical efforts aimed at integrating the work of R&D engineers (who possess technical knowledge) and marketers (who possess market knowledge). The term "knowledge" is rarely mentioned, though in practice, such inter-functional cooperation does contribute to the integration of both kinds of knowledge. This is why, the research output on the R&D-marketing interface can be further developed by drawing complementary insights from the KBV and dynamic capabilities. Moreover, certain gaps and inconsistencies can be identified in the very concept of R&D-marketing integration. The author of this monograph has focused on six aspects, which constitute a considerable *research gap*. Given the research output in this field, the first five aspects concern the concept of R&D-marketing integration, while the last one, which is the most important, relates to all three concepts.

Firstly, results of studies in the field of R&D-marketing integration are not always consistent. The majority of authors (e.g. Griffin & Hauser, 1992; Rafiq & Saxon, 2000; Lu & Yang, 2004; Garrett et al., 2006; Song & Thieme, 2006; Yao et al., 2014) maintain that the integration between R&D and marketing departments is extremely important. This view is supported by numerous empirical studies, which indicate that integration processes enable companies to exploit their technical resources more effectively (Li & Calantone, 1998). Efforts in this area usually improve the performance of products, services or companies themselves (e.g. Song et al., 2000; Leenders & Wierenga, 2002; Song & Song, 2010). However, some authors report negative effects of R&D-marketing integration. There are also opinions suggesting that not all activities require the same level of integration and in some cases excessive integration can harm the company's overall performance. The study by Maltz et al. (2001) showed that the way R&D managers use information provided by the marketing department may lead to inter-functional rivalry and increase pressures to ignore useful marketing information. According to Brettel et al. (2011), effects of integration depend on the level of innovativeness and the process stage. Rubera et al. (2012) found that the level of R&D-marketing integration should depend on the type of new product under development. Moreover, Shim et al. (2016) analysed previous studies regarding the effect of R&D-marketing integration and found that divergent results obtained in some cases could be due to the application of parametric linear models, which are inherently prone to model misspecification.

Secondly, the literature on R&D-marketing integration continues to focus on relationships, cooperation and the transfer of information between R&D and marketing departments (e.g. Rubera et al., 2012; Shim et al., 2016; Homburg et al., 2017; Nijssen & Ordanini, 2020), in other words on aspects that may not always be present in a given company. People involved in R&D (with technical knowledge) and marketing (with market information) may well be working together in various projects.

Thirdly, there are studies on R&D-marketing integration which involved very disparate samples of industries and companies that not only differ considerably in the way they operate and what type of activities they engage in but also represent different categories of R&D intensity, ranging from the lowest to the highest in the classification created by Galindo-Rueda and Verger (2016) (e.g. Sanzo et al., 2012; Homburg et al., 2017; Yongsheng & Jinjie, 2019). Such sample heterogeneity can affect results, given that the role of knowledge and its integration may vary depending on the characteristics of a given industry. For this reason, there is a need for studies that focus on industries which share as many characteristics as possible.

Fourthly, there are relatively few recent publications on R&D-marketing integration. Above all, however, there is a shortage of recent studies involving R&D-intensive firms or even high-technology companies that take a comprehensive approach to the topic. Those that are relatively recent, such as Boles and Link (2017), focus on selected aspects of R&D-marketing integration or only on the high-technology manufacturing companies. The study by Shim et al. (2016) deals only with companies operating in the ICT industry. Li and Chen (2012, 2016) limited their analysis to the semiconductor industry. The approach adopted by Nijssen and Ordanini (2020) was different: they examined the most innovative small and medium enterprises. It can be argued that the majority of their samples were R&D-intensive firms, but, most probably, not all of them. Summing up, it can be concluded that while all these publications generally deal with the subject analysed in this monograph, none of them presents an up-to-date and comprehensive picture of how R&D-marketing integration in R&D-intensive companies affects their innovativeness and business performance.

Fifthly, so far, even in relatively recent studies on R&D-marketing integration, the analytical approaches and measurement tools date back to the 1990s or even

1980s (e.g. Song & Song, 2010; Eng & Ozdemir, 2014; Ali & Matsuno, 2018; Nijssen & Ordanini, 2020). Those approaches are not suited to modern realities because they do not account for new methods of work and practices employed in companies, which have gained much popularity in R&D-intensive industries (e.g. Scrum methodology).

Sixthly, there is currently no approach to R&D-marketing integration that would account for market and technical knowledge. In contrast, the problem of knowledge integration was addressed in the KBV (cf. Grant, 1996a, 1996b, 1997) and in the concept of dynamic capabilities (cf. Verona & Ravasi, 2003). Both of these theoretical perspectives differ from the concept of R&D-marketing integration in some important respects. For one thing, because both of them originate from the RBV, they focus on resources, which are generally overlooked in studies on R&D-marketing integration, with few exceptions (e.g. Ali & Matsuno, 2018). It should be pointed out that the problem of knowledge integration in an organisation was not comprehensively investigated in studies conducted from the perspective of the KBV or dynamic capabilities, especially with regard to the integration of market and technical knowledge. Researchers studying R&D-marketing integration have analysed the impact of efforts to integrate R&D employees (implicitly, those with technical knowledge) with people from marketing departments (implicitly, those with market knowledge) on various aspects of company performance (e.g. Wang & Lee, 2014; Li & Chen, 2016; Homburg et al., 2017), but without explicitly taking into account those two kinds of knowledge and their development. At the same time, a number of authors recognised the importance of market and technical knowledge for innovativeness and business performance of companies without analysing the integration of these two resources. For instance, Giuliani (2008) notes that technical knowledge is essential for the creation of innovation, especially in the case of companies operating in R&D-intensive industries. According to Atuahene-Gima (2005), in order to innovate, companies also need market knowledge, which is necessary, among other things, to identify emerging opportunities. Bohlmann et al. (2013) stress the importance of information about customer needs (which is part of market knowledge—see definitions in Chapter 2) in the context of new product development. Li and Cavusgil (1999) found a direct, positive effect of customer knowledge and competitor knowledge (components of market knowledge—see definitions in Chapter 2) on the performance of high-technology companies. A similar correlation has been found to exist in the case of technical knowledge. Consequently, findings from the rich body of research in the field of R&D-marketing integration can be exploited in a more comprehensive approach that addresses the need for studies accounting for the development of market and technical knowledge in an organisation together with activities aimed at integrating these two resources. The emphasis on the development of these two resources is important because efforts to integrate outdated market and technical knowledge will not bring expected results in the form of the firm's better innovativeness and business performance. This view is shared by Hitt et al. (2009), who highlight the importance of novel knowledge for companies and He and Wang (2009), who point out that innovative knowledge resources are the key determinant of the company's economic performance.

To fill the *research gap* outlined above, it is necessary to employ a comprehensive approach to the problem of knowledge integration, which, above all, consists of examining activities that lead to the integration of both kinds of knowledge, which are particularly valuable to companies operating in R&D-intensive industries. It is also important to explicitly focus on the role of market and technical knowledge development, particularly by examining the main sources of these two kinds of knowledge that R&D-intensive companies rely on.

In the light of the above, the main objective of the monograph is twofold: *to identify factors that determine the integration of market and technical knowledge in R&D-intensive companies and to evaluate the effect of market and technical knowledge integration on innovativeness and business performance of these firms.*

To achieve this goal, the following five research questions have been put forward:

RQ1: What sources of market and technical knowledge are used by R&D-intensive companies?

RQ2: How does the development of market and technical knowledge affect integration of these knowledge resources in R&D-intensive companies and their innovativeness and business performance?

RQ3: How do R&D-intensive companies integrate market and technical knowledge?

RQ4: How does the integration of market and technical knowledge affect business performance and innovativeness of R&D-intensive companies?

RQ5: What recommendations should be made to managers so that they can facilitate the integration of both kinds of knowledge in R&D-intensive companies and, consequently, improve their business performance and innovativeness?

When Grant's opinion (1996a, 1996b) about knowledge integration in the firm, which is a key tenet of the KBV, is restricted to two specific kinds of knowledge, commonly regarded as important for companies (e.g. Deligianni et al., 2015; Suseno & Pinnington, 2018) it can be argued that knowledge integration activities should be supported by the development of market and technical knowledge to achieve the expected integration effects. Following Grant's view (1996a, 1996b) it can further be hypothesised that the activities associated with knowledge integration have a mediating effect between the development of market and technical knowledge and the company's innovativeness and its business performance. According to Shrout and Bolger (2002) "mediation is said to occur when causal effect of some variable X on an outcome Y is explained by some intervening variable M" (p. 422). Furthermore, this mediating effect does not necessarily rule out the possibility that the two explanatory variables directly affect innovativeness and business performance of analysed companies. As noted earlier, the effect of market and technical knowledge on the company's effectiveness is recognised in the literature (e.g. Li & Cavusgil, 1999; Giuliani, 2008; Bohlmann et al., 2013). It is necessary, however, to investigate whether this effect is direct, indirect (mediated through knowledge integration activities) or direct and indirect effects exist in parallel. It can also be expected that all these efforts, namely the development of both kinds of knowledge and their integration, is particularly important for R&D-intensive firms, which are under constant pressure to innovate (Wang & Li, 2017; Pham et al., 2019) and compete with innovative rivals (Avsar, 2018).

In view of the above consideration and the research gap described above, 12 hypotheses of this monograph have been formulated as follows:

H1: The development of market knowledge has a direct positive effect on market and technical knowledge integration activities.
H2: The development of technical knowledge has a direct positive effect on market and technical knowledge integration activities.
H3: Market and technical knowledge integration activities have a positive mediating effect between the development of market knowledge and innovativeness of R&D-intensive firms.
H4: Market and technical knowledge integration activities have a positive mediating effect between the development of technical knowledge and innovativeness of R&D-intensive firms.
H5: Market and technical knowledge integration activities have a positive mediating effect between the development of market knowledge and business performance of R&D-intensive firms.
H6: Market and technical knowledge integration activities have a positive mediating effect between the development of technical knowledge and business performance of R&D-intensive firms.
H7: The development of market knowledge has a direct positive effect on innovativeness of R&D-intensive companies.
H8: The development of technical knowledge has a direct positive effect on innovativeness of R&D-intensive companies.
H9: The development of market knowledge has a direct positive effect on business performance of R&D-intensive companies.
H10: The development of technical knowledge has a direct positive effect on business performance of R&D-intensive companies.
H11: Market and technical knowledge integration activities in R&D-intensive firms have a direct positive effect on innovativeness of these companies.
H12: Market and technical knowledge integration activities in R&D-intensive firms have a direct positive effect on business performance of these companies.

Figure 4.1 shows the conceptual framework of the study, which summarises the monograph's main objective, research questions and hypotheses based on the KBV and also the concepts of dynamic capabilities and R&D-marketing integration.

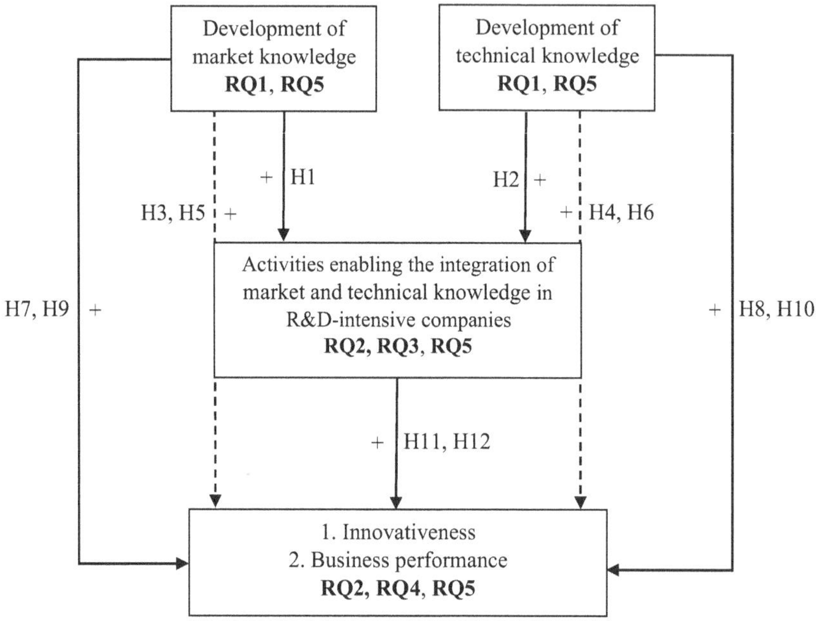

Figure 4.1 Conceptual framework of the study

Note: The solid lines represent hypothesised direct relationships, while the dashed lines represent hypothesised indirect relationships.

The conceptual framework in Figure 4.1 starts with two important elements: the development of market knowledge and the development of technical knowledge. They constitute the basis for further activities, since, as already mentioned, even the best activities designed to integrate market and technical knowledge will not be effective if either of these resources is outdated. Authors of the resource-based approaches, that is the KBV and the concept of dynamic capabilities, have not created models accounting for the integration of market and technical knowledge, while most models developed in relation to R&D-marketing integration (e.g. Wang & Lee, 2014; Li & Chen, 2016; Homburg et al., 2017) fail to take them into consideration. The central element of the conceptual framework is associated with activities enabling the integration of market and technical knowledge, activities which are specific to R&D-intensive companies. The final element of the conceptual framework includes two dependent variables: innovativeness and business performance.

One of the goals of the literature review was to answer RQ1 (What sources of market and technical knowledge are used by R&D-intensive companies?) and RQ3 (How do R&D-intensive companies integrate market and technical knowledge?). The review of the literature has only partly answered these two questions because there is a shortage of studies involving R&D-intensive firms. For example, it cannot be determined which methods of integrating market and technical knowledge analysed in the literature are suitable and implemented in R&D-intensive companies. Moreover, companies in this category can also be using other, modern integration strategies, which have not been studied so far. There are also no studies concerning knowledge sources used by these firms, especially ones in which a distinction is made between market and technical knowledge. Although different sources of market and technical knowledge are mentioned in the literature (cf. Chapter 2), some of them may be irrelevant for R&D-intensive companies and there may be others that such firms rely on but we are not aware of. As a result, the conceptual framework can be perceived as being too general, especially in relation to the activities of market and technical knowledge integration. This is why, answers to RQ1 and RQ3, derived from the literature review, were complemented by the results of a qualitative study conducted among R&D-intensive firms. The findings of this study were used to modify the conceptual framework of the study and served as the basis for the quantitative study, which provided results that were used to answer RQ2 (How does the development of market and technical knowledge affect integration of these knowledge resources in R&D-intensive companies and their innovativeness and business performance?), RQ4 (How does the integration of market and technical knowledge affect business performance and innovativeness of R&D-intensive companies?), and then RQ5 (What recommendations should be made to managers so that they can facilitate the integration of both kinds of knowledge in R&D-intensive companies and, consequently, improve their business performance and innovativeness?).

4.4 Chapter summary

The purpose of this chapter was to review the existing literature on market and technical knowledge integration. One section is devoted to presenting the key aspects and assumptions of the RBV as well as those of the two related perspectives, namely the KBV and the concept of dynamic capabilities. The purpose of the second section was to provide a critical review of research on R&D-marketing integration, which has greatly contributed to the understanding of the problem of market and technical knowledge integration. The main idea of this integration is to facilitate inter-functional interactions in a company, that is between R&D employees (with technical knowledge) and the marketing staff (with market knowledge). The research output on R&D-marketing integration was presented according to the author's division of its historical development.

In the third section, the author describes each of the six aspects of the *research gap* identified after reviewing the literature. This part is followed by the presentation of the conceptual framework of the study, created by combining theoretical insights from the KBV and making reference to the concepts of dynamic capabilities and R&D-marketing integration. Finally, a justification is provided for a qualitative study that was required to modify the conceptual framework.

Chapter 5

Results from a Qualitative Study of Market and Technical Knowledge Integration Activities in R&D-Intensive Companies

The qualitative study was part of the empirical research conducted for the purpose of this monograph. The goal of the study was to get a thorough understanding of the problem of market and technical knowledge integration in R&D-intensive firms and the role of these resources in companies operating in different R&D-intensive industries, especially their impact on business performance and innovativeness. Valuable insights into these aspects, based on opinions and experiences of respondents interviewed during the study, were used to create measures of knowledge integration that were later employed in the quantitative study.

Both the qualitative and the quantitative studies were concerned with companies operating in R&D-intensive industries, which include medium-high and high R&D intensity industries according to the classification created by Galindo-Rueda and Verger (2016). In companies of this kind, R&D expenditures (measured as a percentage of gross value added) exceed 5%. Combined categories have also been used by other authors, for example Brandt (2018), Carbonara et al. (2019) and Dawid and Mitkova (2020). This practice is discussed in more detail in Chapter 1.

The purpose of this chapter is to present the results of the qualitative study, which consisted of 16 in-depth semi-structured interviews conducted with representatives

DOI: 10.1201/9781032642352-5

of 16 R&D-intensive firms. The first part of the analysis deals with the sources of market and technical knowledge used by the companies in the sample. The second part deals with the activities the companies use to integrate both knowledge resources.

5.1 Qualitative research method

As noted at the end of Chapter 4, the literature review provided only a partial answer to the questions about the development and integration of market and technical knowledge in enterprises. Since there are no recent studies that focus on market and technical knowledge integration activities in R&D-intensive enterprises, the author opted for an exploratory sequential research design, which is used when it is necessary to develop new quantitative measurement instruments based on the results of a qualitative study. Hence, the goal of the study was, firstly, to better understand methods that R&D-intensive enterprises use to develop and integrate market and technical knowledge, and secondly, to create new quantitative research instruments. Measurement instruments based on insights from qualitative studies are better rooted in the culture of business entities that are being investigated and are more likely to be perceived as relevant by respondents (Creswell & Plano Clark, 2018). Qualitative data were collected using the method of an in-depth semi-structured interview, which is probably the best choice for this research setup. During interviews of this type, the research tries to find out what respondents know about the topic of interest, elicit their opinions about it and learn how important it is for them (Mears, 2012). A semi-structured interview combines benefits of flexibility and structure (Legard et al., 2003). Unlike a structured interview, it provides an opportunity for dialogue with respondents. In comparison to an unstructured interview, it helps the researcher to investigate aspects that are of interest to him (Brinkmann, 2014).

Respondents were asked open-ended questions, which were designed according to recommendations made by Cook (2008), Yin (2016) or Leavy (2017). Such questions enable respondents to describe a given aspect using their own words. The questions were formulated on the basis of the conceptual framework of the study, the research questions and the literature review. Respondents were asked to talk about the activities of market and technical knowledge integration in their companies, the importance of knowledge integration and specific activities undertaken in this regard and the sources of market and technical knowledge. Questions were also asked about how all of these aspects affected the company's business performance and innovativeness. While the frequency of similar answers was analysed, results of the qualitative study cannot be generalised to the entire population of R&D-intensive companies. The interviews were conducted in Poland between May and September 2019. Respondents included company representatives with a good knowledge of their respective organisations: presidents, executive directors, board members, managers of various levels and heads of R&D departments of 16 R&D-intensive

enterprises. All interviews were recorded, except one, which was conducted on the phone and could not be recorded for technical reasons.[1] The interviews lasted from 1.5 to 2 h. Some of the responding entities agreed to reveal their names, while others chose to remain anonymous. Each interview was personally conducted by the author of this monograph, who had the most comprehensive knowledge of the subject and was able to adequately engage the respondents in conversation and thus elicit more detailed information.

The companies in the sample were quite diverse, though most of them were large firms employing over 250 people. They represented different R&D-intensive industries (Table 5.1) since the purpose of the qualitative study was to collect information

Table 5.1 Profiles of the analysed companies

No.	*Company name*	*Industry*	*Number of employees*
1.	AAA*	Services provided using software developed by the company	Over 250
2.	Cognifide	Development of customised software	Over 250
3.	BBB	Pharmaceutical industry	Over 250
4.	Taskoprojekt	Manufacture of other machinery and equipment	50–249
5.	PamProject	Development of customised software	Under 10
6.	CCC	Manufacture of electronic equipment	Over 250
7.	Kudrycki-Media Service	IT services and other data processing services	20–49
8.	ALVO Medical	Manufacture of medical and dental instruments	Over 250
9.	DDD	Development of customised software	Over 250
10.	Signify	Manufacture of electric equipment	Over 250
11.	EEE	Manufacture of other machinery and equipment	Over 250
12.	n-Educatio	Development of customised software	20–49
13.	FFF	Manufacture of medical and dental instruments	Over 250
14.	GGG	Manufacture of computers, electronics and optical products	Over 250
15.	HHH	Manufacture of air and spacecraft and related machinery	Over 250
16.	Netguru	Development of customised software	Over 250

* *Companies that wanted to remain anonymous are labelled with strings ranging from AAA to HHH.*

about activities that take place in different kinds of R&D-intensive firms and identify the differences between them. Half of the companies were owned by Polish-based entities, and the other half by foreign entities. None was owned by the State Treasury. The majority of the companies offer their products or services exclusively or largely to customers in foreign markets.

The qualitative study is divided into two parts. The first part focuses on the analysis of the sources of market and technical knowledge. The second part deals with the role of each kind of knowledge and the ways of integrating them.

Data collected during the interviews were analysed using the most popular method in qualitative research, namely the constant comparative method, which is used to identify patterns (Merriam & Tisdell, 2016). The raw data included audio recordings and notes taken during the interviews, many of which were held at company premises enabling the researcher to collect additional and useful information by way of observation. The analysis involves searching for repeating elements of the content regarding the sources of market and technical knowledge used by the companies, opinions about market and technical knowledge integration, its role and practical ways of implementing it in the enterprise, as well as ideas on how these integration activities could be improved. The results of the analysis are accompanied by relevant utterances of the respondents.

5.2 Sources of market and technical knowledge

All respondents said that a lot of their market knowledge came from existing and potential customers and explained that such contacts were a crucial way of learning about their needs. One respondent emphasised that this kind of knowledge could not be obtained without maintaining close contacts and building strong relationships with customers. The president of company EEE pointed out that everything was based on direct contact, which is the first and the most essential source of knowledge for a company. A similar view was expressed by a respondent from Signify, who stressed the importance of direct meetings with customers in order to learn what problems they face that need solving. For respondents from Netguru, meetings over coffee with decision makers in certain industries were an important way of finding out what aspects were crucial to making the company's offering attractive for enterprises operating in these sectors. Respondents from Cognifide stressed the importance of getting to know the needs of existing customers in a search for possible ways of expanding the current service offering. Another way by which EEE or Netguru acquire market knowledge from customers is to collect all inquiries from potential customers that the companies are not able to cater for in order to know directions worth developing in the future. A respondent from PamProject also pointed out that customers could be a valuable source of market knowledge, so keeping in touch with them was worth the effort. Some of the analysed companies acquire market knowledge from customers indirectly through their partners, sales representatives or distributors.

In the case of some kinds of products, for example various machines or sophisticated tools, useful knowledge can be obtained from people responsible for service and maintenance, who have direct contact with customers. According to a respondent from ALVO Medical, which manufactures equipment for operating theatres, in this market it is essential to align the needs of distributors with those of end users, which can sometimes be contradictory. It should be emphasised that it may be particularly difficult to learn the exact needs of end users in some markets. ALVO Medical acquires this critical knowledge by having its sales representatives observe surgical operations, sending demonstration products to customers or organising medical consultations in one of its nine Customer Experience Centres located all over the world, including one in Poland. It is not easy for the company to organise such meetings, especially with very busy surgeons, but the company's management is aware that they are worth the effort and are a source of valuable market knowledge.

The analysed companies rarely gain market knowledge from their suppliers, unless they supply products that are complementary to their own products.

Another important source of market knowledge, frequently mentioned by the respondents, are competitors. In contrast to the previous sources, this knowledge is gained mainly through observation. Some larger companies in the sample (e.g. AAA) have dedicated departments tasked with monitoring activities of their competitors.

The analysed companies also acquire market knowledge by collecting qualitative and quantitative data from market research conducted among its existing and potential customers. Such studies are either carried out by the companies themselves or commissioned from specialist market researchers. Many respondents emphasised that market research was an important source of knowledge for them. However, some of the analysed companies, even the big ones, rarely conduct or commission such studies because they are expensive.

Internet search is a practically cost-free alternative, which is exploited by all the companies in the sample. According to a manager from n-Educatio, content published in the Internet is a good indication of industry trends. GGG has its own Internet forum, where partners from all over the world propose ideas for how to improve products. Useful information can also be obtained from certain blogs or Facebook groups. According to a respondent from AAA, Internet-based companies, such as web portals, learn a lot about their target market by analysing traffic on their website and user behaviour.

Market knowledge can also be found in various reports, either those freely available online or those published by large research and consulting firms, like Gartner, Inc., which are rarely used because of their price.

Many of the respondents said they spent a lot of money to send their employees to conferences, seminars and trade fairs. For PamProject, participation in trade conferences is treated as a kind of investment. In addition to being an excellent opportunity for presenting and promoting the company, such events are a source of the most up-to-date market knowledge, which can also be gained from informal conversations between conference participants, by making inferences about current problems and needs. A respondent from HHH also stressed the importance of networking.

Other sources of market knowledge mentioned by some respondents include various industry meetings, which provide opportunities for an exchange of useful information with suppliers and customers concerning the market situation. For example, HHH, which operates in the aerospace industry, obtains a big part of its market knowledge thanks to its membership in the Polish Space Industry Association. Some respondents also mentioned using trade periodicals, but very rarely.

The president of EEE emphasised the importance of megatrends, such as environmental awareness. For some of the analysed companies, market knowledge is associated with certain regulations, national and international (e.g. EU directives).

Various sources of market knowledge mentioned by the respondents are listed in Table 5.2.

It should be noted that while for the majority of the respondents customers were the main source of market knowledge, specific companies used different ways of obtaining this knowledge: for example, the manufacturing firms, rather than getting such knowledge directly from customers, tended to obtain it indirectly through distributors, sales representatives and maintenance and service providers. Some sources of market knowledge can be very expensive, mainly market research or specialist

Table 5.2 Sources of market knowledge

No.	*Source*
1.	Existing and potential customers
2.	Inquiries from potential customers
3.	Former customers
4.	Maintenance and service providers
5.	Distributors
6.	Competitors
7.	Qualitative and quantitative market research
8.	Analysis of traffic on the company's website
9.	Keeping track of content published on relevant websites
10.	Keeping track of content published on relevant blogs
11.	Following relevant Facebook groups
12.	Industry research reports, which are freely available online and sold by research and data analytics companies
13.	Conferences, seminars and trade fairs
14.	Networking
15.	Industry meetings
16.	National and international regulations

reports created by research and consulting firms. As a result, many of the analysed companies were reluctant to spend money to acquire this kind of knowledge and preferred to rely on freely available sources of knowledge instead.

As far as technical knowledge is concerned, the majority of respondents indicated suppliers and customers as an important source. A respondent from AAA mentioned technical manuals and training courses where participants receive certificates confirming that they have learned how to use tools provided by suppliers. A respondent from DDD said that the company relied on support provided by the Microsoft Community Hub, but added that it can only be accessed by registered users. According to a respondent from ALVO Medical, the firm learns a lot from following market trends regarding materials or new technical solutions. A respondent from EEE said that important knowledge about production materials and components used in machines the company manufactures was obtained from its suppliers.

Technical knowledge can also be acquired from customers, especially in the B2B market, since, as some respondents pointed out, customers often have certain standards and requirements that the companies have to meet. Since information about these requirements cannot be easily found online, it has to be obtained directly from customers.

Meetups are another source of technical knowledge, which has grown increasingly popular in recent years, especially among IT companies. These are meetings for those interested in a particular field or technology. Some of the big companies in the sample (e.g. AAA or Netguru) organised internal meetups for its own employees.

Online sources are obviously used by all analysed companies. These include blogs, knowledge sharing portals, like Stack Overflow, open-source repositories, online courses or newsletters. A board member from PamProject emphasised the importance of being able to search for useful information online using different sources. A respondent from the IT industry noted that because technical knowledge in traditional books becomes outdated fairly quickly, e-books are used more frequently.

Some of the companies, like Netguru, rely mainly on online knowledge although this approach has benefits and drawbacks. On the one hand, knowledge available online is very cheap and up to date. On the other hand, one cannot be sure whether a given methodology is completely error-free and this kind of uncertainty is not well looked upon in corporate settings where there are strict security requirements. Because of the approach adopted by Netguru, IT projects for the government or the army remain out of its reach.

In spite of the availability of digital knowledge resources, personal exchange of knowledge at trade fairs and conferences is an opportunity that many of the analysed companies frequently use to learn about new technical solutions.

Knowledge in specific fields can also be obtained by hiring employees with a particular kind of expertise. Alternatively, an entire company can be taken over together with its experienced employees, who are its most valuable resource. During the period in which the study was conducted, such takeovers were carried out by Netguru. Since having a well-trained workforce is crucial for R&D-intensive companies, many of them count on their employees to learn on their own or have them attend various external courses. For some of the analysed companies, experience accumulated over the years of operation is a very important source of technical knowledge. However, as the president of HHH admitted, without new knowledge such experience would be largely worthless.

Finally, new technical knowledge is also produced as a result of own research and development activities, which are particularly important for manufacturing companies. In addition, some of the companies in the sample cooperate with technical universities and participate in scientific conferences. A respondent from Signify stressed the importance of alliances with other firms that supply complementary solutions. A respondent from HHH said that, as in the case of market knowledge, the company gains useful technical knowledge as a member of the Polish Space Industry Association by participating in specialist training courses. It also values its cooperation with international organisations, such as the European Space Agency.

Various sources of technical knowledge mentioned by the respondents are listed in Table 5.3.

Table 5.3 Sources of technical knowledge

No.	*Source*
1.	Customers
2.	Suppliers
3.	Meetups
4.	Blogs
5.	Knowledge sharing portals, e.g. Stack Overflow
6.	Open-source repositories
7.	Traditional and online courses
8.	Newsletters
9.	E-books
10.	Trade fairs
11.	Trade conferences
12.	New employees
13.	Takeovers of companies along with all their technical knowledge
14.	Experience accumulated over the years of operation
15.	Own research and development activities
16.	Cooperation with technical universities
17.	Participation in scientific conferences
18.	Alliances with other companies
19.	Membership in trade associations

The main difference regarding ways of acquiring technical knowledge can be observed between manufacturing companies and those that operate in the virtual space. For firms in the first group, knowledge that cannot be easily found online is often crucial. In contrast, companies in the second group take advantage of modern knowledge sharing opportunities, like meetups, or rely on online resources, free and paid, such as open-source repositories, specialist portals, online courses, newsletters or e-books. However, as a board member from Netguru made it clear, reliance on solutions that have not been thoroughly tested disqualifies a company as a potential contractor in projects commissioned by big corporations or the army, which have very strict security requirements.

5.3 Market and technical knowledge integration activities

It should be noted that all respondents regarded market and technical knowledge integration as crucial for innovativeness and business performance of R&D-intensive companies. According to a manager from Cognifide, it was the most important reason why the company made sure that its technological development was aligned with current and future needs of existing and prospective customers. The person emphasised it was important to always keep in mind that the company exists to create products and services for customers and not start thinking that customers are there merely to receive products and services offered to them. When asked about the effectiveness of integration activities, a number of respondents expressed an opinion that there was still a lot of room for improvement in this regard, which is why their companies were greatly interested in this problem.

A respondent from AAA, who had worked in many IT companies, said that Polish and foreign companies differed considerably in how much importance they attached to market knowledge and its integration with technical knowledge: while managers in foreign firms do not need to be convinced that market research was worth the expense, it is not so obvious for their counterparts in Polish companies. According to the executive director of ALVO Medical, products and services used to be designed behind closed doors but things have changed since then, and in his opinion, companies in Poland still have a lot to learn in this regard.

This is not to say that large foreign firms do not encounter problems with the integration or imbalance between the amount of market and technical knowledge. An experienced president of a large international company (EEE) said that despite having much technical knowledge German companies were not able to exploit it because they could not integrate it with market knowledge.

The majority of respondents indicated that both kinds of knowledge were equally important and one was worthless without the other. The executive director of ALVO Medical said that both kinds of knowledge were intertwined: both were required to function properly and they should be closely correlated. According to Marcin

Stańczyk from Cognifide, proportions between each kind of knowledge may differ, with market knowledge accounting for 80% and technical knowledge only 20%. What matters is that both kinds are treated as important and both are developed.

According to the respondents, what their companies need is more market knowledge rather than more technical knowledge. A manager from one of the IT companies (DDD) said that situations in which they did not know what to do were more frequent than those in which they knew what to do but they did not know how. A manager of the development department of a large medical equipment company (FFF) said that the company's export manager spends a third of the year on business trips to acquire market knowledge from customers, distributors and manufacturers. Sometimes such relationships last for years. According to a manager from Kudrycki-Media Service, which mainly provides IT services for Volkswagen Poznań, it is not technical knowledge that is crucial for the company's business performance but a very good knowledge of its customers.

A board member from PamProject pointed out that technical knowledge could sometimes be an obstacle: technical specialists tend to see many problems connected with a particular application, while experienced employees (without extensive technical knowledge) can sometimes find a simple solution.

All of the analysed companies need their technical knowledge to operate but they cannot achieve their goals without market knowledge, which is critical because it is much more difficult to acquire.

According to a manager from AAA (IT company), it is important to create teams including employees with technical and market knowledge (sometimes referred to as business knowledge), who provide knowledge about what users and/or customers expect. The goal is to strike a balance between what customers want and what is technically possible, which can sometimes be difficult. This is why both sides need to discuss things and convince one another. There was a time when persons with business (or market) knowledge and software developers worked separately in IT companies. Nowadays, they cooperate continuously. The same respondent said it was important to ask questions to clarify frequent misunderstandings between the two groups. A similar view on interdisciplinary relationships was expressed by the executive director of ALVO Medical, who stressed the importance of consultation with end users and observation of how they normally work. He pointed out that there was a time when new ideas were created behind closed doors of the R&D department but with time it became clear that it was necessary to address real needs. The company's management realised that the goal was to decrease the number of surgical site infections; a number of studies had been conducted involving surgeons as well as members of staff responsible for managing or cleaning the operating theatre. According to the same respondent, the acquisition of market knowledge is not easy: one cannot just come up to a user and ask what they need. End users, in this case doctors or surgeons, are usually too busy to list their needs or expectations. Instead, they need to be curious enough to ask questions themselves. A manager from Cognifide emphasised the importance of team diversity, in terms of education, experience or personality traits; it is also important that this diversity should be seen as an asset, otherwise it may cause problems. According to one respondent, an engineer will always have an engineer's perspective, so someone who is not an engineer can potentially contribute to product development by offering a different point of view. What matters is that the exchange of perspectives is perceived as valuable. An interdisciplinary team should cultivate a healthy dialogue and strive to solve problems. The executive director of ALVO Medical admitted that it was difficult to run an interdisciplinary group and that such structures need to be open and internalised by its members to enable dialogue between representatives of different disciplines; for example, the R&D department should include people who do not specialise in technology. Also, a lot in this regard depends on the company culture: to what extent it fosters an open mindset and encourages engineers to get out of their comfort zone. The same respondent said that persons connected with technology tended to keep within the limits of their own discipline and are reluctant to adopt the perspective of an end user. According to a board member from n-Educatio, employees with technical education are very reluctant to become more familiar with market-related aspects and they prefer to stick to their own discipline. If they were able to grasp various market factors themselves, they could set up their own companies and would not have to work for someone else. For the president of CCC, what matters is openness and understanding between employees responsible for market-related and technical aspects. A manager from GGG emphasised the importance of regular project meetings attended by people representing different departments, either face-to-face, which is preferable, or using various videoconferencing tools.

The respondents mentioned a number of factors which inhibit the integration of market and technical knowledge. One of them is the fact that engineers and marketers often have different perspectives on the same problems. The first group is mainly concerned with developing the best possible product, while the main goal of the second group is to make sure that the product can be sold. According to the president of CCC, sales representatives often do not have sufficient amount of technical knowledge about the product. At some fundamental level, there will always be a lack of understanding between both groups resulting from their different goals, for example when it comes to the available range of products: from the perspective of sales, it should be as broad as possible to cater for different customer needs. In contrast, engineers prefer the number of products to be smaller because this makes production easier and limits production costs. The same respondent said it was necessary to find a healthy trade-off in this respect: if a company loses to its competitors, it is a sign that the trade-off was bad.

Knowledge integration is much easier for small firms, where the exchange of information is much better and often takes place during informal conversations. According to a board member from PamProject, close cooperation between employees and quick exchange of market and technical knowledge are what distinguish their company from large foreign firms.

Knowledge integration is greatly facilitated by a flat organisational structure. In the case of some of the analysed companies, there are many intermediaries between people with market and technical knowledge. According to a respondent from BBB, both kinds of knowledge are practically integrated only at the top of the firm's organisational hierarchy, that is between its board members.

A large group of firms in the sample create customised products and services. Respondents from these companies emphasised the importance of close cooperation with each client. In many of these companies this cooperation is maintained by a business analyst, project manager or project owner. According to a manager from DDD, a person in this position should ideally have market and technical knowledge. The EEE company has a list of technical questions that a project manager puts to a client to obtain knowledge enabling the company to manufacture a machine to required specifications. The company also makes sure that internally knowledge flows both ways: from project managers to engineers and vice versa.

As far as market knowledge is concerned, according to a manager who has worked in a number of companies that develop custom software, customer knowledge is crucial for firms that provide customised products or services. In many cases, the acquisition of this kind of knowledge poses a challenge, since customers are not always able or willing to share vital market knowledge. In other situations, customers underestimate the importance of market knowledge, usually because they lack experience in this regard. According to a number of respondents, the biggest problem faced by companies in this group is to make sure that customers specify their requirements appropriately and to keep close contact with them.

According to the president of EEE, many problems result from misunderstandings caused by the differences in how sales people and engineers use language: representatives of the first group tend to be less precise. Another problem mentioned by the same respondent is cultural differences encountered in foreign markets. A manager from Signify pointed out that customers were often not able to translate general requirements into technical ones, which means that company is faced with the challenge of eliciting them from the customer. The president of EEE added that employees involved in a given project should be informed about its outcome; this kind of feedback help project participants to draw valuable conclusions for the future.

Nowadays, to prevent problems of this kind, many companies, especially in the IT industry, use Agile methodologies, such as Scrum, where project teams, in addition to programmers, include members with other roles, such as product owners or product managers, who represent the client, as well as product testers and a Scrum master who provide support. Moreover, the work of the project team is divided into segments, called sprints, whose results are discussed with clients every two weeks. In Scrum projects, the customer does not pay for the end result but for work aimed at implementing certain functionalities. Many respondents said they had tried using the Scrum methodology in their companies but did not find it useful. Others prefer to use certain elements of this methodology, for example having a project manager who liaises between clients and the technical team.

While the Agile methodology certainly helps to integrate market and technical knowledge in many companies, it does not solve all problems. According to a manager from DDD, regardless of the method, the client needs to have a person dedicated to work with the project team, someone who is always there to pick up the phone; the biggest waste of resources happens when the project team does not know specific details.

It can therefore be concluded that the integration of market and technical knowledge is greatly facilitated when the exchange of both kinds of knowledge happens within interdisciplinary teams at low levels of the organisational hierarchy. According to a respondent from AAA, in well-established companies, often foreign ones, top managers responsible for marketing and technical development work on new products side by side. A respondent from Signify pointed out that in his company both kinds of knowledge were integrated at all levels of the organisational hierarchy.

The respondents proposed a number of ways in which the integration of market and technical knowledge could be improved. According to a manager from Signify, in addition to understanding the client's needs, which is the most important thing, the integration activities should be well structured to be repeatable. This is why the company's management tries to describe the activities in the best possible manner. The president of EEE also emphasised the importance of procedures which must be developed collaboratively by all participants of information exchange. Another thing mentioned by the same respondent are good habits that are promoted by people who are deeply committed to their work. According to a manager from GGG, it is important that all employees speak the same language, in the sense of technical and marketing terms, and know they are striving to achieve a common goal.

Another aspect of critical importance for market and technical knowledge integration is how communicative employees are. A respondent from AAA recalled meeting programmers who were so focused on their work they had to set an alarm clock to know when it was time to go home. According to a respondent from Kudrycki-Media Service, companies need people with communication skills and they cannot be easily acquired. The value of communication was also stressed by the president of EEE, who noted that it was not always possible to test a candidate's ability to share knowledge and that their HR department tries to recruit people who are willing to learn. The biggest emphasis on communication skills was placed by Netguru, a custom software development company founded in 2008, which has been growing very quickly. In 2019, the company employed 600 people. According to respondents from Netguru, communication skills of the technical staff are crucial for the company and are carefully evaluated during the recruitment process. A member of Netguru's board went as far as to say that the company suffered from over-communication: the number of posts appearing on various internal blogs is so big that the really important ones need to be highlighted. During the implementation of a project, interdisciplinary teams are created, which in addition to employees from the marketing department include clients. Direct contact between clients and programmers is maintained via a dedicated Slack channel, where the intensity of communication between the two groups is very high. Because all Netguru programmers are willing to share their knowledge, it can sometimes be difficult to book a presentation room in the company's Warsaw office. In addition, the company organises frequent internal conferences, where employees share knowledge.

5.4 Findings from the qualitative study in the context of previous studies

In summary, it can be concluded that the acquisition of market knowledge is far from easy. Existing or potential clients are often not interested in sharing this kind of knowledge for various reasons, for example because they do not have the time or are not able to communicate their requirements precisely. This is why the analysed companies rely on other sources, though customers always remain the most important source of market knowledge, which can be tapped in various ways, depending on the kind of activity undertaken by the company. While the acquisition of technical knowledge is also associated with certain difficulties, it is comparatively easier, probably because the analysed companies are more focused on this resource and are more aware of its importance. Much of the technical knowledge these companies need comes from human resources.

One problem that some of the firms face is that they underestimate the role of market knowledge and, as a result, are reluctant to allocate enough resources to obtain it. Moreover, a number of companies in the sample feel a shortage of market knowledge. As one respondent put it, both kinds of knowledge are indispensable, though, depending on the project, they may be required in different proportions.

A company cannot efficiently integrate market and technical knowledge if its stock of each resource is not sufficient. Therefore, every company should strive not only to keep its technical knowledge up to date but also try to acquire market knowledge. This requires a good understanding of the needs of customers, and sometimes even customers' customers. When a custom product is being developed, it is important to maintain close cooperation with the client to know their needs and expectations regarding the final product. In the case of products created for a larger group of customers (e.g. for a particular market segment), it is more difficult to obtain market knowledge but efforts to acquire it should be equally intensive, for example through market research or market observation.

The sources of market knowledge and technical knowledge used by R&D-intensive firms are, to some extent, similar to those used by companies in general or those operating in other types of industries (e.g. Caloghirou et al., 2004; Keupp & Gassmann, 2009; Tsai & Wang, 2009; Fletcher & Harris, 2011; Dolnicar & Grün, 2013; Rakthin et al., 2016; Chen & Liu, 2019; Paschen et al., 2019). Nevertheless, there are some differences. For example, companies in R&D-intensive industries rarely rely on suppliers to obtain market knowledge. Instead, they maintain contacts with customers, even former ones. While recognising the importance of market research, these enterprises use it infrequently because of its high cost. As far as technical knowledge is concerned, in addition to providing their employees with education opportunities and encouraging them to learn on their own, R&D-intensive companies hire new experienced employees with necessary skills.

The interviews with respondents from the selected companies indicate that knowledge integration needs to be conducted tactfully to make sure that cooperation between teams consisting of people with different personalities and educational backgrounds runs without unnecessary tensions or conflicts. Employees with technical backgrounds do not always understand the way marketers look at things, and vice versa. However, it is essential that the two groups do not stop cooperating and try to convince each other using rational arguments. Nowadays, cooperation within such interdisciplinary teams is unavoidable because firms operate in a highly competitive market, often involving players from around the world, and need to create innovative products; this requires different perspectives and different kinds of knowledge, especially a very good understanding of customer needs and market requirements. It is, therefore, the task of the managerial staff to create an atmosphere in which market and technical knowledge are recognised as equally important and to encourage engineers and marketers to effectively cooperate to find optimal solutions and reach healthy compromises. It should also be noted that the integration cannot be limited to the top of the organisational hierarchy, but must take place at all its levels because the absence of integration activities is particularly evident at the lowest levels. The importance of cross-functional teams for the integration of market and technical knowledge has been recognised in the literature (e.g. Maltz et al., 2001) but has been analysed from a different perspective or only partially (e.g. Verona & Ravasi, 2003).

The results of the qualitative study indicate that companies develop faster when their employees responsible for the technical development of new products take into account market knowledge, appreciate its importance and can easily access it. This positive effect is best exemplified in the case of Netguru, which started as a small company in 2008 and after less than a decade of fast growth was recognised as one of the world's 1000 fastest growing companies in 2017 (Stabe et al., 2017). According to a respondent from Signify, the more market knowledge a company acquires, the better its financial results are.

As regards the concept of dynamic capabilities, particularly the capability to integrate market and technical knowledge, the results presented above confirm the view expressed by Helfat and Winter (2011), namely that organisational capabilities can have operational and dynamic applications. An operational application can be associated with, for example, the creation of new software using the Scrum methodology, while it is manifested as a dynamic capability, for example during the development of a new innovative product or service.

It should be noted that many aspects associated with the integration of market and technical knowledge that the respondents mentioned are consistent with previous studies, for example the role of information technology (Song & Song, 2010), the importance of the organisational structure (Wang & Lee, 2014) and the role of the managerial staff (Li & Chen, 2016). The main difference is the fact that most of those studies focused almost exclusively on activities aimed at integrating R&D and marketing departments (e.g. Shaw & Shaw, 1998; Wang et al., 2014; Li & Chen, 2012, 2016; Homburg et al., 2017) rather than on activities intended to improve the functioning of a company by introducing interdisciplinary teams. The fact that many more recent articles on this topic (e.g. Eng & Ozdemir, 2014; Ali & Matsuno, 2018; Nijssen & Ordanini, 2020) continue this approach can be put down to the fact that they are largely based on older publications, such as Gupta et al. (1986b), Moenaert and Souder (1990), Li and Calantone (1998) or Song et al. (1998), and rely on research tools created many years ago.

5.5 Chapter summary

The purpose of this chapter was to present the results of the qualitative study involving 16 R&D-intensive companies. The analysis started with a description of the study method and the characteristics of the companies in the sample. The presentation of the findings started with the results concerning the sources of market and technical knowledge used by the analysed firms. The second part was devoted to activities these R&D-intensive companies use to integrate market and technical knowledge as well as respondents' ideas on how they can be improved. Finally, the findings derived from the interviews were compared with those reported by other researchers.

While many sources of market and technical knowledge and integration practices employed in the analysed firms are consistent with those described in the literature, there are some differences. R&D-intensive companies rarely depend on suppliers for market knowledge, which they mainly obtain from customers they maintain close relationships with. The most important technical knowledge source for these firms are their own employees, whose skills need to be constantly improved and updated. In the case of knowledge integration, the biggest and crucial difference between the present and previous studies is the general approach to integration activities. Until now, especially in studies of R&D-marketing integration, the focus had been on the integration of R&D and marketing departments, whereas many respondents in the qualitative study described in the chapter emphasised the importance of creating interdisciplinary teams consisting of employees with technical and market knowledge.

Note

1 According to Ward et al. (2015), a qualitative interview conducted over the telephone can also yield valuable information, which is comparable to that obtained through face-to-face interviews.

Chapter 6

Quantitative Results Regarding the Influence of Market and Technical Knowledge Integration on Innovativeness and Business Performance of R&D-Intensive Companies

The purpose of this chapter is to analyse data from the quantitative study by applying the PLS-SEM method and two research models. The models are based on the conceptual framework of the study, literature review and qualitative study. The quantitative analysis consists of two parts: The first part focuses on the effect of market and technical knowledge integration activities on the innovativeness of R&D-intensive companies and the second one deals with the influence of integration activities on their business performance.

DOI: 10.1201/9781032642352-6

6.1 Presentation of latent variables and research models

Under the conceptual framework of the study (see Chapter 4, Figure 4.1), created after a review of the literature, the development of market and technical knowledge is assumed to shape knowledge integration activities, which affect the innovativeness and business performance of R&D-intensive companies. Furthermore, market and technical knowledge development are assumed to have a direct effect on innovativeness and business performance of aforementioned firms. The conceptual framework, created after reviewing the literature, was elaborated using data from the qualitative study, whose results are described in Chapter 5. Presented below are latent variable (constructs) that make up the research models, which represent elaborated versions of the conceptual framework of the study.

After reviewing the literature on the integration of market and technical knowledge, described in Chapter 4, and considering the results from the qualitative study, described in Chapter 5, two constructs were identified that enable effective integration of both kinds of knowledge in R&D-intensive firms:

- Primary: "Diverse, interdisciplinary project teams" (DIPT)
- Secondary: "New product development in cooperation with customers" (NPDC)

The most important construct is called "diverse, interdisciplinary project teams" (DIPT). The inclusion of this latent variable is mainly motivated by the results of the qualitative study described in the previous chapter (the importance of DIPTs was emphasised by respondents from AAA, Cognifide or ALVO Medical) although the role of cross-functional teams has been mentioned by a number of authors. For example, in the context of dynamic capabilities, Verona and Ravasi (2003) reported the example of Oticon, which used cross-functional teams consisting of engineers and marketers, but this aspect was not studied in more detail. Maltz et al. (2001) found that cross-functional teams could improve "R&D's use of information supplied by marketing personnel" (p. 69) by reducing inter-functional rivalry. A decade earlier, Gupta and Wilemon (1990, 1991) reported the results of two studies, in which representatives of R&D and marketing departments were asked how to improve inter-functional relations. The suggestion to encourage teamwork appeared high on the list of ideas proposed by each group. While respondents in those studies may not have specifically thought about cooperation in the form of cross-functional teams, their suggestions clearly indicate that people dealing with market and technical knowledge want to cooperate more closely, and cross-functional teams can be one of the most effective forms of such collaboration. Another thing that should be considered in this context are characteristics of such teams, which determine how effectively they perform. Many respondents interviewed in the qualitative study emphasised the importance of diversity, experience, educational background and personality. Another aspect mentioned in this context, especially by respondents from AAA and Netguru, was the technical staff's ability to share knowledge and communicate effectively, which should be considered and tested during the recruitment stage. The result is consistent with Jemielniak's study (2008) of programmers, in which one respondent stressed how important it is that programmers working together form a well-functioning team.

The secondary construct, namely "new product development in cooperation with customers" (NPDC), emphasises the role of close cooperation between technical employees and customers to better understand their points of view and needs. The best example of this practice is ALVO Medical, which has nine Customer Experience Centres located all over the world, where the company's technical personnel can directly interact with doctors and surgeons and watch them at work in order to be able to create innovative equipment that meets the needs of end users. These centres are sources of unique market knowledge for ALVO Medical. A number of respondents, for example from DDD and FFF, pointed out that when it comes to the creation of innovation and improvement of the company's business performance, market knowledge was even more valuable and sought after than technical knowledge, because, as a manager from DDD said, situations when they did not know what to do were more frequent than those where they knew what to do but they did not know how.

Similarly, as in case of two previous constructs, using insights from the literature and findings from the qualitative study, the author identified constructs concerning the development of market and technical knowledge in R&D-intensive enterprises:

- "Market knowledge development" (MKD)
- "Technical knowledge development" (TKD)

As mentioned in Chapter 4, the decision to focus on the development of both types of knowledge rather than their level at a given moment was motivated by the fact that R&D-intensive firms operate in rapidly changing markets, which means that their market and technical knowledge needs to be frequently updated. It should also be noted that it is difficult to objectively measure the company's existing level of knowledge. Therefore, information about the company's activities aimed at developing both kinds of knowledge is a better indication of the level of these resources in R&D-intensive companies. The most important knowledge sources for enterprises were identified using the literature—in the case of market knowledge (Zhou & Li, 2012; Dolnicar & Grün, 2013; Rakthin et al., 2016; Paschen et al., 2019) and in the case of technical knowledge (Caloghirou et al., 2004; Tsai & Wang, 2009; Fletcher & Harris, 2011; Chen & Liu, 2019; Wu et al., 2020). That said, the author primarily relied on his qualitative study, as it focused on specific types of enterprises, in contrast to studies described in the literature. The MKD construct focuses on customers, in particular their changing needs, and efforts to develop relations with them and continuously monitor market trends and other economic phenomena that are relevant to the company. The qualitative study showed that when it comes to technical knowledge development (TKD) in R&D-intensive companies, qualified employees are crucial, which is why the construct places emphasis on employing well-educated and experienced technical staff and on continuously investing in the development of their skills. Another important activity is investing in the latest technologies since technology in R&D-intensive industries quickly becomes outdated.

The effects of the activities associated with the explanatory constructs described above are measured using the last two constructs created on the basis of the literature review:

- "Innovativeness" (INN)
- "Business Performance" (BPER)

Survey questions referring to each latent variable are presented in Section 6.2.

The conceptual framework of the study was operationalised in the form of two more detailed research models based on the insights from the literature and findings from the qualitative study (see Chapter 5). This kind of approach is commonly used nowadays by many authors (e.g. Cheng et al., 2018; Tu, 2018; Shi et al., 2020). Figure 6.1 shows the relationships between the more abstract conceptual framework of the study, created after reviewing the literature (Figure 4.1, Chapter 4), and the two models designed to verify its validity. The difference in the level of abstraction between the conceptual framework and the models is particularly evident with respect to knowledge integration activities, which were investigated in more detail during the qualitative study. The research models consist of two kinds of latent variables concerning knowledge integration, which are described above, namely primary (diverse, interdisciplinary project teams—DIPT) and secondary (new product development in cooperation with customers—NPDC).

The decision to use two separate research models is motivated by the fact that the effectiveness of operation of R&D-intensive firms is measured by two different dependent variables: their innovativeness and business performance. By using two separate models it is possible to better capture the effect of the analysed constructs on the dependent variables.

It also implies having to split the two hypotheses, H1 and H2, into two corresponding pairs of sub-hypotheses, each containing the same paths, namely H1.IN and H1.BP as well as H2.IN and H2.BP (Table 6.1). Although the repeated analysis of the same paths may seem redundant, both hypotheses (H1 and H2) and the paths that comprise them are components of a different research model containing one different dependent variable (construct)—either INN (innovativeness) in model 1 or BPER (business performance) in model 2. In the PLS-SEM method, a change of even one component in the model can affect relationships between other constructs. This means that all model paths need to be analysed again.

It should also be noted that in contrast to a more general conceptual framework, the research models include two constructs related to market and technical knowledge integration, primary (diverse, interdisciplinary project teams—DIPT) and secondary (new product development in cooperation with customers—NPDC). As a result, in order to validate some hypotheses or sub-hypotheses, for example H3, H4 or H11, not one but two model paths need to verified (Table 6.1). Additionally, in the case of hypotheses 1 and 2 both sub-hypotheses assigned to them must be verified to be accepted.

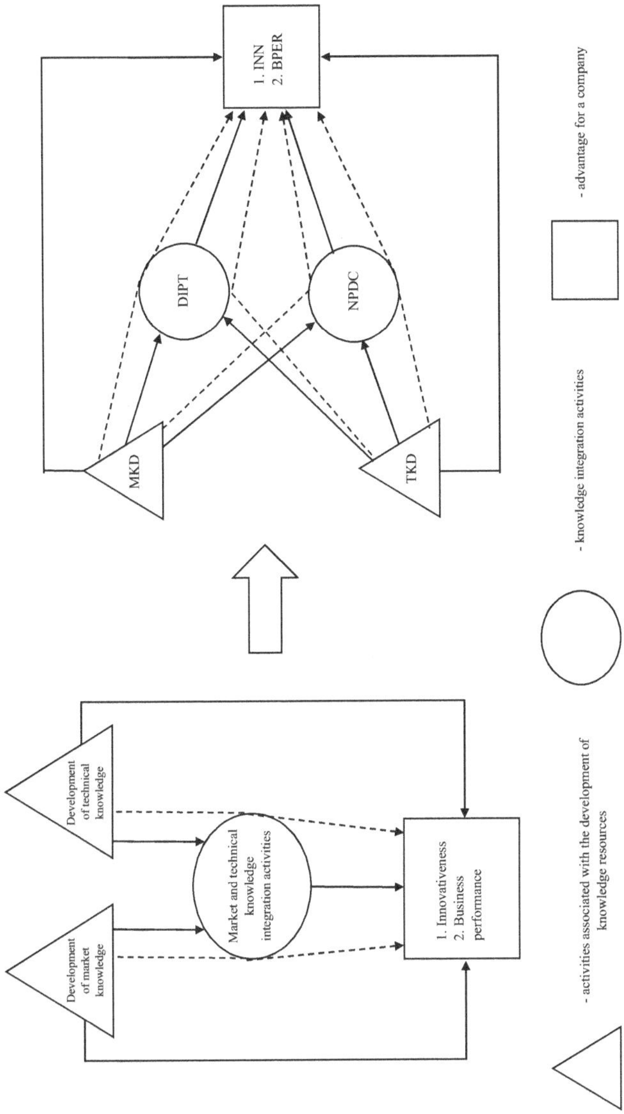

Figure 6.1 The relationship between the conceptual framework of the study (based on the review of the literature) and the research models (based on the review of the literature and findings from the qualitative study)*

Legend: DIPT—Diverse, interdisciplinary project teams; NPDC—New product development in cooperation with customers; MKD—Development of market knowledge; TKD—Development of technical knowledge; INN—Innovativeness; and BPER—Business performance.

** The solid lines represent hypothesised direct relationships, while the dashed lines represent hypothesised indirect relationships.*

Table 6.1 Paths analysed under each hypothesis/sub-hypothesis in both research models

Research Model	*Hypothesis/ sub-hypothesis*	*Path(s)*
Model 1—innovativeness	H1.IN	MKD -> DIPT
		MKD -> NPDC
	H2.IN	TKD -> DIPT
		TKD -> NPDC
	H3	MKD -> DIPT -> INN
		MKD -> NPDC -> INN
	H4	TKD -> DIPT -> INN
		TKD -> NPDC -> INN
	H7	MKD -> INN
	H8	TKD -> INN
	H11	DIPT -> INN
		NPDC -> INN
Model 2—business performance	H1.BP	MKD -> DIPT
		MKD -> NPDC
	H2.BP	TKD -> DIPT
		TKD -> NPDC
	H5	MKD -> DIPT -> BPER
		MKD -> NPDC -> BPER
	H6	TKD -> DIPT -> BPER
		TKD -> NPDC -> BPER
	H9	MKD -> BPER
	H10	TKD -> BPER
	H12	DIPT -> BPER
		NPDC -> BPER

6.2 Quantitative research method

6.2.1 Sample selection method and sample description

The quantitative study, commissioned by the author from the Indicator company, was conducted in April and May 2020 using computer-assisted telephone interviewing (CATI). To exclude the effect of the Covid-19 pandemic, all respondents were informed that the survey concerned 2019. The Bisnode database was used as the sampling frame. According to information provided by Indicator, the database has a smaller coverage error than databases maintained by Statistics Poland. A total of 3528 entities were selected and information about them was transferred into the CADAS software, which used a randomisation algorithm to ensure that each company had an equal probability of being sampled. Fifteen interviewers were employed to conduct the survey, which was stopped after 520 interviews were completed. 798 entities refused to participate and 12 interviews were interrupted. The sample included manufacturing and non-manufacturing companies from medium-high and high R&D intensity industries, according to the classification proposed by Galindo-Rueda and Verger (2016), which are characterised in detail in Chapter 1. The composition of the sample by industry and other sample characteristics are presented in Tables 6.2 and 6.3.

Table 6.2 Number of sampled companies by industry

High R&D intensity manufacturing industries		
Industry	*Number of companies*	*Share in the sample*
Air and spacecraft and related machinery	17	3.3%
Pharmaceuticals	40	7.7%
Computer, electronic and optical products	37	7.1%
Total:	94	18.1%
High R&D intensity non-manufacturing industries		
Scientific research and development	30	5.8%
Software publishing*	–	–
Services provided using software developed by the company	16	3.1%
Development of software according to customer specification	13	2.5%
Development and sale of software	13	2.5%
Total:	72	13.8%
Medium-high R&D intensity manufacturing industries		
Weapons and ammunition	7	1.3%
Motor vehicles, trailers and semi-trailers	41	7.9%
Medical and dental instruments	27	5.2%
Machinery and equipment n.e.c.**	79	15.2%
Chemicals and chemical products	71	13.7%
Electrical equipment	29	5.6%

(Continued)

Table 6.2 (Continued)

Medium-high R&D intensity manufacturing industries		
Industry	*Number of companies*	*Share in the sample*
Railroad, military vehicles and transport n.e.c.	29	5.6%
Total:	283	54.4%
Medium-high R&D intensity non-manufacturing industries		
IT and other information services	71	13.7%
Total:	71	13.7%
Total—all industries in the sample:	520	100%

* *The division into three subcategories was suggested by respondents in the qualitative study.*

** *n.e.c.—not elsewhere classified.*

Table 6.3 Characteristics of sampled companies and respondents

Types of companies /respondents	*Medium-high R&D intensity industries*	*Share in the sample*	*High R&D intensity industries*	*Share in the sample*	*Total*	*Share in the sample*
Number of employees						
1–9	86	16.5%	42	8.1%	128	24.6%
10–49	91	17.5%	41	7.9%	132	25.4%
50–250	80	15.4%	49	9.4%	129	24.8%
More than 250	97	18.7%	34	6.5%	131	25.2%
Total:	354	68.1%	166	31.9%	520	100.0%
General description of activities						
Creation of standard or slightly customised products/ services	239	46.0%	100	19.2%	339	65.2%
High level of product/service customisation according to customers' specifications	115	22.1%	66	12.7%	181	34.8%
Total:	354	68.1%	166	31.9%	520	100.0%

(Continued)

Table 6.3 (Continued)

Types of companies /respondents	*Medium-high R&D intensity industries*	*Share in the sample*	*High R&D intensity industries*	*Share in the sample*	*Total*	*Share in the sample*
Dominant form of ownership						
Polish privately owned	239	46.0%	101	19.4%	340	65.4%
Polish state-owned	6	1.2%	3	0.6%	9	1.7%
Foreign-owned	109	21.0%	62	11.9%	171	32.9%
Total:	354	68.1%	166	31.9%	520	100.0%
Operation in foreign markets						
Company operates abroad	189	36.3%	81	15.6%	270	51.9%
Company does not operate abroad	165	31.7%	85	16.3%	250	48.1%
Total:	354	68.1%	166	31.9%	520	100.0%
Management level of respondents						
Lower (operational)	13	2.5%	7	1.3%	20	3.8%
Medium	161	31.0%	73	14.0%	234	45.0%
Higher	180	34.6%	86	16.5%	266	51.2%
Total:	354	68.1%	166	31.9%	520	100.0%

As can be seen in Table 6.2, nearly three quarters of entities in the sample (72.5%) are manufacturing enterprises; medium-high R&D intensity companies account for 68.1% of the sample. Among high R&D intensity firms, the three most represented sectors include software publishing (8.1%), pharmaceuticals (7.7%) and computer, electronic and optical products (7.1%). Among medium-high R&D intensity enterprises, sectors with the biggest shares in the sample include machinery and equipment n.e.c. (15.2%), chemicals and chemical products (13.7%) and IT and other information services (13.7%).

Table 6.3 shows some characteristics of sampled companies and respondents. As can be seen, the sample composition is well-balanced in terms of company size. Almost two thirds of companies in the sample (65.2%) focus on creating standard products or services, while the remaining specialise in creating products according to customer specifications. It should be pointed out, however, that the share of individualised products in high R&D intensity industries is greater than in medium-high R&D intensity industries. 65.4% of the companies in the sample are Polish private-owned entities. The second largest group are foreign-owned enterprises (32.9%), while Polish state-owned firms account for only 1.7%. Over a half of the surveyed firms operate abroad (51.9%), while the remaining 48.1% cater exclusively to the domestic market. Over half of all respondents were representatives of senior management (51.2%). The second largest group were middle management employees (45%), and respondents from lower management accounted for only 3.8% of the sample. In this case, the proportions between medium-high R&D and high R&D intensity companies were similar.

6.2.2 Survey questionnaire

The survey questionnaire was created after reviewing the literature and accounting for the results of the qualitative study conducted by the author. Individual items (survey questions) relating to each latent variable are presented later in the chapter.

Although, the survey questions concerning the primary latent variable associated with knowledge integration, namely diverse, interdisciplinary project teams, were largely based on the literature review, their final form was heavily influenced by the qualitative study. The author took into account results of a study conducted by Lucas and Bush (1988), which suggests that the number of new products that companies create and their market success depend on characteristics of their employees. The importance of recruiting the right kind of people was also emphasised by Cohen (1988), who observed that the best candidates were "not necessarily outstanding scientists but practical problem solvers and team players" (pp. 48–49). The survey questions concerning diverse, interdisciplinary project teams were also influenced by the results of the study by Maltz et al. (2001), which indicate that the presence of cross-functional teams helped to improve the R&D's use of information supplied by marketing personnel by mitigating inter-functional rivalry between the two departments. It can therefore be inferred that market and technical knowledge integration is greatly facilitated by close, regular cooperation between employees from R&D and marketing departments in the form of interdisciplinary teams whose members have an opportunity to collaborate, get to know each other and build a sufficient level of mutual trust. The survey questions connected with the secondary construct, namely new product development in cooperation with customers, are based exclusively on the results of the qualitative study. Indeed, the idea to include this construct in the model was inspired by the results of the qualitative study.

The questions concerning the development of market and technical knowledge were based mainly on the results of the qualitative study to account for the specific nature of knowledge sources used by the surveyed enterprises, but the results of existing studies were also taken into consideration, particularly with regard to the development of market knowledge through market research, which was emphasised, among others, by Gupta and Wilemon (1990, 1991); moreover, one of the survey questions came from the questionnaire used by Hooley et al. (2000).

Measures of innovativeness and business performance were created on the basis of the literature including Hooley et al. (2000), Deshpandé et al. (1993), Joshi and Sharma (2004), Fonfara (2009), Donate and de Pablo (2015) and Koohang et al. (2017). To measure the company's business performance and innovativeness, the author used comparisons to its nearest competitors, which is an approach used by a number of authors, for example by Hooley et al. (2000), Fonfara (2009, 2012), Rhee et al. (2010), Oehmichen and Puck (2016) and Ratajczak-Mrozek (2017).

Listed below are items (indicators) relating to each latent variable.

Diverse, interdisciplinary project teams (DIPT)

1 Project teams in our company are interdisciplinary, that is in addition to employees with technical expertise (or experience), they include people with other backgrounds, for example in economic sciences or humanities. (DIPT-1)
2 We believe that in our company project teams should not only include people with different educational backgrounds but also be diverse in terms of personality, sex and nationality. (DIPT-2)
3 When we recruit people for technical positions, we pay special attention to their ability to communicate and soft skills. (DIPT-3)

New product development in cooperation with customers (NPDC)

1 New product development in our company involves developing and testing many new ideas. (NPDC-1)
2 We learn a lot about our clients' preferences by working with them on successive versions of new products. (NPDC-2)
3 In our company, technical employees working on new products or improving existing ones have direct contact with clients. (NPDC-3)

Market knowledge development (MKD)

1 Our commitment to serving customer needs is constantly monitored. (MKD-1)
2 Top managers regularly visit important customers. (MKD-2)
3 Customer satisfaction is frequently assessed. (MKD-3)
4 Our company spends a considerable amount of money to monitor the market in search of trends and economic phenomena that are relevant for the company. (MKD-4)

Technical knowledge development (TKD)

1 Our company has well-educated and experienced technical employees. (TKD-1)
2 Our company uses latest technologies and technical solutions available in the industry. (TKD-2)

3 The development of technical knowledge is our company's priority. (TKD-3)
4 Our company invests in developing employees' technical knowledge. (TKD-4)

Innovativeness (INN)

1 Compared to our closest competitors, we introduce more products or services that are completely new (for the company). (INN-1)
2 Compared to our closest competitors, we introduce more product or service modifications. (INN-2)
3 The number of new or modified products or services we introduce to the market continues to increase. (INN-3)

Business performance (BPER)

1 Our company's rate of growth compared to that of our closest competitors. (BPER-1)
2 Our company's total sales revenue compared to that of our closest competitors. (BPER-2)
3 Our company's market share compared to that of our closest competitors. (BPER-3)

For each item, respondents were asked to select one of five options on a 5-point Likert scale, where each value represented the following responses: 1—completely disagree; 2—disagree; 3—do not disagree or agree; 4—agree; 5—completely agree. Because the level of business performance was measured in relation to closest competitors, the options on the Likert scale were as follows: 1—much lower; 2—lower; 3—comparable; 4—higher; 5—much higher.

6.2.3 Data analysis

Data collected in the survey were analysed by applying partial least squares structural equation modelling (PLS-SEM) using the PLS algorithm implemented in SmartPLS 3 (Ringle et al., 2015).

Structural equation modelling methods can be divided into CB-SEM and PLS-SEM, which are regarded as complementary (Sarstedt et al., 2014). Covariance-based SEM is a parametric method and assumes normally distributed data, while PLS-SEM is a non-parametric method, which can also be applied to data that are not normally distributed (Hair Jr. et al., 2017b). PLS-SEM is particularly useful when the goal of the study is to explain or predict the variance of key constructs, for example the company's success, by explanatory constructs, for instance sources of competitive advantage (Hair et al., 2012). It can therefore be concluded that this method is suitable for analysing data collected in the survey.

The use of PLS-SEM is associated with certain requirements. Hypothesis testing can only be performed after conducting a series of analyses. What kind of analyses are required depends on whether the latent variables used in the model are measured reflectively or formatively (Hair et al., 2019). According to Fornell and Bookstein (1982), "reflective indicators are typical of classical test theory and factor analysis models; they are invoked in an attempt to account for observed variances or covariances" (p. 441); "formative indicators, in contrast, are not designed to account for observed variables; they are used to minimize residuals in the structural relationship" (p. 441). All latent variables included in the two research models are reflective. The constructs were measured reflectively because it was assumed that observable, strongly correlated indicators, measured by specific test items, were "caused" by unobservable phenomena (constructs). No attempt was made to test a formative measurement model because it was not assumed that observable indicators could "cause" the phenomena of interest. In the case of reflective measurement models, the following requirements must be satisfied: indicator reliability, internal consistency reliability, convergent validity and discriminant validity (Hulland, 1999; Hair et al., 2019).

Indicator reliability is tested by analysing indicator loadings, which "determine an item's absolute contribution to its assigned construct" (Hair Jr. et al., 2021, p. 186). Indicator loadings indicate "how much of each indicator's variance is explained by its construct" (Hair Jr. et al., 2021, p. 77). Indicator loadings of at least 0.7 are recommended (Hulland, 1999), though slightly lower values are sometimes also acceptable (Birkinshaw et al., 1995; Hair et al., 2011).

Internal consistency reliability "determines whether the items measuring a construct are similar in their scores (i.e. if the correlations between items are strong)" (Hair Jr. et al., 2021, pp. 186–187). It can be checked using two measures: Cronbach's alpha and composite reliability rho_c (CR) (Hair et al., 2019). According to Hair et al. (2019), the first measure is a lower-bound estimate of reliability, while the second is its upper-bound estimate. The values of these two measures should range from 0.7 to 0.95 (Hair et al., 2019).

Convergent validity indicates "the degree to which a reflectively specified construct explains the variance of its indicators" (Hair Jr. et al., 2021, p. 183), which is evaluated by the average variance extracted (AVE) for all indicators assigned to each construct. The AVE for each construct should be above 0.50 (Hair et al., 2019, 2021; Sarstedt et al., 2021).

Discriminant validity indicates "the extent to which a construct is empirically distinct from other constructs in the model" (Hair Jr. et al., 2021, p. 184), that is shows a phenomenon not captured by other constructs (Hair Jr., et al., 2014). Discriminant validity is assessed by ensuring that the square root of each construct's AVE is greater than the correlation between that construct and all other reflectively measured constructs, which is known as the Fornell–Larcker criterion (Fornell & Larcker, 1981; Chin, 2010; Koohang et al., 2017).

Detailed information regarding discriminant validity can be obtained by examining cross-loadings, which involves checking whether each indicator has been assigned to the right construct. It is important that each indicator (item) should be strongly correlated with the construct it is assigned to and weakly correlated with any other construct included in the model. Otherwise, it will not be possible to determine if a given indicator (item) is not associated with a construct other than the one it was originally supposed to measure (Chin, 2010).

Although the Fornell–Larcker criterion along with the examination of cross-loadings are popular tools used for assessing discriminant validity (e.g. Bauer & Matzler, 2014), it has recently been criticised because of its unacceptably low sensitivity (Henseler et al., 2015). An alternative form of assessment is therefore recommended, namely the heterotrait-monotrait ratio of correlations (HTMT). HTMT is defined as "a ratio of the average [indicator] correlations between constructs to the geometric mean of the average correlations within items of the same constructs" (Voorhees et al., 2016, p. 124). Henseler et al. (2015) recommend a threshold value of 0.9 for path models with conceptually similar constructs and a more conservative value of 0.85 for models including constructs that are conceptually more distinct. If HTMT values do not exceed the selected threshold, the model is believed to have discriminant validity.

In PLS-SEM analysis, it is also necessary to examine the coefficient of determination (R^2) of dependent variables (constructs), which indicates how much of the variance of each dependent variable (construct) is explained by its predictor constructs. In other words, R^2 values determine the explanatory power of the model (Shmueli & Koppius, 2011; Hair Jr. et al., 2021). Authors differ in their opinions regarding the satisfactory level of R^2. For instance, according to Falk and Miller (1992), it should be at least 10% to be considered meaningful.

After the above tests have been passed, it is possible to start hypothesis testing. Hypotheses are accepted or rejected depending on the values of the *t*-test. The critical *t*-value at the significance level of 0.05 is $t = \pm 1.96$ (Hair et al., 2011; Koohang et al., 2017).

The following quantitative data analysis is divided into two parts, each concerning one research model. The first model was used to analyse the effect of market and technical knowledge development and integration activities involving both types of knowledge on innovativeness of R&D-intensive companies, while the second one on their business performance.

6.3 Effect of market and technical knowledge integration on the innovativeness of R&D-intensive companies

The assessment of model validity began with analysing reflective indicator loadings for each construct (Table 6.4). As already mentioned, indicator loadings must be at least 0.7 (Hulland, 1999). All indicators satisfy this requirement. Next, internal consistency reliability was verified. Cronbach's alpha and composite reliability rho_c must range from 0.7 to 0.95 (Moores & Chang, 2006; Hair et al., 2019). Since both values of the selected measures for all latent variables meet the requirements, the model can be said to have internal consistency reliability. The assessment of convergent validity involves analysing each construct's AVE. The values of AVE must be higher than

Table 6.4 Assessment of measurement model 1

Construct/indicator	*Loadings*	*AVE*	*Composite reliability*	*Cronbach's alpha*
Market knowledge development (MKD)		0.57	0.84	0.75
Our commitment to serving customer needs is constantly monitored (MKD-1)	0.81			
Top managers regularly visit important customers (MKD-2)	0.70			
Customer satisfaction is frequently assessed (MKD-3)	0.75			
Our company spends a considerable amount of money to monitor the market (MKD-4)	0.74			
Technical knowledge development (TKD)		0.57	0.84	0.75
Our company has well-educated and experienced technical employees (TKD-1)	0.73			
Our company uses latest technologies and technical solutions available in the industry (TKD-2)	0.84			
The development of technical knowledge is our company's priority (TKD-3)	0.75			
Our company invests in developing employees' technical knowledge (TKD-4)	0.70			
Diverse, interdisciplinary project teams (DIPT)		0.64	0.84	0.72
Project teams in our company are interdisciplinary (DIPT-1)	0.79			
We believe that in our company project teams should be diverse in terms of personality, sex and nationality (DIPT-2)	0.81			
When we recruit people for technical positions, we pay special attention to their ability to communicate and soft skills (DIPT-3)	0.80			

(Continued)

Table 6.4 (Continued)

Construct/indicator	*Loadings*	*AVE*	*Composite reliability*	*Cronbach's alpha*
New product development in cooperation with customers (NPDC)		0.72	0.89	0.80
New product development in our company involves developing and testing many new ideas (NPDC-1)	0.79			
We learn a lot about our clients' preferences by working with them on successive versions of new products (NPDC-2)	0.84			
In our company, technical employees working on new products or improving existing ones have direct contact with clients (NPDC-3)	0.92			
Innovativeness (INN)		0.66	0.85	0.74
Compared to our closest competitors, we introduce more products or services that are completely new (for the company) (INN-1)	0.79			
Compared to our closest competitors, we introduce more product or service modifications (INN-2)	0.88			
The number of new or modified products or services we introduce to the market continues to increase (INN-3)	0.75			

0.5 (Hair Jr. et al., 2021). Since the values of AVE for every latent variable meet this requirement, it can be concluded that model 1 is characterised by convergent validity.

The Fornell–Larcker criterion was used to determine the existence of discriminant validity—Table 6.5. As can be seen, bolded square roots of the AVEs in the diagonal are higher than inter-construct correlations. As far as cross-loadings in Table 6.6 are concerned, the strongest correlations exist between indicators assigned to their appropriate constructs, which means that model 1 can be said to have discriminant validity.

As already mentioned, the use of the Fornell–Larcker criterion along with the examination of cross-loadings to assess discriminant validity has recently been criticised (Henseler et al., 2015). For this reason, additionally, the HTMT criterion was used and

Table 6.5 Research model 1—Fornell–Larcker criterion

Construct	*DIPT*	*INN*	*MKD*	*NPDC*	*TKD*
DIPT	**0.80**				
INN	0.45	**0.81**			
MKD	0.51	0.35	**0.75**		
NPDC	0.30	0.30	0.37	**0.85**	
TKD	0.33	0.23	0.23	0.23	**0.75**

Table 6.6 Research model 1—cross-loadings

Indicator	*DIPT*	*INN*	*MKD*	*NPDC*	*TKD*
MKD-1	0.28	0.24	**0.81**	0.35	0.14
MKD-2	0.53	0.30	**0.70**	0.24	0.18
MKD-3	0.19	0.15	**0.75**	0.27	0.10
MKD-4	0.41	0.30	**0.74**	0.25	0.22
TKD-1	0.24	0.19	0.16	0.10	**0.73**
TKD-2	0.30	0.16	0.24	0.28	**0.84**
TKD-3	0.21	0.13	0.10	0.11	**0.75**
TKD-4	0.24	0.20	0.17	0.17	**0.70**
DIPT-1	**0.79**	0.36	0.36	0.21	0.26
DIPT-2	**0.81**	0.33	0.41	0.20	0.23
DIPT-3	**0.80**	0.39	0.45	0.29	0.31
NPDC-1	0.24	0.30	0.27	**0.79**	0.19
NPDC-2	0.27	0.20	0.36	**0.84**	0.23
NPDC-3	0.25	0.26	0.30	**0.92**	0.18
INN-1	0.34	**0.79**	0.30	0.19	0.14
INN-2	0.44	**0.88**	0.29	0.29	0.21
INN-3	0.29	**0.75**	0.25	0.23	0.21

its results are shown in Table 6.7. The most conservative (highest) HTMT value, recommended by Henseler et al. (2015) for models with constructs that are conceptually more distinct, is 0.85. As can be seen, none of the values in Table 6.7 exceeds this threshold, so it can be concluded that the model's discriminant validity has been confirmed.

Figure 6.2 presents the first model with the corresponding results calculated on the basis of the survey data. Values shown along the paths, known as path coefficients, represent the strength of influence that each latent variable has on the other latent variables. They represent the strength of direct relationships (solid lines) and indirect ones (dashed lines) between individual latent variables. As can be seen, all effects are positive. The values shown inside each construct (circle or square) in Figure 6.2 represent what proportion of its variance (R^2) is explained by its predictor constructs.

The statistical significance of the results was assessed using bootstrap validation involving 3000 samples. Bootstrap provides an estimate of the spread, bias and

Table 6.7 Model 1—the heterotrait-monotrait ratio of correlations (HTMT)

Construct	*DIPT*	*INN*	*MKD*	*NPDC*	*TKD*
DIPT					
INN	0.60				
MKD	0.63	0.44			
NPDC	0.38	0.38	0.47		
TKD	0.44	0.31	0.27	0.28	

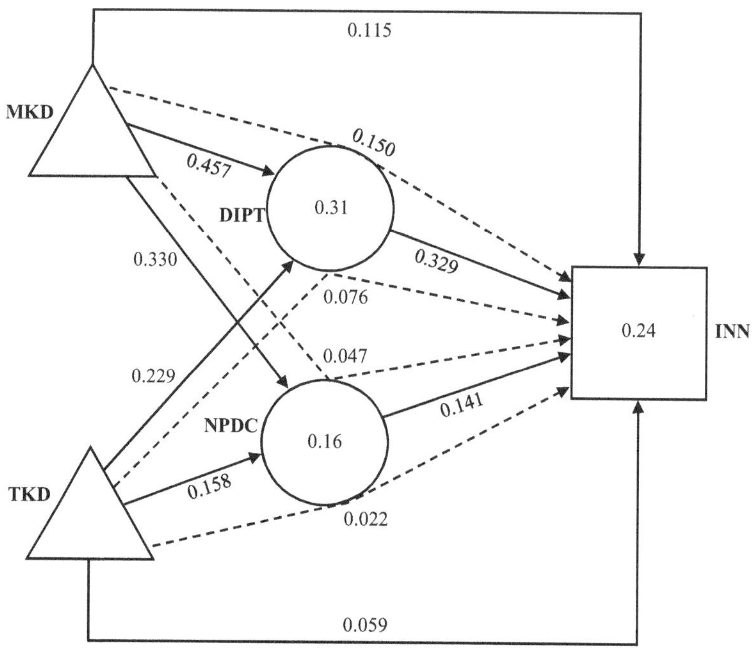

Figure 6.2 Research model 1—the effect of the studied constructs on the company's innovativeness—results

Notes:

1. *The solid lines denote direct effects, while the dashed lines denote indirect effects.*
2. *Values inside circles/square—the proportion of the construct's variance (R^2) explained by its predictor constructs.*
3. *Values along the lines—path coefficients.*

shape of a sampling distribution on the basis of a large, pre-defined number of bootstrap samples, where each one is treated as a sample from the population. The number of cases in each bootstrap sample should be the same as in the original sample. Cases for each bootstrap sample are randomly drawn from the original sample with replacement (Henseler et al., 2009).

Bootstrap validation was used to examine the significance of direct and indirect effects (Table 6.8) and to calculate confidence intervals for the effects (Table 6.9).

As can be seen in Table 6.8, six out of seven hypotheses and sub-hypotheses analysed were accepted. The standard deviations for the accepted hypotheses and sub-hypotheses are very low. The strength of direct and indirect effects for individual model paths can be compared by analysing their confidence intervals, shown in Table 6.9. If confidence intervals for different model paths do not overlap, differences between the strength of their effects are statistically significant. Otherwise, any such differences are not statistically significant (O'Brien & Yi, 2016).

As regards the effects on the primary construct associated with knowledge integration—diverse, interdisciplinary project teams (DIPT)—the strongest effect can

Table 6.8 Model 1—acceptance or rejection of the hypotheses and sub-hypotheses

Hypothesis/ sub-hypothesis	*Path*	β_o	*Bootstrap results*				*Hypothesis/ sub-hypothesis accepted or rejected*
			β_m	*SD*	*t-value*	*p-value*	
H1.IN	MKD -> DIPT	0.457	0.459	0.032	14.306	<0.001	Accepted
	MKD -> NPDC	0.330	0.331	0.040	8.323	<0.001	
H2.IN	TKD -> DIPT	0.229	0.231	0.034	6.722	<0.001	Accepted
	TKD -> NPDC	0.158	0.159	0.044	3.584	<0.001	
H3	MKD -> DIPT -> INN	0.150	0.151	0.024	6.170	<0.001	Accepted
	MKD -> NPDC -> INN	0.047	0.047	0.016	2.919	<0.01	
H4	TKD -> DIPT -> INN	0.076	0.076	0.015	4.981	<0.001	Accepted
	TKD -> NPDC -> INN	0.022	0.023	0.010	2.265	<0.05	
H7	MKD -> INN	0.115	0.116	0.047	2.429	<0.05	Accepted
H8	TKD -> INN	0.059	0.062	0.049	1.211	>0.05	Rejected
H11	DIPT -> INN	0.329	0.329	0.046	7.101	<0.001	Accepted
	NPDC -> INN	0.141	0.142	0.046	3.098	<0.01	

Note: β_o*—original sample;* β_m*—sample mean; SD—standard deviation.*

Table 6.9 Model 1—confidence intervals

Hypothesis/ sub-hypothesis	*Path*	β_o	β_m	*2.5%*	*97.5%*
1.IN	MKD -> DIPT	0.457	0.459	0.394	0.520
	MKD -> NPDC	0.330	0.331	0.252	0.408
2.IN	TKD -> DIPT	0.229	0.231	0.163	0.298
	TKD -> NPDC	0.158	0.159	0.070	0.243
H3	MKD -> DIPT -> INN	0.150	0.151	0.106	0.201
	MKD -> NPDC -> INN	0.047	0.047	0.017	0.080
H4	TKD -> DIPT -> INN	0.076	0.076	0.049	0.109
	TKD -> NPDC -> INN	0.022	0.023	0.006	0.045
H7	MKD -> INN	0.115	0.116	0.022	0.209
H8	TKD -> INN	0.059	0.062	–0.038	0.155
H11	DIPT -> INN	0.329	0.329	0.240	0.420
	NPDC -> INN	0.141	0.142	0.052	0.233

Note: β_o*—original sample;* β_m*—sample mean.*

be observed in the case of market knowledge development (MKD) (β_m = 0.46; p<0.001; 95% CI[0.39–0.52]), a considerably weaker effect is associated with technical knowledge development (TKD) (β_m = 0.23; p<0.001; 95% CI[0.16–0.30]). Similarly, as for the effects on the second latent variable related to knowledge integration, namely new product development in cooperation with customers (NPDC), the strongest effect exists for market knowledge development (MKD) (β_m = 0.33; p<0.001; 95% CI[0.25–0.41]), and weaker for technical knowledge development (TKD) (β_m = 0.16; p<0.001; 95% CI[0.07–0.24]). All of these differences in effect strength are statistically significant because confidence intervals of these paths do not overlap. As regards the effects of knowledge integration on innovativeness (INN) it is split between two latent variables—diverse, interdisciplinary project teams (DIPT) and new product development in cooperation with customers (NPDC). The effect is statistically stronger in the case of DIPT (β_m = 0.33; p<0.001; 95% CI[0.24–0.42]) than in the case of NPDC (β_m = 0.14; p<0.01; 95% CI[0.05–0.23]).

As regards the effect of the market knowledge development (MKD) construct on innovativeness (INN), there are three paths in the model: a direct one and two indirect ones. DIPT is a more powerful mediator between the two latent variables since the indirect path MKD -> DIPT -> INN (β_m = 0.15; p<0.001; 95% CI[0.11–0.20]) is statistically stronger than MKD -> NPDC -> INN (β_m = 0.05; p<0.01; 95% CI[0.02–0.08]). The effect of the direct path MKD -> INN does not differ significantly from the effect of the two indirect paths, since the confidence interval for the path MKD -> INN (β_m = 0.12; p<0.05; 95% CI[0.02–0.21]) overlaps two other indirect paths, namely MKD -> DIPT -> INN (β_m = 0.15; p<0.001; 95% CI[0.11–0.20]) and MKD -> NPDC -> INN (β_m = 0.05; p<0.01; 95% CI[0.02–0.08]).

As regards the effect of the technical knowledge development (TKD) construct on innovativeness (INN), there are only two statistically significant paths in the model. Both of them are indirect. The path TKD -> DIPT -> INN (β_m = 0.08; $p<0.001$; 95% CI[0.05–0.11]) is statistically stronger than TKD -> NPDC -> INN (β_m = 0.02; $p<0.05$; 95% CI[0.01–0.05]) but the statistical significance of this difference is borderline.

While the direct effect of TKD -> INN was found to be statistically insignificant (Table 6.8), it should be noted that TKD has a statistically significant effect on INN, which is mediated through knowledge integration constructs—DIPT and NPDC, as stated in hypothesis 4 (Table 6.8). This outcome shows the importance of the mediating variables in the case of TKD, which are also a key component of the research model.

It is possible that the statistically significant direct effect of TKD on INN would have been detected in a model that does not account for the mediating variables, since the inclusion of such variables suppresses the direct effect, which is partly converted into the indirect effects TKD -> DIPT -> INN and TKD -> NPDC -> INN. A similar situation may have occurred with the direct MKD -> INN effect. Although it is significant in model 1, its strength can still be partially suppressed by mediators—DIPT and NPDC. To test this hypothesis, an alternative version of model 1 was created (1A), which did not include any latent variables associated with knowledge integration; more specifically, it did not include the mediating variables DIPT and NPDC. Model 1A (Figure 6.3) consisted of just two hypotheses:

H1A.1: Market knowledge development (MKD) has a positive effect on innovativeness (INN)

H1A.2: Technical knowledge development (TKD) has a positive effect on innovativeness (INN)

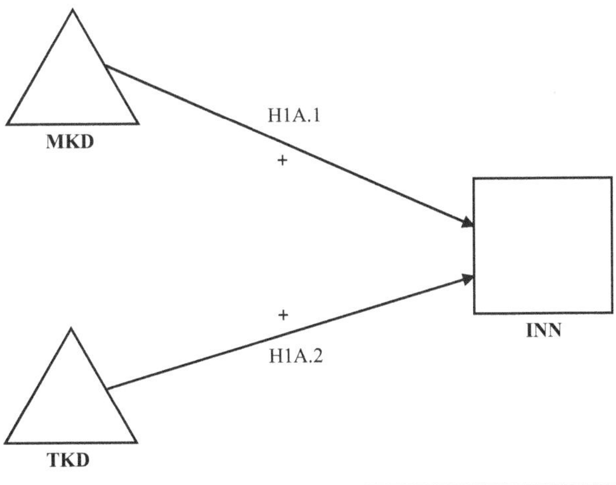

Figure 6.3 Model 1A—the direct effect of the studied constructs on the company's innovativeness

Table 6.10 shows the measurement properties of model 1A, all of which satisfy the requirements: indicator loadings are above 0.7 (Hulland, 1999), AVE values are above 0.5, and the values of Cronbach's alpha and composite reliability rho_c are within the range of 0.7–0.95 (Moores & Chang, 2006; Hair et al., 2019).

Table 6.10 Assessment of measurement model 1A

Construct/indicator	*Loadings*	*AVE*	*Composite reliability*	*Cronbach's alpha*
Market knowledge development (MKD)		0.57	0.84	0.75
Our commitment to serving customer needs is constantly monitored (MKD-1)	0.80			
Top managers regularly visit important customers (MKD-2)	0.70			
Customer satisfaction is frequently assessed (MKD-3)	0.74			
Our company spends a considerable amount of money to monitor the market (MKD-4)	0.76			
Technical knowledge development (TKD)		0.57	0.84	0.75
Our company has well-educated and experienced technical employees (TKD-1)	0.76			
Our company uses latest technologies and technical solutions available in the industry (TKD-2)	0.78			
The development of technical knowledge is our company's priority (TKD-3)	0.74			
Our company invests in developing employees' technical knowledge (TKD-4)	0.73			
Innovativeness (INN)		0.66	0.85	0.74
Compared to our closest competitors, we introduce more products or services that are completely new (for the company) (INN-1)	0.73			

(Continued)

Table 6.10 (Continued)

Construct/indicator	*Loadings*	*AVE*	*Composite reliability*	*Cronbach's alpha*
Compared to our closest competitors, we introduce more product or service modifications (INN-2)	0.82			
The number of new or modified products or services we introduce to the market continues to increase (INN-3)	0.83			

Table 6.11 Model 1A—Fornell–Larcker criterion

Construct	*INN*	*MKD*	*TKD*
INN	**0.81**		
MKD	0.35	**0.75**	
TKD	0.23	0.22	**0.75**

Table 6.12 Model 1A—cross-loadings

Indicator	*INN*	*MKD*	*TKD*
INN-1	**0.80**	0.31	0.14
INN-2	**0.86**	0.30	0.21
INN-3	**0.77**	0.25	0.21
MKD-1	0.25	**0.81**	0.13
MKD-2	0.30	**0.70**	0.18
MKD-3	0.15	**0.74**	0.10
MKD-4	0.30	**0.76**	0.22
TKD-1	0.19	0.16	**0.76**
TKD-2	0.16	0.24	**0.78**
TKD-3	0.13	0.10	**0.74**
TKD-4	0.20	0.17	**0.73**

The model's discriminant validity was also confirmed. As required by the Fornell–Larcker criterion, square roots of the AVEs in the diagonal are higher than inter-construct correlations (Table 6.11). The examination of cross-loadings (Table 6.12) indicates that the strongest correlations exist between indicators assigned to their appropriate constructs.

As in the case of model 1, discriminant validity of model 1A was also confirmed by the HTMT criterion with the most conservative threshold value of 0.85, since all values in Table 6.13 are lower.

The results obtained for model 1A are presented in Figure 6.4. It is worth noting that, compared to model 1, the two predictor constructs (MKD and TKD) explain a smaller proportion of the variance in INN: 0.15, compared to 0.24 in model 1. This means that model 1A, which does not include constructs associated with knowledge integration, has a weaker explanatory power than model 1.

The statistical significance of the results was assessed using bootstrap validation involving 3000 samples (Tables 6.14 and 6.15).

As can be seen in Tables 6.14 and 6.15, values of the path coefficients are higher after removing the mediating variables associated with knowledge

Table 6.13 Model 1A—the heterotrait-monotrait ratio of correlations (HTMT)

Construct	*INN*	*MKD*	*TKD*
INN			
MKD	0.44		
TKD	0.31	0.27	

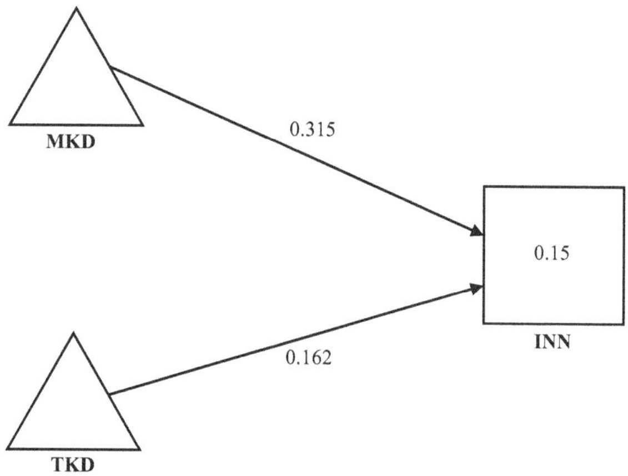

Figure 6.4 Model 1A—the direct effect of the studied constructs on the company's innovativeness—results

Notes:

1. *Value inside the square—the proportion of the construct's variance (R^2) explained by its predictor constructs.*
2. *Values along the lines—path coefficients.*

Table 6.14 Model 1A—direct effects—acceptance or rejection of the hypotheses

Hypothesis	*Path*	β_o	*Bootstrap results*				*Hypotheses accepted or rejected*
			β_m	*SD*	*t-value*	*p-value*	
H1A.1	MKD -> INN	0.315	0.319	0.038	8.287	<0.001	Accepted
H1A.2	TKD -> INN	0.162	0.168	0.046	3.561	<0.001	Accepted

Note: β_o*—original sample;* β_m*—sample mean; SD—standard deviation.*

Table 6.15 Model 1A—direct effects—confidence intervals

Hypothesis	*Path*	β_o	β_m	*2.5%*	*97.5%*
H1A.1	MKD -> INN	0.315	0.319	0.243	0.391
H1A.2	TKD -> INN	0.162	0.168	0.075	0.256

Note: β_o*—original sample;* β_m*—sample mean.*

integration—DIPT and NPDC. In model 1, the path coefficient for MKD -> INN is β_m = 0.12 ($p<0.001$; 95% CI[0.02–0.21]), compared to β_m = 0.32 ($p<0.001$; 95% CI[0.24–0.39]) in model 1A. The corresponding confidence intervals for this path in both models do not overlap, so it can be concluded that the direct effect of MKD on INN in model 1A, is significantly stronger than that in model 1. In model 1, the path coefficient for TKD -> INN is β_m = 0.06 ($p>0.05$; 95% CI[-0.04–0.16]) and its effect was not found to be statistically significant, while in model 1A it is β_m = 0.17 ($p<0.001$; 95% CI[0.08–0.26]) and is statistically significant.

The most important conclusion from the analysis of model 1A is that the direct effect of TKD on INN without the presence of the mediating variables DIPT and NPDC is statistically significant (Table 6.14), which confirms the mediating effect of DIPT and NPDC along the indirect paths TKD -> DIPT -> INN and TKD -> NPDC -> INN, causing the suppression of the direct path TKD -> INN and making it statistically insignificant. A similar effect can be observed for the direct effect of market knowledge development (MKD) on innovativeness (INN), but in this case, the direct path MKD -> INN, though suppressed by the mediating effect of DIPT and NPDC, remains statistically significant. This result also confirms the importance of DIPT and NPDC in the mediating effect of MKD on INN.

In addition to its effect on innovativeness, market and technical knowledge integration can also affect the company's business performance. Therefore, the next section describes an analysis that focuses on this very factor.

6.4 Effect of market and technical knowledge integration on business performance of R&D-intensive companies

The same measures were used to assess indicator reliability, internal consistency reliability and convergent validity of the second model. The results shown in Table 6.16 confirm that all the requirements were satisfied: indicator loadings of each construct are at least 0.7, AVE values are greater than 0.5, and the values of composite reliability rho$_c$ and Cronbach's alpha range from 0.7 to 0.95 (Hulland, 1999; Moores & Chang, 2006; Hair et al., 2017a, 2019).

Table 6.16 Assessment of measurement model 2

Construct/indicator	*Loadings*	*AVE*	*Composite reliability*	*Cronbach's alpha*
Market knowledge development (MKD)		0.56	0.84	0.75
Our commitment to serving customer needs is constantly monitored (MKD-1)	0.81			
Top managers regularly visit important customers (MKD-2)	0.72			
Customer satisfaction is frequently assessed (MKD-3)	0.74			
Our company spends a considerable amount of money to monitor the market (MKD-4)	0.74			
Technical knowledge development (TKD)		0.57	0.84	0.75
The company has well-educated and experienced technical employees (TKD-1)	0.73			
Our company uses latest technologies and technical solutions available in the industry (TKD-2)	0.83			
The development of technical knowledge is our company's priority (TKD-3)	0.74			
Our company invests in developing employees' technical knowledge (TKD-4)	0.71			

(Continued)

Table 6.16 (Continued)

Construct/indicator	*Loadings*	*AVE*	*Composite reliability*	*Cronbach's alpha*
Diverse, interdisciplinary project teams (DIPT)		0.64	0.84	0.72
Project teams in our company are interdisciplinary (DIPT-1)	0.79			
We believe that in our company project teams should be diverse in terms of personality, sex and nationality (DIPT-2)	0.82			
When we are recruiting people for technical positions, we pay special attention to their ability to communicate and soft skills (DIPT-3)	0.79			
New product development in cooperation with customers (NPDC)		0.72	0.89	0.80
New product development in our company involves developing and testing many new ideas (NPDC-1)	0.79			
We learn a lot about our clients' preferences by working with them on successive versions of new products (NPDC-2)	0.84			
In our company technical employees working on new products or improving existing ones have direct contact with clients (NPDC-3)	0.92			
Business performance (BPER)		0.80	0.92	0.87
Our company's rate of growth compared to that of our closest competitors (BPER-1)	0.85			
Our company's total sales revenue compared to that of our closest competitors (BPER-2)	0.91			
Our company's market share compared to that of our closest competitors (BPER-3)	0.92			

Table 6.17 shows the results of the analysis of the Fornell–Larcker criterion. As can be seen, the bolded square roots of the AVE values in the diagonal are higher than inter-construct correlations. Moving on to cross-loadings in Table 6.18, the strongest correlations exist between indicators assigned to their appropriate constructs, which means that model 2 can be said to have discriminant validity.

The model's discriminant validity was also confirmed by the HTMT criterion (Table 6.19), since none of the values in the table exceeds the threshold of 0.85 (Henseler et al., 2015).

Table 6.17 Model 2—Fornell–Larcker criterion

Construct	*BPER*	*DIPT*	*MKD*	*NPDC*	*TKD*
BPER	**0.89**				
DIPT	0.55	**0.80**			
MKD	0.44	0.51	**0.75**		
NPDC	0.34	0.30	0.36	**0.85**	
TKD	0.25	0.33	0.23	0.23	**0.75**

Table 6.18 Model 2—cross-loadings

Indicator	*BPER*	*DIPT*	*MKD*	*NPDC*	*TKD*
MKD-1	0.27	0.28	**0.81**	0.35	0.14
MKD-2	0.42	0.54	**0.72**	0.24	0.18
MKD-3	0.18	0.19	**0.74**	0.27	0.10
MKD-4	0.36	0.41	**0.74**	0.25	0.22
TKD-1	0.19	0.24	0.16	0.10	**0.73**
TKD-2	0.18	0.30	0.24	0.28	**0.83**
TKD-3	0.13	0.21	0.10	0.11	**0.74**
TKD-4	0.25	0.24	0.17	0.17	**0.71**
DIPT-1	0.42	**0.79**	0.36	0.21	0.26
DIPT-2	0.45	**0.82**	0.42	0.20	0.23
DIPT-3	0.45	**0.79**	0.45	0.29	0.31
NPDC-1	0.33	0.23	0.27	**0.79**	0.19
NPDC-2	0.24	0.27	0.35	**0.84**	0.23
NPDC-3	0.29	0.25	0.30	**0.92**	0.18
BPER-1	**0.85**	0.45	0.36	0.30	0.20
BPER-2	**0.91**	0.45	0.38	0.27	0.21
BPER-3	**0.92**	0.56	0.44	0.33	0.26

Table 6.19 Model 2—the heterotrait-monotrait ratio of correlations (HTMT)

Construct	*BPER*	*DIPT*	*MKD*	*NPDC*	*TKD*
BPER					
DIPT	0.69				
MKD	0.50	0.63			
NPDC	0.40	0.38	0.47		
TKD	0.30	0.44	0.27	0.28	

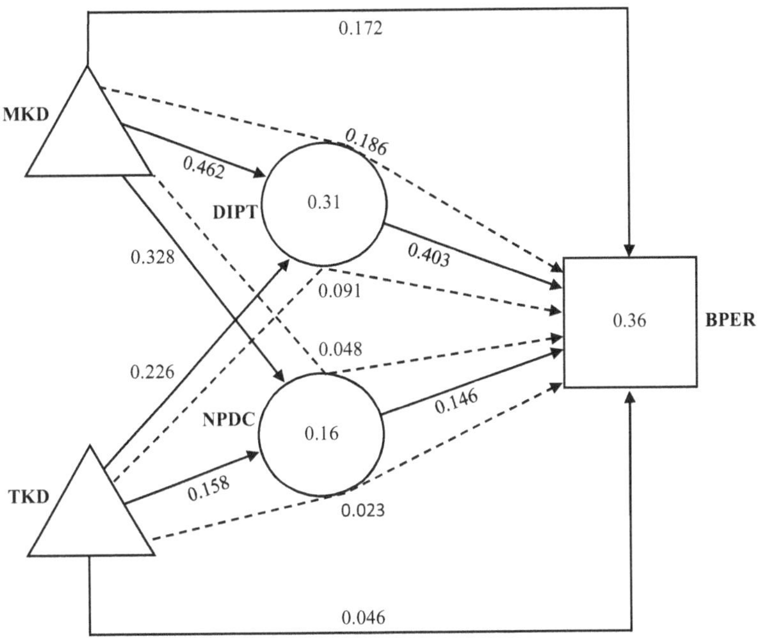

Figure 6.5 Model 2—the effect of the studied constructs on the company's business performance—results

Notes:

1. *The solid lines denote direct effects, while the dashed lines denote indirect effects.*
2. *Values inside the circle/square—the proportion of the construct's variance (R^2) explained by its predictor constructs.*
3. *Values along the lines—path coefficients.*

Figure 6.5 presents the results for the second model. Values shown along the paths, known as path coefficients, represent the strength of influence that each latent variable has on the other latent variables. They represent the strength of direct relationships (solid lines) and indirect ones (dashed lines) between individual latent variables. As can be seen, all effects are positive. Values shown inside each construct (circle or square) in Figure 6.5 represent what proportion of its variance (R^2) is explained by its predictor constructs.

Results of bootstrap validation involving 3000 samples with respect to direct and indirect effects are presented in Table 6.20, and those regarding their corresponding confidence intervals in Table 6.21.

Table 6.20 shows that, as in the case of model 1, six out of seven hypotheses and sub-hypotheses analysed were accepted, with very low standard deviations. The strength and statistical significance of direct and indirect effects for individual model paths were compared by analysing bootstrap confidence intervals, shown in Table 6.21. As already mentioned, the existence of statistically significant differences between observed effects can be confirmed if their corresponding confidence intervals do not overlap (O'Brien & Yi, 2016).

Like in model 1, the strongest, statistically significant direct effect on diverse interdisciplinary project teams (DIPT) is associated with MKD ($\beta_m = 0.46$; $p<0.001$; 95% CI[0.40–0.52]), and a much weaker effect exists for technical knowledge development (TKD) ($\beta_m = 0.23$; $p<0.001$; 95% CI[0.16–0.30]). The difference is

Table 6.20 Model 2—acceptance or rejection of the hypotheses and sub-hypotheses

Hypothesis/ sub-hypothesis	*Path*	β_o	*Bootstrap results*				*Hypothesis/ sub-hypothesis accepted or rejected*
			β_m	*SD*	*t-value*	*p-value*	
H1.BP	MKD -> DIPT	0.462	0.463	0.032	14.397	<0.001	Accepted
	MKD -> NPDC	0.328	0.330	0.040	8.299	<0.001	
H2.BP	TKD -> DIPT	0.226	0.228	0.034	6.625	<0.001	Accepted
	TKD -> NPDC	0.158	0.159	0.045	3.506	<0.001	
H5	MKD -> DIPT -> BPER	0.186	0.187	0.023	8.153	<0.001	Accepted
	MKD -> NPDC -> BPER	0.048	0.048	0.014	3.445	<0.01	
H6	TKD -> DIPT -> BPER	0.091	0.092	0.016	5.593	<0.001	Accepted
	TKD -> NPDC -> BPER	0.023	0.023	0.009	2.520	<0.05	
H9	MKD -> BPER	0.172	0.172	0.041	4.147	<0.001	Accepted
H10	TKD -> BPER	0.046	0.047	0.039	1.185	>0.05	Rejected
H12	DIPT -> BPER	0.403	0.404	0.040	10.095	<0.001	Accepted
	NPDC -> BPER	0.146	0.145	0.039	3.752	<0.001	

Note: β_o*—original sample;* β_m*—sample mean; SD—standard deviation.*

Table 6.21 Model 2—confidence intervals

Hypothesis/ sub-hypothesis	*Path*	β_o	β_m	*2.5%*	*97.5%*
1.BP	MKD -> DIPT	0.462	0.463	0.398	0.524
	MKD -> NPDC	0.328	0.330	0.253	0.406
2.BP	TKD -> DIPT	0.226	0.228	0.162	0.297
	TKD -> NPDC	0.158	0.159	0.071	0.245
H5	MKD -> DIPT -> BPER	0.186	0.187	0.145	0.233
	MKD -> NPDC -> BPER	0.048	0.048	0.021	0.077
H6	TKD -> DIPT -> BPER	0.091	0.092	0.062	0.127
	TKD -> NPDC -> BPER	0.023	0.023	0.008	0.043
H9	MKD -> BPER	0.172	0.172	0.090	0.253
H10	TKD -> BPER	0.046	0.047	-0.030	0.121
H12	DIPT -> BPER	0.403	0.404	0.323	0.480
	NPDC -> BPER	0.146	0.145	0.068	0.223

Note: β_o*—original sample;* β_m*—sample mean.*

statistically significant—confidence intervals of the paths do not overlap. As regards the effects on new product development in cooperation with customers (NPDC), a stronger one is associated with market knowledge development (MKD) (β_m = 0.33; $p<0.001$; 95% CI[0.25–0.41]). A weaker effect exists for technical knowledge development (TKD) (β_m = 0.16; $p<0.001$; 95% CI[0.07–0.25]), but statistical significance of the difference is borderline. Similarly, as in the case of the previous model, the effect of knowledge integration on business performance (BPER) is split between two constructs. The strongest one is associated with diverse, interdisciplinary project teams (DIPT) (β_m = 0.40; $p<0.001$; 95% CI[0.32–0.48]), and a much weaker one exists for new product development in cooperation with customers (NPDC) (β_m = 0.15; $p<0.001$; 95% CI[0.07–0.22]). The confidence intervals of the paths do not overlap; therefore, the difference in the effect strengths is statistically significant.

As regards the effect of the market knowledge development (MKD) construct on business performance (BPER), it consists of three paths—a direct one and two indirect ones. In the case of indirect paths, MKD -> DIPT -> BPER (β_m = 0.19; $p<0.001$; 95% CI[0.15–0.23]) is statistically stronger than MKD -> NPDC -> BPER (β_m = 0.05; $p<0.01$; 95% CI[0.02–0.08]). Similarly, MKD -> BPER (β_m = 0.17; $p<0.001$; 95% CI[0.09–0.25]) is statistically stronger than MKD -> NPDC -> BPER (β_m = 0.05; $p<0.01$; 95% CI[0.02–0.08]) as in both cases the confidence intervals of the compared paths do not overlap. Nevertheless, the effect of the path MKD -> DIPT -> BPER (β_m = 0.19; p<0.001; 95% CI[0.15–0.23]) does not differ significantly from the effect of the path MKD -> BPER (β_m = 0.17; p<0.001; 95% CI[0.09–0.25]) as the confidence intervals of their paths overlap.

In terms of effect of technical knowledge development (TKD) in business performance (BPER), the model includes just two statistically significant, indirect paths. The path TKD -> DIPT -> BPER (β_m = 0.09; p<0.001; 95% CI[0.06–0.13]) is statistically stronger than TKD -> NPDC -> BPER (β_m = 0.02; p<0.05; 95% CI[0.01–0.04]) as the confidence intervals of their paths do not overlap.

The direct effect TKD -> BPER was found to be statistically insignificant (Table 6.20). However, a statistically significant indirect effect described above exists between TKD and BPER, mediated by the DIPT and NPDC constructs. As in the earlier model, this result indicates the relevance of these mediators. To test if the direct effect of TKD on BPER is not suppressed by the mediating variable, an alternative version of model 2 was created (2A), which did not include any latent variables associated with knowledge integration. Model 2A (Figure 6.6) consisted of just two hypotheses:

H2A.1: Market knowledge development (MKD) has a positive effect on business performance (BPER)
H2A.2: Technical knowledge development (TKD) has a positive effect on business performance (BPER)

Table 6.22 presents measurement properties of model 2A, all of which satisfy the requirements: indicator loadings are above 0.7 (Hulland, 1999), AVE values are above 0.5, and the values of Cronbach's alpha and composite reliability rho$_c$ are within the range of 0.7–0.95 (Moores & Chang, 2006; Hair et al., 2019).

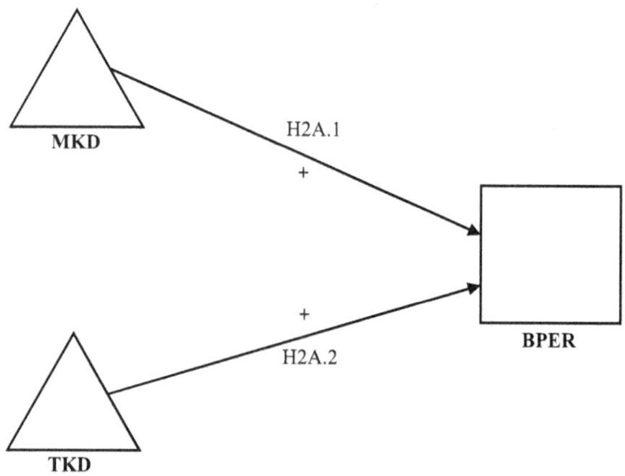

Figure 6.6 Model 2A—the direct effect of the studied constructs on the company's business performance

Table 6.22 Assessment of model 2A

Construct/indicator	*Loadings*	*AVE*	*Composite reliability*	*Cronbach's alpha*
Market knowledge development (MKD)		0.56	0.83	0.75
Our commitment to serving customer needs is constantly monitored (MKD-1)	0.78			
Top managers regularly visit important customers (MKD-2)	0.73			
Customer satisfaction is frequently assessed (MKD-3)	0.72			
Our company spends a considerable amount of money to monitor the market (MKD-4)	0.75			
Technical knowledge development (TKD)		0.56	0.84	0.75
The company has well-educated and experienced technical employees (TKD-1)	0.73			
Our company uses latest technologies and technical solutions available in the industry (TKD-2)	0.78			
The development of technical knowledge is our company's priority (TKD-3)	0.72			
Our company invests in developing employees' technical knowledge (TKD-4)	0.76			
Business performance (BPER)		0.80	0.92	0.87
Our company's rate of growth compared to that of our closest competitors (BPER-1)	0.85			
Our company's total sales revenue compared to that of our closest competitors (BPER-2)	0.91			
Our company's market share compared to that of our closest competitors (BPER-3)	0.92			

The model's discriminant validity was confirmed. As required by the Fornell–Larcker criterion, square roots of the AVEs in the diagonal are higher than inter-construct correlations (Table 6.23). Cross-loadings in Table 6.24 indicate that the strongest correlations exist between indicators assigned to their appropriate constructs.

In addition, discriminant validity of model 2A was also confirmed by the HTMT criterion: all values in Table 6.25 are below the threshold value of 0.85.

The results obtained for model 2A are presented in Figure 6.7. As was the case with model 1 and 1A, after removing constructs associated with knowledge integration, the explanatory power of model 2A is lower than that of model 2, since the two predictor constructs (MKD and TKD) explain a smaller proportion of the variance (R^2) in BPER: 0.23 versus 0.36 in model 2.

Table 6.23 Model 2A—Fornell–Larcker criterion

Construct	*BPER*	*MKD*	*TKD*
BPER	**0.89**		
MKD	0.45	**0.75**	
TKD	0.26	0.23	**0.75**

Table 6.24 Model 2A—cross-loadings

Indicator	*BPER*	*MKD*	*TKD*
BPER-1	**0.85**	0.37	0.20
BPER-2	**0.91**	0.38	0.22
BPER-3	**0.92**	0.45	0.27
MKD-1	0.27	**0.78**	0.14
MKD-2	0.42	**0.73**	0.19
MKD-3	0.18	**0.72**	0.10
MKD-4	0.36	**0.75**	0.22
TKD-1	0.19	0.16	**0.73**
TKD-2	0.18	0.24	**0.78**
TKD-3	0.13	0.10	**0.72**
TKD-4	0.25	0.17	**0.76**

Table 6.25 Model 2A—the heterotrait-monotrait ratio of correlations (HTMT)

Construct	*BPER*	*MKD*	*TKD*
BPER			
MKD	0.50		
TKD	0.30	0.27	

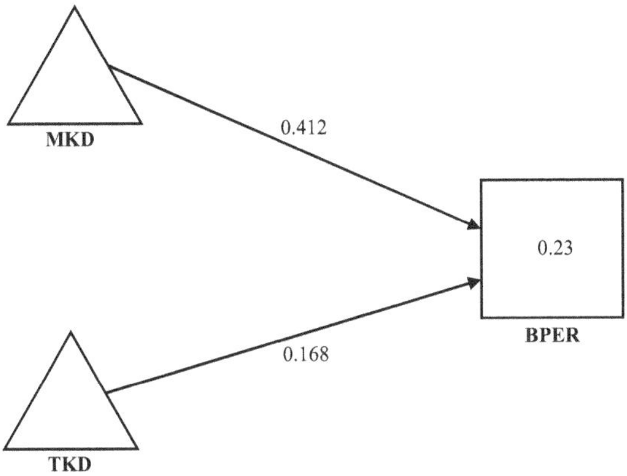

Figure 6.7 Model 2A—the direct effect of the studied constructs on the company's business performance—results

Notes:
1. *Value inside the square—the proportion of the construct's variance (R^2) explained by its predictor constructs.*
2. *Values along the lines—path coefficients.*

Table 6.26 Model 2A—direct effects—acceptance or rejection of hypotheses

Hypothesis	*Path*	β_o	*Bootstrap results*				*Hypotheses accepted or rejected*
			β_m	*SD*	*t-value*	*p-value*	
H2A.1	MKD -> BPER	0.412	0.414	0.032	12.978	<0.001	Accepted
H2A.2	TKD -> BPER	0.168	0.173	0.039	4.299	<0.001	Accepted

Note: β_o*—Original Sample;* β_m*—Sample Mean; SD—Standard Deviation.*

Table 6.27 Model 2A—direct effects—confidence intervals

Hypothesis	*Path*	β_o	β_m	*2.5%*	*97.5%*
H1A.1	MKD -> BPER	0.412	0.414	0.351	0.474
H1A.2	TKD -> BPER	0.168	0.173	0.094	0.247

Note: β_o*—original sample;* β_m*—sample mean.*

The statistical significance of the results was assessed using bootstrap validation involving 3000 samples (Tables 6.26 and 6.27).

As can be seen in Tables 6.26 and 6.27, values of the path coefficients in model 2A are higher than the corresponding ones in model 2. The path coefficient for MKD -> BPER in model 2 is $\beta_m = 0.17$ ($p<0.001$; 95% CI[0.09–0.25]), while in model 2A it is $\beta_m = 0.41$ ($p<0.001$; 95% CI[0.35–0.47]). The corresponding confidence intervals for this path in both models do not overlap, so it can be concluded that the direct effect of MKD on BPER in model 2A is significantly stronger than that in model 2. In model 2, the path coefficient for TKD -> BPER is $\beta_m = 0.05$ ($p>0.05$; 95% CI[-0.03–0.12]), and the effect was not found to be statistically significant. The corresponding path coefficient in model 2A is $\beta_m = 0.17$ ($p<0.001$; 95% CI[0.09–0.25]) and the effect is statistically significant.

As in the case of model 1A, the most important conclusion from the analysis of model 2A is that the direct effect of TKD on BPER without the presence of the mediating variables DIPT and NPDC is statistically significant (Table 6.26). This confirms the importance of the knowledge integration constructs DIPT and NPDC as mediators, as the effect is transferred to the indirect paths TKD -> DIPT -> BPER and TKD -> DIPT -> BPER, as a result the direct path TKD -> BPER is sufficiently suppressed to be statistically insignificant. A similar consequence can be observed for the effect of market knowledge development (MKD) on business performance (BPER), but in this case, the direct path MKD -> BPER, though suppressed by the mediating effect of DIPT and NPDC, as in the case of model 1, remains statistically significant. This result also confirms the importance of DIPT and NPDC in mediating the effect of MKD on BPER.

6.5 Summary of hypotheses validation and analysis of the results in the context of previous studies

Most of the hypotheses were directly verified in the two preceding sections. However, in order to validate hypotheses 1 and 2, the sub-hypotheses assigned to them had to be verified first. As shown in Table 6.28, since all sub-hypotheses were accepted, hypotheses 1 and 2 can also be accepted.

As shown in Table 6.29, 10 out of the 12 hypotheses were accepted. Two hypotheses were rejected, namely:

H8: The development of technical knowledge has a direct positive effect on innovativeness of R&D-intensive companies.

H10: The development of technical knowledge has a direct positive effect on business performance of R&D-intensive companies.

Table 6.28 Verification of hypotheses 1 and 2

Hypothesis	*Hypothesis accepted/rejected*	*Sub-hypothesis*	*Sub-hypothesis accepted/rejected*
Hypothesis 1	Accepted	Sub-hypothesis 1.IN	Accepted
		Sub-hypothesis 1.BP	Accepted
Hypothesis 2	Accepted	Sub-hypothesis 2.IN	Accepted
		Sub-hypothesis 2.BP	Accepted

Table 6.29 Summary of hypotheses verification results

Hypothesis	*Hypothesis accepted/rejected*
Hypothesis 1	Accepted
Hypothesis 2	Accepted
Hypothesis 3	Accepted
Hypothesis 4	Accepted
Hypothesis 5	Accepted
Hypothesis 6	Accepted
Hypothesis 7	Accepted
Hypothesis 8	Rejected
Hypothesis 9	Accepted
Hypothesis 10	Rejected
Hypothesis 11	Accepted
Hypothesis 12	Accepted

As can be seen, both rejected hypotheses are related to the direct impact of technical knowledge development on innovativeness (H8) or business performance (H10) of R&D-intensive companies. Moreover, the validation results confirm the indirect effect of technical knowledge development on innovativeness and business performance in the two main research models (1 and 2), which is mediated through latent variables related to knowledge integration. The analysis of the alternative research models (1A and 2A), which did not include constructs related to knowledge integration revealed a statistically significant direct effect of technical knowledge development on both innovativeness and business performance of R&D-intensive companies. This is because the presence of strong mediators in models 1 and 2 causes a suppression of direct paths, making their effect statistically insignificant. This kind of result provides evidence of the strength and importance of constructs related to market and technical knowledge integration, which act as mediators between technical knowledge development and innovativeness as well as business performance of R&D-intensive enterprises.

This result confirms previous views regarding the importance of market and technical knowledge in the enterprise (e.g. Deligianni et al., 2015; Suseno & Pinnington, 2018). It is also a confirmation of Grant's opinion (1996a, 1996b) about knowledge integration based on the KBV with respect to market and technical knowledge. The result also fills a research gap in this area, as highlighted by Azari et al. (2020).

In view of the above analyses, a number of conclusions can be drawn. The literature emphasises the effect of market and technical knowledge on the company's effectiveness (e.g. Li & Cavusgil, 1999; Giuliani, 2008; Bohlmann et al., 2013). The results of the study described above show that activities involving market and technical knowledge integration are strong mediators between the development of market and technical knowledge and innovativeness and business performance of R&D-intensive enterprises. However, the study has demonstrated that this mediating effect does not necessarily exclude the existence of a direct effect. More specifically, in addition to being mediated through the knowledge integration constructs, the development of market knowledge also has a direct effect on innovativeness and business performance. In the case of the development of technical knowledge, the paths of the direct effect on innovativeness and business performance turned out to be statistically insignificant in the two main models. This result shows the complexity of influences between individual activities of the company and their effects, but, above all, it shows that the development of technical knowledge in R&D-intensive enterprises without integrating it with current market knowledge may not bring the expected effects.

In addition to verifying the research hypotheses by means of the research models, the author identified a number of factors that foster market and technical knowledge integration, which are captured by two constructs related to activities involving knowledge integration in R&D-intensive enterprises, and a number of sources of market and technical knowledge that are particularly valuable for enterprises of this kind. One of them is the creation of cross-functional teams (Maltz et al., 2001). This is the most important component of both research models used in the quantitative study. In particular, the existence of such interdisciplinary teams was found to have a positive effect on innovativeness and business performance of R&D-intensive firms provided that such teams meet additional requirements: technical employees are effective communicators and team members not only represent different areas of expertise (technical and market knowledge) but are also sufficiently diverse in terms of sex, personality and nationality. These criteria were mentioned by the respondents during the qualitative study and were confirmed by the questionnaire survey. In addition to the key role of diverse, interdisciplinary project teams in both research models, the other identified latent variable that supports the integration of market and technical knowledge is the practice of new product development in cooperation with customers. While this factor was found to be less important than the presence of diverse, interdisciplinary project teams, it is an important complement.

Two other explanatory latent variables included in both research models are associated with the development of market and technical knowledge. As already mentioned, the majority of previous studies on market and technical knowledge integration focused on ways of integrating R&D employees (with technical knowledge) with members of marketing teams (with market knowledge). Market and technical knowledge integration models created in this strand of research, with few exceptions (e.g. Ali & Matsuno, 2018) failed to specifically account for the company's knowledge resources and their development. The results of the quantitative study obtained for both models indicate that the development of each analysed kind of knowledge is an important element that should be accounted for in models describing market and technical knowledge integration. This is because these constructs have a strong positive effect on knowledge integration constructs and on the final variables explained by such models. In this monograph, the literature review was used to identify knowledge sources—for example regarding market knowledge (e.g. Zhou & Li, 2012; Dolnicar & Grün, 2013; Rakthin et al., 2016; Paschen et al., 2019) and technical knowledge (e.g. Caloghirou et al., 2004; Tsai & Wang, 2009; Fletcher & Harris, 2011; Chen & Liu, 2019; Wu et al., 2020). Nevertheless, the literature in many cases did not identify specific market and technical knowledge sources that are useful for R&D-intensive companies. That is why the qualitative study was the key source in this respect. It was found that the company's market knowledge should be developed, first of all, by activities involving close cooperation with customers. It is also important to spend adequate amounts of money to monitor the market in search of trends and economic phenomena that are relevant for the company. The best way to acquire valuable technical knowledge is to employ well-educated and experienced specialists, but companies should also invest in training their employees and provide them with access to the latest technological solutions available in the industry.

It is also worth noting that findings from the quantitative study contribute valuable insights to the literature on dynamic capabilities. They provide empirical evidence supporting the existence of a more specific dynamic capability, namely market and technical knowledge integration capability, which was discussed in Chapter 4. While one case study analysed by Verona and Ravasi (2003) contains some elements indicative of market and technical knowledge integration, the authors did not focus on this aspect and provided only a very general definition of knowledge integration capability, which does not make a distinction between different kinds of knowledge. Therefore, this monograph can be regarded as the first publication to explicitly propose the existence of a market and technical knowledge integration capability in the strand of research on dynamic capabilities and to provide empirical evidence supporting its importance for the company's performance. It was found that enterprises should try to develop both kinds of knowledge while implementing integration activities. It needs be pointed out, however, that the empirical results only support the importance of this new capability for R&D-intensive firms. Nonetheless, they are sufficiently conclusive to identify a new capability that could be taken into account in future research concerning other groups of companies.

In summary, it can be concluded that the results obtained by the author are consistent with the findings reported by the majority of previous studies on the integration of market and technical knowledge (e.g. Garrett et al., 2006; Song & Thieme, 2006; Song & Song, 2010; Yao et al., 2014). Even so, the research models provide additional details regarding aspects that remained previously unexplained, particularly with respect to diverse, interdisciplinary project teams and their composition. Because both models were created to represent specific characteristics of companies operating in R&D-intensive industries (the category includes medium-high and high R&D intensity companies, according to the classification proposed by Galindo-Rueda and Verger (2016)), their components represent activities that are particularly important for the performance of such companies. The research models provide an indication for R&D-intensive firms as to what activities regarding the development and integration of market and technical knowledge should be prioritised in order to improve their innovativeness and business performance. It can therefore be concluded they are an important contribution to the literature on the activity of companies operating in R&D-intensive industries.

However, the quantitative survey conducted in the study has some limitations. Its first limitation is connected with the sample size (520 entities), which affects the degree of certainty with which the results can be generalised to the whole population of R&D-intensive firms.

The second limitation is connected with the data collection method (CATI). Although the anonymity of respondents was guaranteed, it is possible that not all answers were entirely truthful, especially when considering sensitive information. Another problem is that some statements called for respondents' subjective assessments, which may have not reflected the actual facts.

Reservations can also be raised regarding the method of measuring the latent variables. To measure some completely new concepts, it was necessary to create indicators based on ideas described in the literature and the results of the qualitative study.

6.6 Chapter summary

The purpose of the chapter was to analyse quantitative data using the PLS-SEM method and the two research models, one of which was designed to analyse the effect of the studied factors on innovativeness, while the other to analyse the effect on the business performance of R&D-intensive enterprises. The chapter starts with a description of the latent variables included in each model. Two key constructs representing the integration of market and technical knowledge were created based on the literature and the results of the qualitative study conducted by the author. Later in the chapter, the 12 hypotheses presented in Section 4.3 were developed into paths that need to be tested in order to confirm particular hypotheses. This approach can be explained by the fact that the detailed research models, as opposed to a more general conceptual framework, include two constructs related to market and technical knowledge: the primary one (diverse, interdisciplinary project teams) and the secondary one (new product development in cooperation with customers). The way in which the research models were derived from the conceptual framework is illustrated in a diagram. The analysed research models are largely based on insights from studies on R&D-marketing integration, especially the key role of cross-functional teams reported by Maltz et al. (2001). This aspect was further developed in this monograph by taking into account the findings from the qualitative study. The following quantitative study confirmed the effectiveness of such interdisciplinary teams provided they meet additional requirements, such as good communication skills of technical employees. Another construct related to knowledge integration, namely new product development with customers, showed the importance of close cooperation between the company's employees and its customers during the improvement or development of completely new products. In addition to confirming the innovativeness and business performance of R&D-intensive firms can be improved by knowledge integration activities, the analyses revealed benefits associated with the development of both kinds of knowledge. Since knowledge development is closely connected with knowledge integration activities, R&D-intensive firms should pay equal attention to both activities in pursuit of the end result, namely a high level of innovativeness and business performance. It is worth remembering that the aspect of knowledge development was practically ignored in the strand of research on R&D-marketing integration.

The next part of the chapter described the quantitative research procedure with information about the method of data collection, descriptive statistics about the sample consisting of 520 enterprises, the list of questionnaire items and the basic assumptions of the PLS-SEM. The data collected in the survey were analysed using SmartPLS 3 software. The purpose of the analyses was to validate the research models and test the hypotheses.

The measurement properties of the research models were found to satisfy the requirements: the indicator variables were sufficiently reliable and internally consistent while the constructs met the requirements for convergent and discriminant validity. The analysis of the measurement model confirmed the effect of latent variables on observable indicators. In the process of hypotheses validation, 10 out of the 12 hypotheses were confirmed. Two hypotheses regarding the direct effect of technical knowledge development on innovativeness (model 1) and on business performance (model 2) were rejected. However, one must note that the indirect effect of technical knowledge development on innovation and business performance in research models 1 and 2 mediated through constructs related to knowledge integration was positively verified. In order to analyse this issue more thoroughly, two alternative research models were created—1A and 2A—which did not include the latent variables related to knowledge integration. Both models revealed a statistically significant direct effect of technical knowledge on both innovativeness and business performance of R&D-intensive companies. As a result, it can be concluded that the constructs related to the integration of market and technical knowledge present in models 1 and 2 suppress the direct paths of influence of technical knowledge on innovativeness and business performance to a statistically insignificant level. This can be treated as evidence that knowledge integration activities are strong mediators between the development of technical knowledge and innovativeness and business performance. It also means that the development of technical knowledge in R&D-intensive companies without activities designed to integrate this knowledge with current market knowledge may not lead to better innovativeness and business performance. In contrast, the development of market knowledge in the case of models 1 and 2 was found to affect innovativeness and business performance of enterprises, both directly and indirectly, through knowledge integration activities. This is indicative of the complexity of influences that occur when R&D-intensive enterprises develop and integrate market and technical knowledge.

The results of the study confirm the importance of market and technical knowledge for enterprises, which has been postulated in the literature by Deligianni et al. (2015) and Suseno and Pinnington (2018). They also fill the research gap regarding the integration of both types of knowledge, which has been identified, among others, by Azari et al. (2020). The findings of the quantitative study are consistent with the opinion expressed by Grant (1996a, 1997) with reference to the KBV, namely that knowledge integration is the company's main task. They are also an important contribution to the literature on the activity of R&D-intensive companies in that they provide empirical evidence confirming the beneficial effect of activities aimed at developing and integrating market and technical knowledge on innovativeness and business performance.

Chapter 7

Conclusion

The main objective of the monograph was twofold: *to identify factors that determine the integration of market and technical knowledge in R&D-intensive companies and to evaluate the effect of market and technical knowledge integration on innovativeness and business performance of these firms.*

The purpose of the literature review presented in Chapters 1, 2, 3 and 4 was to systematise the research output regarding

- classifications and typologies of industries by level of technology, especially those based on the criterion of R&D expenditures;
- market and technical knowledge;
- the RBV, the KBV and the concept of dynamic capabilities and their use in the context of the main topic of this monograph;
- the concept of R&D-marketing integration;
- innovation, its types and innovativeness of companies; and
- business performance of companies.

The literature review and the identified research gap served as the basis for the five research questions, the 12 hypotheses of this monograph and the conceptual framework of the study.

Empirical research was conducted using a mixed-method approach and an exploratory sequential design. Because appropriate measurement instruments were not available in the literature, it was necessary to develop a new measurement instrument for the quantitative study that would be perceived as relevant by the target population of companies. To collect such information, the author carried out semi-structured in-depth interviews with respondents from 16 firms representing different R&D-intensive industries. Insights from the interviews were used to create two more detailed research models based on the conceptual framework of the study. The

DOI: 10.1201/9781032642352-7

models were validated using data from a survey of 520 R&D-intensive companies. The quantitative data were analysed by applying the PLS-SEM method. The indicator variables used for measuring the constructs were found to be sufficiently reliable and internally consistent, and the constructs met the requirements for convergent and discriminant validity. The statistical significance of the results was confirmed using bootstrap validation.

Ten out of the twelve hypotheses were verified. The two rejected hypotheses concerned the direct effect of technical knowledge development on innovativeness (model 1) and on business performance (model 2). It should be pointed out, however, that the hypothesised indirect effect of technical knowledge development on both innovativeness and business performance, mediated by the latent variables related to knowledge integration, was confirmed. To further explore the issue of the direct impact of technical knowledge development on innovativeness and business performance, two alternative research models 1A and 2A were created, which did not include constructs related to knowledge integration. After analysing models 1A and 2A, the direct effect of technical knowledge development on both innovativeness and business performance of R&D-intensive companies was found to be statistically significant. The analyses of models 1 and 2 and their alternative versions 1A and 2A confirm the existence of constructs related to the integration of market and technical knowledge, which act as strong mediators that suppress the direct effect of technical knowledge development on innovativeness and business performance to a statistically insignificant level. A similar situation can be observed in the case of the direct effect of market knowledge development on innovativeness and business performance, which is also suppressed by the aforementioned mediators but remains statistically significant. This result demonstrates that market and technical knowledge integration activities in R&D-intensive companies serve as mediators, especially between technical knowledge development and innovativeness and business performance of analysed companies.

The results presented in this monograph fill the *research gap* described in Chapter 4 and arising from the lack of studies seeking to account for the development of market and technical knowledge together with the activities aimed at integrating these knowledge resources as well as the effect of these activities on the company's innovativeness and business performance.

7.1 Theoretical contribution

There are seven aspects of this monograph that can be regarded as its theoretical contribution:

1 First of all, the contribution to the stream of research concerning market and technical knowledge integration. The KBV, together with the concepts of dynamic capabilities and R&D-marketing integration were used to develop

the conceptual framework of the study. Then results of the qualitative study were used to create two more detailed versions of the conceptual framework: research models describing the effect of market and technical knowledge integration in R&D-intensive firms on their innovativeness and business performance. These models were validated by applying the PLS-SEM method to quantitative data using SmartPLS 3 software. In addition to proving most of the effects mentioned in the hypotheses, the models show how to effectively integrate and develop market and technical knowledge under the current conditions in order to improve the efficiency of the studied companies. The models focused on interpersonal relations in the context of market and technical knowledge integration, in other words, on activities associated with interactions between different groups of employees that facilitate the integration of both kinds of knowledge. It should be emphasised that in the past, research on R&D-marketing integration (which until now has contributed the most to our understanding of how to integrate market and technical knowledge) focused on the integration of the departments of R&D and marketing. The study described in this monograph has demonstrated that people from these departments must constantly collaborate to achieve a higher level of mutual understanding and effectiveness. This finding prompted the author to further develop the idea of cross-functional teams, which was investigated by Maltz et al. (2001). In this monograph, these cross-functional teams are referred to as "diverse, interdisciplinary project teams". Given their importance, they are the key latent variable in each research model. The results of the quantitative study indicate that the existence of such interdisciplinary teams has a particularly positive effect on innovativeness and business performance of R&D-intensive firms when these teams meet additional requirements: good communication skills of technical employees and a high degree of diversity, not only with respect to professional expertise (technical and market knowledge) but also in terms of sex, personality and nationality. These characteristics are essential if interdisciplinary teams of employees with different backgrounds are to cooperate effectively and be creative. While these teams are the main component of both research models, because of their essential role in the integration of market and technical knowledge, they are not the only factor that contributes to knowledge integration. Both models include a secondary construct, associated with new product development, which should be conducted in cooperation with customers if it is to have a positive effect on innovativeness and business performance. This is because customer knowledge is essential for the ultimate success of new product development. Quantitative analyses have also demonstrated that knowledge integration is very complex and interdisciplinary teams together with the secondary construct—new product development with customers—are not the only elements that should be taken into consideration. A component which is often ignored by authors interested in this field (with few exceptions, e.g. Ali and Matsuno (2018)) is the development of market and technical knowledge. Until now, the majority of studies have focused on ways of integrating employees equipped with the two kinds of knowledge (e.g. Fain & Wagner, 2014; Boles & Link, 2017; Yongsheng & Jinjie, 2019). The study described in this monograph has shown that the development of market and technical knowledge is a crucial form of support that benefits the work of both knowledge integration constructs. Moreover, the study has demonstrated that both constructs related to knowledge integration are strong mediators between the development of market and technical knowledge and innovativeness and business performance of R&D-intensive enterprises. In the case of market knowledge development, this mediating effect does not exclude the existence of a direct effect on both dependent variables. On the other hand, the absence of a statistically significant direct impact of the development of technical knowledge on innovativeness and business performance can be taken to mean that without integrating technical knowledge with current market knowledge, its development may not bring the expected results.

2 A contribution to the concept of dynamic capabilities, which has been used to analyse the problem of knowledge integration. Knowledge integration capability has been previously identified in the literature though it has been differently defined: in some cases, rather generally, as integration of any kind of knowledge (e.g. Verona & Ravasi, 2003; Martinelli et al., 2018); in others, more specifically, as integration of external knowledge (Villar et al., 2014). For this reason, the author has identified a new, more specific kind of capability, which refers to the integration of market and technical knowledge. This new capability is also dynamic because it enables companies to adapt to current market trends and create innovative products. It can also be viewed as an operational capability, for example when viewed in the context of the Scrum methodology, in which a person keeping in touch with customers and having a good understanding of the market, known as a product owner or product manager, cooperates with programmers in the development of an application according to the customers' specifications. The lack of a clear distinction between dynamic and operational capabilities was already recognised by Helfat and Winter (2011), but this aspect is particularly evident in the case of the market and technical knowledge integration capability.

3 A contribution to the KBV, which assumes that new product development requires different kinds of knowledge. According to the KBV, the principal reason why companies exist is to create conditions for employees to specialise and develop narrow, in-depth knowledge in a given field (Grant, 1997), while the main task of a company is to integrate knowledge resources (Grant, 1996b, 1997). Moreover, the KBV is a development of the RBV, in which emphasis was placed on the role of the company's intangible knowledge-based resources and capabilities in value creation (Grant, 1997; DeCarolis & Deeds, 1999; Theriou et al., 2009; Kim et al., 2014) and on the recognition that different kinds of knowledge have specific properties (Kaplan et al., 2001). The results

presented in this monograph provide empirical evidence supporting the above-mentioned arguments concerning knowledge advanced by the authors of the KBV. What is more, the empirical study conducted by the author proves that the integration of market and technical knowledge in R&D-intensive firms is crucial for their innovativeness and business performance, which is an important contribution to the KBV.

4 A contribution to research on R&D-marketing integration. So far, studies conducted in this strand of research have mainly focused on the integration of market and technical knowledge understood as the integration of employees from R&D departments (with technical knowledge) with marketing specialists (with market knowledge). Empirical studies reported in this monograph identify a number of new activities associated with the integration of people with market and technical knowledge used by modern R&D-intensive companies.
5 A comprehensive and systematic review of the literature on R&D-marketing integration. The scientific output in this field was divided into three periods: up to 1986—relatively little interest in R&D-marketing integration; from 1987 to 2000—growing interest in R&D-marketing integration; since 2001—the number of publications on R&D-marketing integration has been relatively stable. The literature review revealed a number of research gaps, one of which was the existence of relatively few recent publications on R&D-marketing integration, especially studies involving R&D-intensive firms or even high-technology companies. The review and the division created by the author can be useful for future research, especially as far as the existing research gaps are concerned. While some have been filled by this monograph, there are still areas that need to be investigated.
6 A systematic overview of classifications and typologies of industries by level of technology in terms of R&D intensity as well as other similar criteria. The author has identified crucial differences between various classifications and typologies and between R&D-intensive companies and high-technology companies, which are often ignored in the literature but can have an effect on the results of studies owing to the inclusion or exclusion of specific industries. Thanks to the systematic review of the literature in this respect, other authors will now be able to choose a classification or typology that is most appropriate for studies concerning specific sectors of the economy. The lack of such an overview was a considerable gap in the literature.
7 A systematic overview of definitions regarding key concepts: knowledge, innovation, organisational innovativeness, business performance and dynamic capabilities. The definitions have been analysed in terms of key words. In addition, the author has proposed his own typology of definitions of organisational innovativeness. The overview covers a number of different approaches to the respective concepts and can help other authors choose a definition that best satisfies their requirements.

7.2 Practical contribution

A number of recommendations for companies in R&D-intensive industries can be derived from the results of the study. The key takeaway for this category of firms is that activities associated with market and technical knowledge integration are crucial for their innovativeness and business performance. The ultimate success of knowledge integration largely depends on the existence of diverse, interdisciplinary project teams and their effective collaboration, because they play a key role in knowledge integration. It is not easy to satisfy this requirement since technical employees have a tendency to be focused on their own work and are not particularly communicative. For this reason, HR departments should pay special attention to communication skills of candidates applying for technical positions. Failure to take this aspect into consideration may lead to problems in the functioning of interdisciplinary project teams and undermine their expected benefits. Another activity related to the integration of market and technical knowledge, which supplements activities of interdisciplinary project teams, is the continuous development of new products, which should take place in cooperation with customers.

Companies should facilitate market and technical knowledge integration at different levels of the organisational hierarchy, particularly at lower levels, where information sharing is not always intensive enough. The results of qualitative research indicate that in some firms integration activities are only undertaken at the highest levels of their hierarchy. This kind of approach is likely to be ineffective since the firm's valuable human resources are not involved in the process. Market and technical knowledge integration is particularly crucial in projects. When a project team includes an appropriately selected, diverse group of employees, they can complement each other's skills and areas of expertise and contribute their different perspectives on problems encountered while working on the project. It is also easier for them to apply this integrated knowledge in the development of a specific task, product or service created for a given customer or market in comparison to people higher in the hierarchy, especially the company's management.

The ultimate success of market and technical knowledge integration also requires that both these resources should be as up to date as possible. As far as technical knowledge is concerned, its most valuable source are the company's employees, who should be given opportunities for continuous professional development. Although the results of the survey indicate that constant development of technical knowledge is generally high on the agenda, efforts should always be monitored and facilitated. Both qualitative and quantitative results have revealed that market knowledge in R&D-intensive firms is in much shorter supply than technical knowledge and has a greater impact on their innovativeness and business performance. For this reason, R&D-intensive companies should maintain close relationships with their customers to better understand their needs and know when they start to change. While this may often be quite a challenging task, this kind of knowledge can be invaluable. Market knowledge about current market trends and the needs of potential customers can also be obtained from market research, either conducted by companies themselves or commissioned from external firms. While this kind of knowledge is usually rather expensive and not as commonly used by R&D-intensive enterprises, the results of the quantitative study indicate that it is extremely useful.

7.3 Limitations and suggestions for further research

Data in the questionnaire survey were collected using the computer-assisted telephone interviewing (CATI) method, which may raise concerns about data reliability. Although the anonymity of respondents was guaranteed, as recommended by many authors (e.g. Podsakoff et al., 2003), it is possible that not all answers were entirely truthful, especially when they concerned sensitive information.

In the future it would be useful to employ other forms of measurement. Qualitative and quantitative data analysed in this monograph were collected in cross-sectional studies, which reflect the state of affairs at a particular point in time. A longitudinal study could therefore provide additional insights about the problem of market and technical knowledge integration.

This monograph provides results concerning companies from R&D-intensive firms. While this sector is an important part of the economy, research should also focus on the market and technical knowledge integration activities in other sectors, especially in low R&D intensity industries, to fill the research gap concerning this category of companies.

Whereas this monograph focuses on the effect of market and technical knowledge integration on innovativeness and business performance of R&D-intensive enterprises, there are other kinds of knowledge that are also worth investigating, for example financial knowledge (Sáenz et al., 2012) or internationalisation knowledge (Deligianni et al., 2015). Future studies could attempt to analyse the effects of integrating different kinds of knowledge or integrating them with market and technical knowledge, for example by developing models proposed in this monograph.

The results presented in this monograph reflect business realities before the outbreak of the Covid-19 pandemic. As is well known, companies all over the world, in practically every industry, have been affected by the consequences of the pandemic and many have changed the way they operate. For example, as a result of a dramatic rise in the popularity of remote work, interpersonal relations within companies and with customers have been weakened. This monograph focuses on the importance of team work and the value of diverse, interdisciplinary project teams but it can safely be assumed that the growing preference for remote work and less frequent in-person meetings have affected the way such teams function nowadays. It would therefore be a good idea to examine what impact such changes have had on the effectiveness of cross-functional project teams and, more generally, on market and technical knowledge integration in companies.

Another important factor affecting the effectiveness of cooperation is trust. For example, the effect of this factor on organisational performance was demonstrated by Paliszkiewicz et al. (2015), and its effect on innovativeness was confirmed by Paliszkiwicz (2019). Given the role of project teams and interpersonal relations in knowledge integration, demonstrated in this monograph, it would be worthwhile to investigate in more depth how trust affects the effectiveness of efforts to integrate market and technical knowledge.

While this monograph has provided empirical evidence for the effectiveness of certain activities undertaken by companies to facilitate market and technical knowledge integration, efforts should be continued to develop new, more effective ways of integrating these two important resources. The author hopes that this monograph and the results confirming the effect of market and technical knowledge integration on innovativeness and business performance will prompt further research in this area.

References

Abbott, T., McGuckin, R., Herrick, P., & Norfolk, L. (1989, January). *Measuring the trade balance in advanced technology products* (Center for Economic Studies, U.S. Census Bureau Working Paper No. 89-1). http://industrialpolicy.us/resources/TechnologyTheory/DefiningHighTechnology.pdf

Abernathy, W. J., & Clark, K. B. (1985). Innovation: Mapping the winds of creative destruction. *Research Policy, 14*(1), 3–22. https://doi.org/10.1016/0048-7333(85)90021-6

Acedo, F. J., Barroso, C., & Galan, J. L. (2006). The resource-based theory: Dissemination and main trends. *Strategic Management Journal, 27*(7), 621–636. https://doi.org/10.1002/smj.532

Acharya, C., Ojha, D., Gokhale, R., & Patel, P. C. (2022). Managing information for innovation using knowledge integration capability: The role of boundary spanning objects. *International Journal of Information Management, 62*. https://doi.org/10.1016/j.ijinfomgt.2021.102438

Ackoff, R. L. (1989). From data to wisdom. *Journal of Applied Systems Analysis, 16*, 3–9.

Acs, Z. J., Audretsch, D. B., & Lehmann, E. E. (2013). The knowledge spillover theory of entrepreneurship. *Small Business Economics, 41*(4), 757–774. https://doi.org/10.1007/s11187-013-9505-9

Adel, H. M., Mahrous, A. A., & Hammad, R. (2020). Entrepreneurial marketing strategy, institutional environment, and business performance of SMEs in Egypt. *Journal of Entrepreneurship in Emerging Economies, 12*(5), 727–746. https://doi.org/10.1108/JEEE-11-2019-0171

Aghasi, K., Colombo, M. G., & Rossi-Lamastra, C. (2017). Acquisitions of small high-tech firms as a mechanism for external knowledge sourcing: The integration-autonomy dilemma. *Technological Forecasting and Social Change, 120*, 334–346. https://doi.org/10.1016/j.techfore.2017.02.010

Ahmadi, H., O'Cass, A., & Miles, M. P. (2014). Product resource–capability complementarity, integration mechanisms, and first product advantage. *Journal of Business Research, 67*(5), 704–709. https://doi.org/10.1016/j.jbusres.2013.11.031

Alavi, M., & Leidner, D. E. (2001). Review: Knowledge management and knowledge management systems: Conceptual foundations and research issues. *MIS Quarterly, 25*(1), 107–136. https://doi.org/10.2307/3250961

Algeo, C. (2014). Exploring project knowledge acquisition and exchange through action research. *Project Management Journal, 45*(3), 46–56. https://doi.org/10.1002/pmj.21417

Ali, A., & Matsuno, K. (2018). Mediating roles of capabilities between R&D-marketing integration and business performance. *Journal of Asia Business Studies, 12*(1), 81–98. https://doi.org/10.1108/JABS-09-2015-0165

Ali, M., Kan, K. A. S., & Sarstedt, M. (2016). Direct and configurational paths of absorptive capacity and organizational innovation to successful organizational performance. *Journal of Business Research, 69*(11), 5317–5323. https://doi.org/10.1016/j.jbusres.2016.04.131

Allee, V. (1997). *The knowledge evolution: Expanding organizational intelligence.* Butterworth-Heinemann.

Alvesson, M., & Kärreman, D. (2001). Odd couple: Making sense of the curious concept of knowledge management. *Journal of Management Studies, 38*(7), 995–1018. https://doi.org/10.1111/1467-6486.00269

Amabile, T. M., Conti, R., Coon, H., Lazenby, J., & Herron, M. (1996). Assessing the work environment for creativity. *Academy of Management Journal, 39*(5), 1154–1184. https://doi.org/10.5465/256995

Ambrosini, V., Bowman, C., & Collier, N. (2009). Dynamic capabilities: An exploration of how firms renew their resource base. *British Journal of Management, 20*(1), S9–S24. https://doi.org/10.1111/j.1467-8551.2008.00610.x

Amit, R., & Schoemaker, P. J. (1993). Strategic assets and organizational rent. *Strategic Management Journal, 14*(1), 33–46. https://doi.org/10.1002/smj.4250140105

Antonelli, C., & Crespi, F. (2012). Matthew effects and R&D subsidies: Knowledge cumulability in high-tech and low-tech industries. *Giornale degli Economisti e Annali di Economia, 71*(125), 5–31. www.jstor.org/stable/23645846

Antunes, H. D. J. G., & Pinheiro, P. G. (2020). Linking knowledge management, organizational learning and memory. *Journal of Innovation & Knowledge, 5*(2), 140–149. https://doi.org/10.1016/j.jik.2019.04.002

Archibugi, D., Evangelista, R., & Simonetti, R. (1994). On the definition of and measurement of product and process innovations. In Y. Shionoya, & M. Perlman (Eds.), *Innovation in technology industries, and institutions. Studies in Schumpeterian perspectives* (pp. 7–24). The University of Michigan Press.

Argote, L., McEvily, B., & Reagans, R. (2003). Managing knowledge in organizations: An integrative framework and review of emerging themes. *Management Science, 49*(4), 571–582. https://doi.org/10.1287/mnsc.49.4.571.14424

Armbrecht, F. M. R., Chapas, R. B., Chappelow, C. C., Farris, G. F., Friga, P. N., Hartz, C. A., McIlvaine, M. E., Postle, S. R., & Whitwell, G. E. (2001). Knowledge management in research and development. *Research Technology Management, 44*(4), 28–48. www.jstor.org/stable/24134029

Arundel, A. (2001). The relative effectiveness of patents and secrecy for appropriation. *Research Policy, 30*(4), 611–624. https://doi.org/10.1016/S0048-7333(00)00100-1

Atuahene-Gima, K. (2005). Resolving the capability–rigidity paradox in new product innovation. *Journal of Marketing, 69*(4), 61–83. https://doi.org/10.1509/jmkg.2005.69.4.61

Augusto, M., & Coelho, F. (2009). Market orientation and new-to-the-world products: Exploring the moderating effects of innovativeness, competitive strength, and environmental forces. *Industrial Marketing Management, 38*(1), 94–108. https://doi.org/10.1016/j.indmarman.2007.09.007

Austin, D. H. (2006, October). *Research and development in the pharmaceutical industry.* Congress of the United States, Congressional Budget Office. www.cbo.gov/sites/default/files/109th-congress-2005-2006/reports/10-02-drugr-d.pdf

Aven, T. (2013). A conceptual framework for linking risk and the elements of the data–information–knowledge–wisdom (DIKW) hierarchy. *Reliability Engineering & System Safety, 111*, 30–36. https://doi.org/10.1016/j.ress.2012.09.014

Avsar, V. (2018). R&D intensity, financing cost and antidumping. *Applied Economics, 50*(39), 4275–4285. https://doi.org/10.1080/00036846.2018.1441524

Ayatse, F. A., Kwahar, N., & Iyortsuun, A. S. (2017). Business incubation process and firm performance: An empirical review. *Journal of Global Entrepreneurship Research, 7*(2), 1–17. https://doi.org/10.1186/s40497-016-0059-6

Azari, M. J., Aspelund, A., & Eide, A. E. (2020). Knowledge integration in international SMEs–The effects on firm innovation and performance. *Cogent Business & Management, 7.* https://doi.org/10.1080/23311975.2020.1849890.

Bailey, K. D. (1994). *Typologies and taxonomies. An introduction to classification techniques.* Sage Publications.

Bakhtiari, S. (2021). Government financial assistance as catalyst for private financing. *International Review of Economics & Finance, 72,* 59–78. https://doi.org/10.1016/j.iref.2020.11.003

Baldwin, J. R., & Hanel, P. (2003). *Innovation and knowledge creation in an open economy. Canadian industry and international implications.* Cambridge University Press.

Bao, Y., Sheng, S., & Zhou, K. Z. (2012). Network-based market knowledge and product innovativeness. *Marketing Letters, 23,* 309–324. https://doi.org/10.1007/s11002-011-9155-0

Baregheh, A., Rowley, J., & Sambrook, S. (2009). Towards a multidisciplinary definition of innovation. *Management Decision, 47*(8), 1323–1339. https://doi.org/10.1108/00251740910984578

Barney, J. B. (1986). Strategic factor markets: Expectations, luck, and business strategy. *Management Science, 32*(10), 1231–1241. https://doi.org/10.1287/mnsc.32.10.1231

Barney, J. B. (1991). Firm resources and sustained competitive advantage. *Journal of Management, 17*(1), 99–120. https://doi.org/10.1177/014920639101700108

Barney, J. B. (1995). Looking inside for competitive advantage. *Academy of Management Perspectives, 9*(4), 49–61. https://doi.org/10.5465/ame.1995.9512032192

Barney, J. B. (2001). Is the resource-based "view" a useful perspective for strategic management research? Yes. *Academy of Management Review, 26*(1), 41–56. https://doi.org/10.5465/amr.2001.4011938

Barney, J. B. (2014). *Gaining and sustaining competitive advantage.* Pearson.

Barney, J. B., & Hesterly, W. S. (2012). *Strategic management and competitive advantage.* Pearson Education.

Barney, J. B., Ketchen Jr, D. J., & Wright, M. (2011). The future of resource-based theory: Revitalization or decline? *Journal of Management, 37*(5), 1299–1315. https://doi.org/10.1177/0149206310391805

Barney, J. B., & Mackey, A. (2016). Text and metatext in the resource-based view. *Human Resource Management Journal, 26*(4), 369–378. https://doi.org/10.1111/1748-8583.12123

Barreto, I. (2010). Dynamic capabilities: A review of past research and an agenda for the future. *Journal of Management, 36*(1), 256–280. https://doi.org/10.1177/0149206309350776

Battisti, E., Nirino, N., Leonidou, E., & Thrassou, A. (2022). Corporate venture capital and CSR performance: An extended resource based view's perspective. *Journal of Business Research, 139,* 1058–1066. https://doi.org/10.1016/j.jbusres.2021.10.054

Bauer, F., & Matzler, K. (2014). Antecedents of M&A success: The role of strategic complementarity, cultural fit, and degree and speed of integration. *Strategic Management Journal, 35*(2), 269–291. https://doi.org/10.1002/smj.2091

Bayraktutan, Y., Bıdırdı, H., & Kutlar, A. (2018). Research and development and high technology exports in selected countries at different development stages: A panel co-integration and causality analysis. In F. Bakırcı, T. Heupel, O. Kocagöz, & Ü. Özen (Eds.), *German-Turkish perspectives on IT and innovation management: Challenges and approaches* (pp. 43–72). Springer Gabler.

Beamish, P. W., & Chakravarty, D. (2021). Using the resource-based view in multinational enterprise research. *Journal of Management, 47*(7), 1861–1877. https://doi.org/10.1177/0149206321995575

Beck, K., Beedle, M., van Bennekum, A., Cockburn, A, Cunningham, W., Fowler, M., Grenning, J., Highsmith, J., Hunt, A., Jeffries, R., Kern, J., Marick, B., Martin, R. C., Mellor, S., Schwaber, K., Sutherland, J., & Thomas, D. (2001). *Manifesto for agile software development.* http://agilemanifesto.org/iso/en/manifesto.html

Becker, J., Johannesen, N., & Riedel, N. (2020). Taxation and the allocation of risk inside the multinational firm. *Journal of Public Economics, 183*, 1–20. https://doi.org/10.1016/j.jpubeco.2020.104138

Becker, M. C., & Lillemark, M. (2006). Marketing/R&D integration in the pharmaceutical industry. *Research Policy, 35*(1), 105–120. https://doi.org/10.1016/j.respol.2005.09.005

Berkun, S. (2010). *The myths of innovation.* O'Reilly Media, Inc.

Bessant, J., Lamming, R., Noke, H., & Phillips, W. (2005). Managing innovation beyond the steady state. *Technovation, 25*(12), 1366–1376. https://doi.org/10.1016/j.technovation.2005.04.007

Bessant, J., & Tidd, J. (2015). *Innovation and entrepreneurship.* John Wiley & Sons Ltd.

Bierly, P., & Chakrabarti, A. (1996). Generic knowledge strategies in the US pharmaceutical industry. *Strategic Management Journal, 17*(S2), 123–135. https://doi.org/10.1002/smj.4250171111

Bigliardi, B., & Galati, F. (2018). An open innovation model for SMEs. In W. Vanhaverbeke, F. Frattini, N. Roijakkers, & M. Usman (Eds.), *Researching open innovation in SMEs* (pp. 71–113). World Scientific Publishing.

Birkinshaw, J., Morrison, A., & Hulland, J. (1995). Structural and competitive determinants of a global integration strategy. *Strategic Management Journal, 16*(8), 637–655. https://doi.org/10.1002/smj.4250160805

Bissell, H. D. (1971). Research and marketing—rivals or partners? *Research Management, 14*(3), 65–73. https://doi.org/10.1080/00345334.1971.11756068

Blümm, C. (2002). *Die Bedeutung impliziten Wissens im Innovationsprozess—Zum Aufbau dynamischer Wettbewerbsvorteile.* Springer.

Bocquet, R., Le Bas, C., Mothe, C., & Poussing, N. (2017). CSR, innovation, and firm performance in sluggish growth contexts: A firm-level empirical analysis. *Journal of Business Ethics, 146*(1), 241–254. https://doi.org/10.1007/s10551-015-2959-8

Bogers, M., Foss, N. J., & Lyngsie, J. (2018). The "human side" of open innovation: The role of employee diversity in firm-level openness. *Research Policy, 47*(1), 218–231. https://doi.org/10.1016/j.respol.2017.10.012

Bohlmann, J. D., Spanjol, J., Qualls, W. J., & Rosa, J. A. (2013). The interplay of customer and product innovation dynamics: An exploratory study. *Journal of Product Innovation, 30*(2), 228–244. https://doi.org/10.1111/j.1540-5885.2012.00962.x

Bohn, R. E. (1994). Measuring and managing technological knowledge. *Sloan Management Review, 36*(1), 61–73.

Boisot, M., & Canals, A. (2004). Data, information and knowledge: Have we got it right? *Journal of Evolutionary Economics, 14*, 43–67. https://doi.org/10.1007/s00191-003-0181-9

Boles, J., & Link, A. N. (2017). On the R&D/marketing interface in knowledge intensive entrepreneurial firms. *International Entrepreneurship and Management Journal, 13*(3), 943–952. https://doi.org/10.1007/s11365-016-0429-0

Bolisani, E., & Bratianu, C. (2018). *Emergent knowledge strategies. Strategic thinking in knowledge management.* Springer.

Bollinger, A. S., & Smith, R. D. (2001). Managing organizational knowledge as a strategic asset. *Journal of Knowledge Management, 5*(1), 8–18. https://doi.org/10.1108/13673270110384365

Bonnet, D. C. (1986). Nature of the R&D/marketing co-operation in the design of technologically advanced new industrial products. *R&D Management, 16*(2), 117–126. https://doi.org/10.1111/j.1467-9310.1986.tb01165.x

Bontis, N. (2001). Assessing knowledge assets: A review of the models used to measure intellectual capital. *International Journal of Management Reviews, 3*(1), 41–60. https://doi.org/10.1111/1468-2370.00053

Brandt, N. (2018). *Strengthening innovation in Poland* (OECD Economics Department Working Papers No. 1479). https://doi.org/10.1787/abf2c877-en

Bresciani, S., & Ferraris, A. (2016). Innovation-receiving subsidiaries and dual embeddedness: Impact on business performance. *Baltic Journal of Management, 11*(1), 108–130. https://doi.org/10.1108/BJM-11-2014-0200

Brettel, M., Heinemann, F., Engelen, A., & Neubauer, S. (2011). Cross-functional integration of R&D, marketing, and manufacturing in radical and incremental product innovations and its effects on project effectiveness and efficiency. *Journal of Product Innovation Management, 28*(2), 251–269. https://doi.org/10.1111/j.1540-5885.2011.00795.x

Brinkmann, S. (2014). Unstructured and semi-structured interviewing. In P. Leavy (Ed.), *The Oxford handbook of qualitative research* (pp. 277–299). Oxford University Press.

Brockhoff, K., & Chakrabarti, A. K. (1988). R&D/marketing linkage and innovation strategy: Some West German experience. *IEEE Transactions on Engineering Management, 35*(3), 167–174. https://doi.org/10.1109/17.7436

Brouthers, K. D. (2013). A retrospective on: Institutional, cultural and transaction cost influences on entry mode choice and performance. *Journal of International Business Studies, 44*(1), 14–22. https://doi.org/10.1057/jibs.2012.23

Burgers, J. H., Van Den Bosch, F. A. J., & Volberda, H. W. (2008). Why new business development projects fail: Coping with the differences of technological versus market knowledge. *Long Range Planning, 41*(1), 55–73. https://doi.org/10.1016/j.lrp.2007.10.003

Burgin, M. (2010). *Theory of information. Fundamentality, diversity and unification.* World Scientific.

Calantone, R. J., Cavusgil, S. T., & Zhao, Y. (2002). Learning orientation, firm innovation capability, and firm performance. *Industrial Marketing Management, 31*(6), 515–524. https://doi.org/10.1016/S0019-8501(01)00203-6

Caloghirou, Y., Kastelli, I., & Tsakanikas, A. (2004). Internal capabilities and external knowledge sources: Complements or substitutes for innovative performance? *Technovation, 24*(1), 29–39. https://doi.org/10.1016/S0166-4972(02)00051-2

Cameron, G., Proudman, J., & Redding, S. (2005). Technological convergence, R&D, trade and productivity growth. *European Economic Review, 49*(3), 775–807. https://doi.org/10.1016/S0014-2921(03)00070-9

Campi, M., Dueñas, M., Barigozzi, M., & Fagiolo, G. (2019). Intellectual property rights, imitation, and development. The effect on cross-border mergers and acquisitions. *The Journal of International Trade & Economic Development, 28*(2), 230–256. https://doi.org/10.1080/09638199.2018.1518477

Carbonara, E., Gianfreda, G., Santarelli, E., & Vallanti, G. (2019, May). *The impact of intellectual property rights on labor productivity: Do constitutions matter?* (Luiss Lab of European Economics Working Paper No. 151). https://economiaefinanza.luiss.it/sites/economiaefinanza.luiss.it/files/19151.pdf

Carneiro, A. (2000). How does knowledge management influence innovation and competitiveness? *Journal of Knowledge Management, 4*(2), 87–98. https://doi.org/10.1108/13673270010372242

Carrillo-Carrillo, F., & Alcalde-Heras, H. (2020). Modes of innovation in an emerging economy: A firm-level analysis from Mexico. *Innovation, 22*(3), 334–352. https://doi.org/10.1080/14479338.2020.1735395

Carroad, P. A., & Carroad, C. A. (1982). Strategic interfacing of R&D and marketing. *Research Management, 25*(1), 28–33. https://doi.org/10.1080/00345334.1982.11756709

Carroll, P., Pol, E., & Robertson, P. L. (2000). Classification of industries by level of technology: An appraisal and some implications. *Prometheus, 18*(4), 417–436. https://doi.org/10.1080/08109020020008523

Carter, C. R., Kosmol, T., & Kaufmann, L. (2017). Toward a supply chain practice view. *Journal of Supply Chain Management, 53*(1), 114–122. https://doi.org/10.1111/jscm.12130

Cavaleri, S., & Seivert, S. (2005). *Knowledge leadership. The art and science of knowledge-based organization.* Elsevier Butterworth-Heinemann.

Chapple, K., Markusen, A., Schrock, G., Yamamoto, D., & Yu, P. (2004). Gauging metropolitan "high-tech" and "I-tech" activity. *Economic Development Quarterly, 18*(1), 10–29. https://doi.org/10.1177/0891242403257948

Chatterjee, S., Chaudhuri, R., Vrontis, D., & Thrassou, A. (2023). Revisiting the resource-based view (RBV) theory: From cross-functional capabilities perspective in post COVID-19 period. *Journal of Strategic Marketing, 20*(23), 1–16. https://doi.org/10.1080/0965254X.2023.2182447

Chechurin, L. (2016). Open questions about open innovations. In A. L. Mention & M. Torkkeli (Eds.), *Open innovation: A multifaceted perspective* (pp. 19–31). World Scientific.

Chen, K.-Y., & Lee, C.-F. (2017). Market knowledge of the travel industry from knowledge-based view: A case of two Taiwanese travel agencies. *Asia Pacific Journal of Tourism Research, 22*(7), 781–797. https://doi.org/10.1080/10941665.2017.1331922

Chen, Q., & Liu, Z. (2019). How does openness to innovation drive organizational ambidexterity? The mediating role of organizational learning goal orientation. *IEEE Transactions on Engineering Management, 66*(2), 156–169. https://doi.org/10.1109/TEM.2018.2834505

Cheng, X., Fu, S., & de Vreede, G. J. (2018). A mixed method investigation of sharing economy driven car-hailing services: Online and offline perspectives. *International Journal of Information Management, 41*, 57–64. https://doi.org/10.1016/j.ijinfomgt.2018.03.005

Chin, W. W. (2010). How to write up and report PLS analyses. In V. E. Vinzi, W. W. Chin, J. Hensler, & H. Wang (Eds.), *Handbook of partial least squares. Concepts, methods and applications* (pp. 655–690). Springer.

Chirico, F., & Salvato, C. (2008). Knowledge integration and dynamic organizational adaptation in family firms. *Family Business Review, 21*(2), 169–181. https://doi.org/10.1111/j.1741-6248.2008.00117.x

Chirumalla, K., Oghazi, P., & Parida, V. (2018). Social media engagement strategy: Investigation of marketing and R&D interfaces in manufacturing industry. *Industrial Marketing Management, 74*, 138–149. https://doi.org/10.1016/j.indmarman.2017.10.001

Cho, E., & Hahn, M. (2004). Antecedents and consequences of the sociocultural differences between R&D and marketing in Korean high-tech firms. *International Journal of Technology Management, 28*(7–8), 801–819. https://doi.org/10.1504/IJTM.2004.005784

Cho, H. J., & Pucik, V. (2005). Relationship between innovativeness, quality, growth, profitability, and market value. *Strategic Management Journal, 26*(6), 555–575. https://doi.org/10.1002/smj.461

Cho, Y. H., & Lee, J. H. (2018). Entrepreneurial orientation, entrepreneurial education and performance. *Asia Pacific Journal of Innovation and Entrepreneurship, 12*(2), 124–134. https://doi.org/10.1108/APJIE-05-2018-0028

Choi, S. B., & Williams, C. (2016). Entrepreneurial orientation and performance: Mediating effects of technology and marketing action across industry types. *Industry and Innovation, 23*(8), 673–693. https://doi.org/10.1080/13662716.2016.1208552

Chollet, B., Géraudel, M., Khedhaouria, A., & Mothe, C. (2016). Market knowledge as a function of CEOs' personality: A fuzzy set approach. *Journal of Business Research, 69*(7), 2567–2573. https://doi.org/10.1016/j.jbusres.2015.10.137

Choo, C. W. (2006). *The knowing organization: How organizations use information to construct meaning, create knowledge, and make decisions.* Oxford University Press.

Cillo, P. (2005). Fostering market knowledge use in innovation: The role of internal brokers. *European Management Journal, 23*(4), 404–412. https://doi.org/10.1016/j.emj.2005.06.008

Clarysse, B., Wright, M., & Van de Velde, E. (2011). Entrepreneurial origin, technological knowledge, and the growth of spin-off companies. *Journal of Management Studies, 48*(6), 1420–1442. https://doi.org/10.1111/j.1467-6486.2010.00991.x

Claudy, M. C., Peterson, M., & Pagell, M. (2016). The roles of sustainability orientation and market knowledge competence in new product development success. *Journal of Product Innovation Management, 33*(S1), 72–85. https://doi.org/10.1111/jpim.12343

Coff, R. (2003). Bidding wars over R&D-intensive firms: Knowledge, opportunism, and the market for corporate control. *Academy of Management Journal, 46*(1), 74–85. https://doi.org/10.5465/30040677

Cohen, A. B. (1988). The IRI medalist's address: Innovation at Du Pont—a real-time perspective. *Research-Technology Management, 31*(6), 47–52. https://doi.org/10.1080/08956308.1988.11670560

Conner, K. R. (1991). A historical comparison of resource-based theory and five schools of thought within industrial organization economics: Do we have a new theory of the firm? *Journal of Management, 17*(1), 121–154. https://doi.org/10.1177/014920639101700109

Conner, K. R., & Prahalad, C. K. (1996). A resource-based theory of the firm: Knowledge versus opportunism. *Organization Science, 7*(5), 477–501. https://doi.org/10.1287/orsc.7.5.477

Cook, K. E. (2008). In-depth interview. In L. M. Given (Ed.), *The SAGE encyclopedia of qualitative research methods* (pp. 422–423). Sage Publications.

Creswell, J. W., & Plano Clark, V. L. (2018). *Designing and conducting mixed methods research.* Sage Publications.

Croteau, A. M., Solomon, S., Raymond, L., & Bergeron, F. (2001, January). Organizational and technological infrastructures alignment. In *Proceedings of the 34th Annual Hawaii International Conference on System Sciences,* Maui, HI. IEEE. https://doi.org/10.1109/HICSS.2001.927162

Cyfert, S., & Krzakiewicz, K. (2019). *Dynamiczne zdolności polskich przedsiębiorstw.* Wydawnictwo Naukowe PWN S.A.

Czakon, W. (2010). Zasobowa teoria firmy w krzywym zwierciadle. *Przegląd organizacji, 843*(4), 8–12. https://doi.org/10.33141/po.2010.04.02

Czerniachowicz, B. (2012). Budowanie konkurencyjności przedsiębiorstwa w podejściu zasobowym na podstawie firmy "a". *Studia i Prace Wydziału Nauk Ekonomicznych i Zarządzania Uniwersytetu Szczecińskiego, 25,* 287–302. http://wneiz.pl/nauka_wneiz/sip/sip25-2012/SiP-25-287.pdf

Damanpour, F. (1987). The adoption of technological, administrative, and ancillary innovations: Impact of organizational factors. *Journal of Management, 13*(4), 675–688. https://doi.org/10.1177/014920638701300408

Damanpour, F. (1991). Organizational innovation: A meta-analysis of effects of determinants and moderators. *Academy of Management Journal, 34*(3), 555–590. https://doi.org/10.5465/256406

Damanpour, F., & Schneider, M. (2006). Phases of the adoption of innovation in organizations: Effects of environment, organization and top managers. *British Journal of Management, 17*(3), 215–236. https://doi.org/10.1111/j.1467-8551.2006.00498.x

Danneels, E. (2002). The dynamics of product innovation and firm competences. *Strategic Management Journal, 23*(12), 1095–1121. https://doi.org/10.1002/smj.275

Darroch, J. (2005). Knowledge management, innovation and firm performance. *Journal of Knowledge Management, 9*(3), 101–115. https://doi.org/10.1108/13673270510602809

Davenport, T. H., De Long, D. H., & Beers, M. C. (1998). Successful knowledge management projects. *Sloan Management Review, 39*(2), 43–57.

Davenport, T. H., & Prusak, L. (1998). *Working knowledge.* Harvard Business Review Press.

Dawid, H., & Mitkova, M. (2020, April). *Sectoral employment shifts and the role of R&D: A cross country comparison for manufacturing and service* (Bielefeld Working Papers in Economics and Management No. 02–2020). http://dx.doi.org/10.2139/ssrn.3586254

DeCarolis, D. M., & Deeds, D. L. (1999). The impact of stocks and flows of organizational knowledge on firm performance: An empirical investigation of the biotechnology industry. *Strategic Management Journal, 20*(10), 953–968. https://doi.org/10.1002/(SICI)1097-0266(199910)20:10<953::AID-SMJ59>3.0.CO;2-3

Delgado-Verde, M., Martín-de Castro, G., & Navas-López, J. E. (2011). Organizational knowledge assets and innovation capability: Evidence from Spanish manufacturing firms. *Journal of Intellectual Capital, 12*(1), 5–19. https://doi.org/10.1108/14691931111097890

Deligianni, I., Voudouris, I., & Lioukas, S. (2015). Growth paths of small technology firms: The effects of different knowledge types over time. *Journal of World Business, 50*(3), 491–504. https://doi.org/10.1016/j.jwb.2014.08.006

De Luca, L. M., & Atuahene-Gima, K. (2007). Market knowledge dimensions and cross-functional collaboration: Examining the different routes to product innovation performance. *Journal of Marketing, 71*(1), 95–112. https://doi.org/10.1509/jmkg.71.1.095

Denis, J.-E., & Depelteau, D. (1985). Market knowledge, diversification and export expansion. *Journal of International Business Studies, 16*, 77–90. https://doi.org/10.1057/palgrave.jibs.8490460

Department of Economic and Social Affairs Statistics Division, United Nations. (2008). *International standard industrial classification of all economic activities. Revision 4*. https://unstats.un.org/unsd/publication/seriesM/seriesm_4rev4e.pdf

Deshpandé, R., Farley, J. U., & Webster Jr., F. E. (1993). Corporate culture, customer orientation, and innovativeness in Japanese firms: A quadrad analysis. *Journal of Marketing, 57*(1), 23–37. https://doi.org/10.1177/002224299305700102

DeVol, R. C., Wong, P., Catapano, J., & Robitshek, G. (1999). *America's high-tech economy: Growth, development, and risks for metropolitan areas*. Milken Institute.

Dewar, R. D., & Dutton, J. E. (1986). The adoption of radical and incremental innovations: An empirical analysis. *Management Science, 32*(11), 1422–1433. https://doi.org/10.1287/mnsc.32.11.1422

Di Benedetto, C. A., & Song, M. (2003). The relationship between strategic type and firm capabilities in Chinese firms. *International Marketing Review, 20*(5), 514–533. https://doi.org/10.1108/02651330310498762

Dierickx, I., & Cool, K. (1989). Asset stock accumulation and sustainability of competitive advantage. *Management Science, 35*(12), 1504–1511. https://doi.org/10.1287/mnsc.35.12.1504

Dijkstra, T. K., & Henseler, J. (2015). Consistent partial least squares path modeling. *MIS Quarterly, 39*(2), 297–316. www.jstor.org/stable/26628355

Distanont, A., & Khongmalai, O. (2020). The role of innovation in creating a competitive advantage. *Kasetsart Journal of Social Sciences, 41*(1), 15–21. https://doi.org/10.1016/j.kjss.2018.07.009

Dodgson, M., Gann, D. M., & Phillips, N. (2014). Perspectives on innovation management. In M. Dodgson, D. M. Gann, & N. Phillips (Eds.), *The Oxford handbook of innovation management* (pp. 3–25). Oxford University Press.

Dolnicar, S., & Grün, B. (2013). "Translating" between survey answer formats. *Journal of Business Research, 66*(9), 1298–1306. https://doi.org/10.1016/j.jbusres.2012.02.029

Donate, M. J., & de Pablo, J. D. S. (2015). The role of knowledge-oriented leadership in knowledge management practices and innovation. *Journal of Business Research, 68*(2), 360–370. https://doi.org/10.1016/j.jbusres.2014.06.022

Dougherty, D. (1992). Interpretive barriers to successful product innovation in large firms. *Organization Science, 3*(2), 179–202. https://doi.org/10.1287/orsc.3.2.179

Dougherty, D., Borrelli, L., Munir, K., & O'Sullivan, A. (2000). Systems of organizational sensemaking for sustained product innovation. *Journal of Engineering and Technology Management, 17*(3–4), 321–355. https://doi.org/10.1016/S0923-4748(00)00028-X

Drucker, P. F. (1994). *Post-capitalist society*. Routledge.

Drucker, P. F. (2014). *Innovation and entrepreneurship: Practice and principles*. Routledge.

Dumay, J., Rooney, J., & Marini, L. (2013). An intellectual capital-based differentiation theory of innovation practice. *Journal of Intellectual Capital, 14*(4), 608–633. https://doi.org/10.1108/JIC-02-2013-0024

Du Plessis, M. (2007). The role of knowledge management in innovation. *Journal of Knowledge Management, 11*(4), 20–29. https://doi.org/10.1108/13673270710762684

Durmuş-Özdemir, E., & Abdukhoshimov, K. (2018). Exploring the mediating role of innovation in the effect of the knowledge management process on performance. *Technology Analysis & Strategic Management, 30*(5), 596–608. https://doi.org/10.1080/09537325.2017.1348495

Edler, J., & Fagerberg, J. (2017). Innovation policy: What, why, and how. *Oxford Review of Economic Policy, 33*(1), 2–23. https://doi.org/10.1093/oxrep/grx001

Eisenhardt, K. M., & Martin, J. A. (2000). Dynamic capabilities: What are they? *Strategic Management Journal, 21*(10–11), 1105–1121. https://doi.org/10.1002/1097-0266(200010/11)21:10/11<1105::AID-SMJ133>3.0.CO;2-E

Eisenstein, E. M., & Hutchinson, J. W. (2006). Action-based learning: Goals and attention in the acquisition of market knowledge. *Journal of Marketing Research, 43*(2), 244–258. https://doi.org/10.1509/jmkr.43.2.244

Eng, T. Y., & Ozdemir, S. (2014). International R&D partnerships and intrafirm R&D–marketing–production integration of manufacturing firms in emerging economies. *Industrial Marketing Management, 43*(1), 32–44. https://doi.org/10.1016/j.indmarman.2013.07.013

Enjolras, M., Camargo, M., & Schmitt, C. (2019). Are high-tech companies more competitive than others? An empirical study of innovative and exporting French SMEs. *Technology Innovation Management Review, 9*(1). https://doi.org/10.22215/timreview/1206

Erden, Z., Von Krogh, G., & Nonaka, I. (2008). The quality of group tacit knowledge. *The Journal of Strategic Information Systems, 17*(1), 4–18. https://doi.org/10.1016/j.jsis.2008.02.002

Erramilli, M. K., & Rao, C. P. (1990). Choice of foreign market entry modes by service firms: Role of market knowledge. *MIR: Management International Review, 30*(2), 135–150. www.jstor.org/stable/40228015

European Commission. (1995). *Green paper on innovation*. https://europa.eu/documents/comm/green_papers/pdf/com95_688_en.pdf

Eurostat. (2023, February 23). *NACE background*. https://ec.europa.eu/eurostat/statistics-explained/index.php/NACE_background#Historical_background_and_legal_context

Evan, W. M. (1966). Organizational lag. *Human Organization, 25*(1), 51–53. https://doi.org/10.17730/humo.25.1.v7354t3822136580

Executive Office of the President Office of Management and Budget. (2022). *North American industry classification system*. www.census.gov/naics/reference_files_tools/2022_NAICS_Manual.pdf

Fagerberg, J. (2004). Innovation: A guide to the literature. In J. Fagerberg, D. C. Mowery, & R. R. Neslon (Eds.), *The Oxford handbook of innovation* (pp. 1–26). Oxford University Press.

Fain, N., Kline, M., & Duhovnik, J. (2011). Integrating R&D and marketing in new product development. *Strojniski Vestnik, 57*(7–8), 599–609. https://doi.org/10.5545/sv-jme.2011.004

Fain, N., & Wagner, B. (2014). R&D-marketing integration in innovation–does culture matter? *European Business Review, 26*(2), 169–187. https://doi.org/10.1108/EBR-09-2013-0121

Falk, R., & Miller, N. (1992). *A primer for soft modeling*. University of Akron Press.

Fallah, M. H., & Lechler, T. G. (2008). Global innovation performance: Strategic challenges for multinational corporations. *Journal of Engineering and Technology Management, 25*(1–2), 58–74. https://doi.org/10.1016/j.jengtecman.2008.01.008

Faucher, J-B. P. L., Everett, A. M., & Lawson, R. (2008). What do we know about knowledge? In A. Koohang, K. Harman, & J. Britz (Eds.), *Knowledge management: Theoretical foundations* (pp. 41–77). Informing Science Press.

Fernando, P. J. S. (2015). Brain circulation at industry-level evidence from the knowledge services industry in Sri Lanka. *Journal of Economics and Development Studies, 3*(2), 50–65. https://doi.org/10.15640/jeds.v3n2a6

Ferrantino, M. J., Koopman, R. B., Wang, Z., & Yinug, F. (2010). The nature of US–China trade in advanced technology products. *Comparative Economic Studies, 52*, 207–224. https://doi.org/10.1057/ces.2010.6

Ferraris, A., Mazzoleni, A., Devalle, A., & Couturier, J. (2019). Big data analytics capabilities and knowledge management: Impact on firm performance. *Management Decision, 57*(8), 1923–1936. https://doi.org/10.1108/MD-07-2018-0825

Ferreira, J. J., Fernandes, C. I., & Ferreira, F. A. (2022). What makes organizations unique? Looking inside the box. *Journal of Business Research, 139*, 664–674. https://doi.org/10.1016/j.jbusres.2021.10.017

Fisch, J. H., & Kertels, K. (2011). Increasing the diversification of technological knowledge through R&D partnerships and foreign subsidiaries. In A. Verbeke, A. T. Tavares-Lehmann, & R. Van Tulder (Eds.), *Entrepreneurship in the global firm (Progress in international business research, Volume 6)* (pp. 275–290). Emerald Group Publishing Limited.

Flavin, M., & Quintero, V. (2018). UK higher education institutions' technology-enhanced learning strategies from the perspective of disruptive innovation. *Research in Learning Technology, 26*. https://doi.org/10.25304/rlt.v26.1987

Fletcher, M., & Harris, S. (2011). Knowledge acquisition for the internationalization of the smaller firm: Content and sources. *International Business Review, 21*(4), 631–647. https://doi.org/10.1016/j.ibusrev.2011.07.008

Fleury, M. T. L., Mauro, M. D., Oliveira, L., Mauerberg Junior, A., & Fleury, A. (2018). Management practices and competitiveness: A multisector study in the Brazilian industry. *BAR-Brazilian Administration Review, 15*(4). https://doi.org/10.1590/1807-7692bar2018180028

Fonfara, K. (2009). Typologia zachowań firm w procesie internacjonalizacji. In K. Fonfara (Ed.), *Zachowanie przedsiębiorstwa w procesie internacjonalizacji. Podejście sieciowe* (pp. 53–68). Polskie Wydawnictwo Ekonomiczne.

Fonfara, K. (2012). The empirical verification of types of company behaviour in the internationalisation process: Results of the 2006–2008 research project. In K. Fonfara (Ed.), *The development of business networks in the company internationalisation process* (pp. 43–50). Poznań University of Economics Press.

Fonfara, K. (2014). Istota i zakres wykorzystania koncepcji marketingu partnerskiego na rynkach zagranicznych. In K. Fonfara (Ed.), *Marketing międzynarodowy. Współczesne trendy i praktyka* (pp. 90–99). PWN.

Fornell, C., & Bookstein, F. L. (1982). Two structural equation models: LISREL and PLS applied to consumer exit-voice theory. *Journal of Marketing Research, 19*(4), 440–452. https://doi.org/10.1177/002224378201900406

Fornell, C., & Larcker, D. F. (1981). Evaluating structural equation models with unobservable variables and measurement error. *Journal of Marketing Research, 18*(1), 39–50. https://doi.org/10.1177/002224378101800104

Foss, K., & Foss, N. J. (2004). The next step in the evolution of the RBV: Integration with transaction cost economics. *Management Revue, 15*(1), 107–121. www.jstor.org/stable/41783453

Foss, N. J., & Ishikawa, I. (2007). Towards a dynamic resource-based view: Insights from Austrian capital and entrepreneurship theory. *Organization Studies, 28*(5), 749–772. https://doi.org/10.1177/0170840607072546

Frankelius, P. (2009). Questioning two myths in innovation literature. *The Journal of High Technology Management Research, 20*(1), 40–51. https://doi.org/10.1016/j.hitech.2009.02.002

Fraumeni, B. M., & Okubo, S. (2005). R&D in the national income and product accounts: A first look at its effect on GDP. In C. Corrado, J. Haltiwanger, & D. Sichel (Eds.), *Measuring capital in the new economy* (pp. 275–322). University of Chicago Press.

Freimane, R., & Bāliņa, S. (2016). Research and development expenditures and economic growth in the EU: A panel data analysis. *Economics and Business, 29*(1), 5–11. https://doi.org/10.1515/eb-2016-0016

Frické, M. (2007). The knowledge pyramid: A critique of the DIKW hierarchy. *Journal of Information Science, 35*(2), 131–142. https://doi.org/10.1177/0165551508094050

Fu, Y., Chen, Z., Liu, Z., & Yang, S. (2020). A comparison of milestone contract and royalty contract under critical value criterion in R&D alliance. *Soft Computing, 24*(4), 2447–2462. https://doi.org/10.1007/s00500-018-03727-0

Galindo-Rueda, F., & Verger, F. (2016). *OECD taxonomy of economic activities based on R&D intensity* (OECD Science, Technology and Industry Working Papers No. 2016/04). https://doi.org/10.1787/5JLV73SQQP8R-EN

Galunic, D. C., & Eisenhardt, K. M. (2001). Architectural innovation and modular corporate forms. *Academy of Management Journal, 44*(6), 1229–1249. https://doi.org/10.5465/3069398

Galunic, D. C., & Rodan, S. (1998). Resource recombinations in the firm: Knowledge structures and the potential for schumpeterian innovation. *Strategic Management Journal, 19*(12), 1193–1201. https://doi.org/10.1002/(SICI)1097-0266(1998120)19:12<1193::AID-SMJ5>3.0.CO;2-F

Gao, J., & Jefferson, G. H. (2007). Science and technology take-off in China?: Sources of rising R&D intensity. *Asia Pacific Business Review, 13*(3), 357–371. https://doi.org/10.1080/13602380701291933

Garavan, T., McCarthy, A., Lai, Y., Murphy, K., Sheehan, M., & Carbery, R. (2020). Training and organisational performance: A meta-analysis of temporal, institutional, and organisational context moderators. *Human Resource Management Journal, 31*(1), 93–119. https://doi.org/10.1111/1748-8583.12284

Garcia, R., & Calantone, R. (2002). A critical look at technological innovation typology and innovativeness terminology: A literature review. *Journal of Product Innovation Management, 19*(2), 110–132. https://doi.org/10.1111/1540-5885.1920110

Garrett, T. C., Buisson, D. H., & Yap, C. M. (2006). National culture and R&D and marketing integration mechanisms in new product development: A cross-cultural study between Singapore and New Zealand. *Industrial Marketing Management, 35*(3), 293–307. https://doi.org/10.1016/j.indmarman.2005.09.007

Garud, R. (1997). On the distinction between know-how, know-what, and know-why. *Advances in Strategic Management, 14*, 81–101.

Gassmann, O., & Keupp, M. M. (2007). The competitive advantage of early and rapidly internationalising SMEs in the biotechnology industry: A knowledge-based view. *Journal of World Business, 42*(3), 350–366. https://doi.org/10.1016/j.jwb.2007.04.006

Gatautis, R., Vaiciukynaite, E., & Tarute, A. (2019). Impact of business model innovations on SME's innovativeness and performance. *Baltic Journal of Management, 14*(4), 521–539. https://doi.org/10.1108/BJM-01-2018-0035

Gault, F. (2018). Defining and measuring innovation in all sectors of the economy. *Research Policy, 47*(3), 617–622. https://doi.org/10.1016/j.respol.2018.01.007

Gaviria-Marin, M., Merigó, J. M., & Baier-Fuentes, H. (2019). Knowledge management: A global examination based on bibliometric analysis. *Technological Forecasting and Social Change, 140*, 194–220. https://doi.org/10.1016/j.techfore.2018.07.006

Gerlach, H., Rønde, T., & Stahl, K. (2009). Labor pooling in R&D intensive industries. *Journal of Urban Economics, 65*(1), 99–111. https://doi.org/10.1016/j.jue.2008.10.001

Gerstenfeld, A., Turk, C. D., Farrow, R. L., & Spicer, R. F. (1969). Marketing and R & D. *Research Management, 12*(6), 409–412. https://doi.org/10.1080/00345334.1969.11755984

Giuliani, E. (2008). Multinational corporations and patterns of local knowledge transfer in Costa Rican high-tech industries. *Development and Change, 39*(3), 385–407. https://doi.org/10.1111/j.1467-7660.2008.00485.x

Glazer, R. (1991). Marketing in an information-intensive environment: Strategic implications of knowledge as an asset. *Journal of Marketing, 55*(4), 1–19. https://doi.org/10.1177/002224299105500401

Gloet, M., & Terziovski, M. (2004). Exploring the relationship between knowledge management practices and innovation performance. *Journal of Manufacturing Technology Management, 15*(5), 402–409. https://doi.org/10.1108/17410380410540390

Goldschlag, N., & Miranda, J. (2016). *Business dynamics statistics of high tech industries* (Center for Economic Studies Working Paper no. 16-55, U.S. Census Bureau). https://www2.census.gov/ces/wp/2016/CES-WP-16-55.pdf

Grant, R. M. (1996a). Toward a knowledge-based theory of the firm. *Strategic Management Journal, 17*(S2), 109–122. https://doi.org/10.1002/smj.4250171110

Grant, R. M. (1996b). Prospering in dynamically-competitive environments: Organizational capability as knowledge integration. *Organization Science, 7*(4), 375–387. https://doi.org/10.1287/orsc.7.4.375

Grant, R. M. (1997). The knowledge-based view of the firm: Implications for management practice. *Long Range Planning, 30*(3), 450–454. https://doi.org/10.1016/S0024-6301(97)00025-3

Grant, R. M. (2002). The knowledge-based view of the firm. The strategic management of intellectual capital and organizational knowledge. In C. W. Choo & N. Bontis (Eds.), *The strategic management of intellectual capital and organizational knowledge* (pp. 133–148). Oxford University Press.

Grant, R. M. (2016). *Contemporary strategy analysis: Text and cases edition*. John Wiley & Sons.

Griffin, A., & Hauser, J. R. (1992). *The marketing and R & D interface*. (Massachusetts Institute of Technology Sloan Working Paper No. 3350-91-MSA). https://dspace.mit.edu/bitstream/handle/1721.1/2377/SWP-3350-26661421.pdf?sequence=1

Griffin, A., & Hauser, J. R. (1996). Integrating R&D and marketing: A review and analysis of the literature. *Journal of Product Innovation Management, 13*(3), 191–215. https://doi.org/10.1111/1540-5885.1330191

Griffith, R. (2000, October). *How important is business R&D for economic growth and should the government subsidise it?* Institute for Fiscal Studies. https://discovery.ucl.ac.uk/id/eprint/14922/1/14922.pdf

Gueler, M. S., & Schneider, S. (2021). The resource-based view in business ecosystems: A perspective on the determinants of a valuable resource and capability. *Journal of Business Research, 133*, 158–169. https://doi.org/10.1016/j.jbusres.2021.04.061

Guellec, D., & Van Pottelsberghe de la Potterie, B. (2002). R&D and productivity growth. *OECD Economic Studies, 33*, 103–126. https://doi.org/10.1787/eco_studies-v2001-art12-en

Guellec, D., & Van Pottelsberghe de la Potterie, B. (2004). From R&D to productivity growth: Do the institutional settings and the source of funds of R&D matter? *Oxford Bulletin of Economics and Statistics*, *66*(3), 353–378. https://doi.org/10.1111/j.1468-0084.2004.00083.x

Gumusluoglu, L., & Ilsev, A. (2009). Transformational leadership, creativity, and organizational innovation. *Journal of Business Research*, *62*(4), 461–473. https://doi.org/10.1016/j.jbusres.2007.07.032

Gupta, A. K., Raj, S. P., & Wilemon, D. (1985). The R&D-marketing interface in high-technology firms. *Journal of Product Innovation Management*, *2*(1), 12–24. https://doi.org/10.1016/0737-6782(85)90012-8

Gupta, A. K., Raj, S. P., & Wilemon, D. (1986a). R&D and marketing managers in high-tech companies: Are they different? *IEEE Transactions on Engineering Management*, *33*(1), 25–32. https://doi.org/10.1109/TEM.1986.6447719

Gupta, A. K., Raj, S. P., & Wilemon, D. (1986b). A model for studying R&D–marketing interface in the product innovation process. *Journal of Marketing*, *50*(2), 7–17. https://doi.org/10.1177/002224298605000201

Gupta, A. K., Tesluk, P. E., & Taylor, M. S. (2007). Innovation at and across multiple levels of analysis. *Organization Science*, *18*(6), 885–897. https://doi.org/10.1287/orsc.1070.0337

Gupta, A. K., & Wilemon, D. (1988). The credibility–cooperation connection at the R&D-marketing interface. *Journal of Product Innovation Management*, *5*(1), 20–31. https://doi.org/10.1111/1540-5885.510020

Gupta, A. K., & Wilemon, D. (1990). Improving R&D/marketing relations: R&D's perspective. *R&D Management*, *20*(4), 277–290. https://doi.org/10.1111/j.1467-9310.1990.tb00718.x

Gupta, A. K., & Wilemon, D. (1991). Improving R&D/marketing relations in technology-based companies: Marketing's perspective. *Journal of Marketing Management*, *7*(1), 25–45. https://doi.org/10.1080/0267257X.1991.9964138

Gur, N., & Avşar, V. (2016). Financial system, R&D intensity and comparative advantage. *The Journal of International Trade & Economic Development*, *25*(2), 213–239. https://doi.org/10.1080/09638199.2015.1045928

Hair Jr., J. F., Black, W. C., Babin, B. J., & Anderson, R. E. (2014). *Multivariate data analysis*. Pearson Education Limited.

Hair, J. F., Hult, G. T. M., Ringle, C. M., & Sarstedt, M. (2017a). *A primer on partial least squares structural equation modeling (PLS-SEM)*. Sage Publication.

Hair Jr., J. F., Hult, T. M., Ringle, C. M., Sarstedt, M., Danks, N. P., & Ray, S. (2021). *Partial least squares structural equation modeling (PLS-SEM) using R*. Springer.

Hair Jr., J. F., Matthews, L. M., Matthews, R. L., & Sarstedt, M. (2017b). PLS-SEM or CB-SEM: Updated guidelines on which method to use. *International Journal of Multivariate Data Analysis*, *1*(2), 107–123. https://doi.org/10.1504/IJMDA.2017.087624

Hair, J. F., Ringle, C. M., & Sarstedt, M. (2011). PLS-SEM: Indeed a silver bullet. *Journal of Marketing Theory and Practice*, *19*(2), 139–152. https://doi.org/10.2753/MTP1069-6679190202

Hair, J. F., Risher, J. J., Sarstedt, M., & Ringle, C. M. (2019). When to use and how to report the results of PLS-SEM. *European Business Review*, *31*(1), 2–24. https://doi.org/10.1108/EBR-11-2018-0203

Hair, J. F., Sarstedt, M., Pieper, T. M., & Ringle, C. M. (2012). The use of partial least squares structural equation modeling in strategic management research: A review of past practices and recommendations for future applications. *Long Range Planning, 45*(5–6), 320–340. https://doi.org/10.1016/j.lrp.2012.09.008

Hall, B. H. (2002). The financing of research and development. *Oxford Review of Economic Policy, 18*(1), 35–51. https://doi.org/10.1093/oxrep/18.1.35

Hall, B. H., Jaffe, A., & Trajtenberg, M. (2005). Market value and patent citations. *The RAND Journal of Economics, 36*(1), 16–38. www.jstor.org/stable/1593752

Hall, B. H., & Lerner, J. (2009, September). *The financing of R&D and innovation* (NBER Working Paper No. 15325). www.nber.org/papers/w15325.pdf

Hart, S. L. (1995). A natural-resource-based view of the firm. *Academy of Management Review, 20*(4), 986–1014. https://doi.org/10.5465/amr.1995.9512280033

Hatzichronoglou, T. (1997). *Revision of the high-technology sector and product classification* (OECD Science, Technology and Industry Working Papers No. 1997/02). https://doi.org/10.1787/134337307632

He, J., & Wang, H. C. (2009). Innovative knowledge assets and economic performance: The asymmetric roles of incentives and monitoring. *Academy of Management Journal, 52*(5), 919–938. https://doi.org/10.5465/amj.2009.44633414

Hecker, D. E. (1999). High-technology employment: A broader view. *Monthly Labor Review, 122*, 18–28. www.bls.gov/mlr/1999/06/art3full.pdf

Hecker, D. E. (2005). High-technology employment: A NAICS-based update. *Monthly Labor Review, 128*, 57–72. https://stats.bls.gov/opub/mlr/2005/07/art6full.pdf

Helfat, C., Finkelstein, S., Mitchell, W., Petraf, M. A., Singh, H., Teece, D. J., & Winter, S. G. (2007). *Dynamic capabilities. Understanding strategic change in organizations.* Blackwell Publishing.

Helfat, C. E., & Winter, S. G. (2011). Untangling dynamic and operational capabilities: Strategy for the (N) ever-changing world. *Strategic Management Journal, 32*(11), 1243–1250. https://doi.org/10.1002/smj.955

Helmers, C., Schulte, C., & Strauss, H. (2009). Business R&D expenditure and capital in Europe. *EIB Papers, 14*(1), 36–61. http://dx.doi.org/10.2139/ssrn.1816426

Hempelmann, F., & Engelen, A. (2015). Integration of finance with marketing and R&D in new product development: The role of project stage. *Journal of Product Innovation Management, 32*(4), 636–654. https://doi.org/10.1111/jpim.12237

Henard, D. H., & McFadyen, M. A. (2006). R&D knowledge is power. *Research-Technology Management, 49*(3), 41–47. https://doi.org/10.1080/08956308.2006.11657377

Henderson, R. M., & Clark, K. B. (1990). Architectural innovation: The reconfiguration of existing product technologies and the failure of established firms. *Administrative Science Quarterly, 35*(1), 9–30. https://doi.org/10.2307/2393549

Henseler, J., Ringle, C. M., & Sarstedt, M. (2015). A new criterion for assessing discriminant validity in variance-based structural equation modeling. *Journal of the Academy of Marketing Science, 43*, 115–135. https://doi.org/10.1007/s11747-014-0403-8

Henseler, J., Ringle, C. M., & Sinkovics, R. R. (2009). The use of partial least squares path modeling in international marketing. In R. R. Sinkovics, & P. N. Ghauri (Eds.), *New challenges to international marketing (advances in international marketing, Vol. 20)* (pp. 277–319). Emerald Group Publishing Limited. https://doi.org/10.1108/S1474-7979(2009)0000020014

Herrero, D., & Rial, A. (2023). Productive linkages in a segmented economy: The role of services in the export performance of German manufacturing. *Economic Systems Research, 35*(2), 183–210. https://doi.org/10.1080/09535314.2022.2026894

Hicks, R. C., Dattero, R., & Galup, S. D. (2006). The five-tier knowledge management hierarchy. *Journal of Knowledge Management, 10*(1), 19–31. https://doi.org/10.1108/13673270610650076

Hill, C. W. L., & Deeds, D. L. (1996). The importance of industry structure for the determination of firm profitability: A neo-Austrian Perspective. *Journal of Management Studies, 33*(4), 429–451. https://doi.org/10.1111/j.1467-6486.1996.tb00163.x

Hill, D. (2020). *Production and trade of knowledge- and technology- intensive industries* (Report No. NSB-2020-5). National Center for Science and Engineering Statistics. Directorate for Social, Behavioral and Economic Sciences, National Science Foundation. https://ncses.nsf.gov/pubs/nsb20205/introduction

Hise, R. T., O'Neal, L., Parasuraman, A., & McNeal, J. U. (1990). Marketing/R&D interaction in new product development: Implications for new product success rates. *Journal of Product Innovation Management, 7*(2), 142–155. https://doi.org/10.1111/1540-5885.720142

Hitt, M. A., King, D., Krishnan, H., Makri, M., Schijven, M., Shimizu, K., & Zhu, H. (2009). Mergers and acquisitions: Overcoming pitfalls, building synergy, and creating value. *Business Horizons, 52*(6), 523–529. https://doi.org/10.1016/j.bushor.2009.06.008

Hjalager, A. M. (2010). A review of innovation research in tourism. *Tourism Management, 31*(1), 1–12. https://doi.org/10.1016/j.tourman.2009.08.012

Ho, T. B. (2012). Knowledge discovery. In Y. Nakamori (Ed.), *Knowledge science. Modeling the knowledge creation process* (pp. 57–80). CRC Press.

Homburg, C., Alavi, S., Rajab, T., & Wieseke, J. (2017). The contingent roles of R&D–sales versus R&D–marketing cooperation in new-product development of business-to-business firms. *International Journal of Research in Marketing, 34*(1), 212–230. https://doi.org/10.1016/j.ijresmar.2016.05.008

Honjo, Y., Doi, N., & Kudo, Y. (2018). The turnover of market leaders in growing and declining industries: Evidence from Japan. *Journal of Industry, Competition and Trade, 18*, 121–138. https://doi.org/10.1007/s10842-017-0254-3

Hooley, G., Cox, T., Fahy, J., Shipley, D., Beracs, J., Fonfara, K., & Snoj, B. (2000). Market orientation in the transition economies of Central Europe: Tests of the Narver and Slater Market Orientation Scales. *Journal of Business Research, 50*(3), 273–285. https://doi.org/10.1016/S0148-2963(99)00105-8

Hoskisson, R. E., Hitt, M. A., Wan, W. P., & Yiu, D. (1999). Theory and research in strategic management: Swings of a pendulum. *Journal of Management, 25*(3), 417–456. https://doi.org/10.1177/014920639902500307

Hou, J. J. (2008). Toward a research model of market orientation and dynamic capabilities. *Social Behavior and Personality: An International Journal, 36*(9), 1251–1268. https://doi.org/10.2224/sbp.2008.36.9.1251

Hovgaard, A., & Hansen, E. (2004). Innovativeness in the forest products industry. *Forest Products Journal, 54*(1), 26–33.

Hsieh, P. H., Mishra, C. S., & Gobeli, D. H. (2003). The return on R&D versus capital expenditures in pharmaceutical and chemical industries. *IEEE Transactions on Engineering Management, 50*(2), 141–150. https://doi.org/10.1109/TEM.2003.810828

Hughes, P., Morgan, R. E., & Kouropalatis, Y. (2008). Market knowledge diffusion and business performance. *European Journal of Marketing*, *42*(11/12), 1372–1395. https://doi.org/10.1108/03090560810903718

Hulland, J. (1999). Use of partial least squares (PLS) in strategic management research: A review of four recent studies. *Strategic Management Journal*, *20*(2), 195–204. https://doi.org/10.1002/(SICI)1097-0266(199902)20:2<195::AID-SMJ13>3.0.CO;2-7

Hult, G. T. M., Hurley, R. F., & Knight, G. A. (2004). Innovativeness: Its antecedents and impact on business performance. *Industrial Marketing Management*, *33*(5), 429–438. https://doi.org/10.1016/j.indmarman.2003.08.015

Hurley, R. F., & Hult, G. T. M. (1998). Innovation, market orientation, and organizational learning: An integration and empirical examination. *Journal of Marketing*, *62*(3), 42–54. https://doi.org/10.1177/002224299806200303

Ilyina, A., & Samaniego, R. (2011). Technology and financial development. *Journal of Money, Credit and Banking*, *43*(5), 899–921. https://doi.org/10.1111/j.1538-4616.2011.00401.x

Inkinen, H. (2016). Review of empirical research on knowledge management practices and firm performance. *Journal of Knowledge Management*, *20*(2), 230–257. https://doi.org/10.1108/JKM-09-2015-0336

Intezari, A., Taskin, N., & Pauleen, D. J. (2017). Looking beyond knowledge sharing: An integrative approach to knowledge management culture. *Journal of Knowledge Management*, *21*(2), 492–515. https://doi.org/10.1108/JKM-06-2016-0216

Jacobs, L., & Herbig, P. (1998). Japanese product development strategies. *Journal of Business & Industrial Marketing*, *13*(2), 132–154. https://doi.org/10.1108/08858629810213351

Jaffe, A. B. (1986, January). *Technological opportunity and spillovers of R&D: Evidence from firms' patents, profits and market value* (National Bureau of Economic Research Working Paper No. 1815). www.nber.org/papers/w1815.pdf

Jakus, G., Milutinović, V., Omerović, S., & Tomažič, S. (2013). *Concepts, ontologies, and knowledge representation*. Springer Science & Business Media.

Jemielniak, D. (2008). *Praca oparta na wiedzy: praca w przedsiębiorstwach wiedzy na przykładzie organizacji high-tech*. Wydawnictwo Akademickie i Profesjonalne.

Jemielniak, D. (2012). Zarządzanie Wiedzą. Podstawowe pojęcia. In D. Jemielniak & A. K. Koźmiński (Eds.), *Zarządzanie wiedzą* (pp. 21–42). Wolters Kluwer.

Jennex, M. E. (2019). Using a revised knowledge pyramid to redefine knowledge management strategy. In M. E. Jennex (Ed.), *Effective knowledge management systems in modern society* (pp. 1–18). IGI Global.

Jin, Z. (2001). The nature of NPD and role flexibility of R&D/marketing in a fast growing high-tech setting. *R&D Management*, *31*(3), 275–285. https://doi.org/10.1111/1467-9310.00216

Jin, Z., Hewitt-Dundas, N., & Thompson, N. J. (2004). Innovativeness and performance: Evidence from manufacturing sectors. *Journal of Strategic Marketing*, *12*(4), 255–266. https://doi.org/10.1080/0965254042000308075

Johannessen, J.-A., Olsen, B., & Lumpkin, G. T. (2001). Innovation as newness what is new, how new, and new to whom. *European Journal of Innovation Management*, *4*(1), 20–31. https://doi.org/10.1108/14601060110365547

Joshi, A. W., & Sharma, S. (2004). Customer knowledge development: Antecedents and impact on new product performance. *Journal of Marketing*, *68*(4), 47–59. https://doi.org/10.1509/jmkg.68.4.47.42722

Kahn, K. B. (2018). Understanding innovation. *Business Horizons*, *61*(3), 453–460. https://doi.org/10.1016/j.bushor.2018.01.011

Kahn, K. B., & McDonough III, E. F. (1997a). An empirical study of the relationships among co-location, integration, performance, and satisfaction. *Journal of Product Innovation Management, 14*(3), 161–178. https://doi.org/10.1111/1540-5885.1430161

Kahn, K. B., & McDonough, E. F. (1997b). Marketing's Integration with R&D and manufacturing: A cross-regional analysis. *Journal of International Marketing, 5*(1), 51–76. https://doi.org/10.1177/1069031X9700500105

Kakabadse, N. K., Kouzmin, A., & Kakabadse, A. (2001). From tacit knowledge to knowledge management: Leveraging invisible assets. *Knowledge and Process Management, 8*(3), 137–154. https://doi.org/10.1002/kpm.120

Kaluzny, A. D., Veney, J. E., & Gentry, J. T. (1974). Innovation of health services: A comparative study of hospitals and health departments. *The Milbank Memorial Fund Quarterly. Health and Society, 52*(1), 51–82. https://doi.org/10.2307/3349503

Kamaşak, R., & Bulutlar, F. (2010). The influence of knowledge sharing on innovation. *European Business Review, 22*(3), 306–317. https://doi.org/10.1108/09555341011040994

Kampf, R. (2013). From data to wisdom: The contribution of intellectual property rights to the knowledge pyramid. In D. Beldiman (Ed.), *Access to information and knowledge: 21st century challenges in intellectual property and knowledge governance* (pp. 235–257). Edward Elgar Publishing.

Kang, N., Kim, J., & Park, Y. (2007). Integration of marketing domain and R&D domain in NPD design process. *Industrial Management & Data Systems, 107*(6), 780–801. https://doi.org/10.1108/02635570710758725

Kaplan, S., Schenkel, A., von Krogh, G., & Weber, C. (2001). *Knowledge-based theories of the firm in strategic management: A review and extension* (Massachusetts Institute of Technology Sloan Working Paper No. 4216-01). https://citeseerx.ist.psu.edu/document?repid=rep1&type=pdf&doi=1a0762442607f602e2458665c892bba6b171b4c5

Kato, M., & Honjo, Y. (2015). Entrepreneurial human capital and the survival of new firms in high-and low-tech sectors. *Journal of Evolutionary Economics, 25*, 925–957. https://doi.org/10.1007/s00191-015-0427-3

Keiningham, T., Aksoy, L., Bruce, H. L., Cadet, F., Clennell, N., Hodgkinson, I. R., & Kearney, T. (2019). Customer experience driven business model innovation. *Journal of Business Research, 116*, 431–440. https://doi.org/10.1016/j.jbusres.2019.08.003

Kerzner, H. (2019). *Innovation project management: Methods, case studies, and tools for managing innovation projects.* John Wiley & Sons.

Ketchen Jr, D. J., Hult, G. T. M., & Slater, S. F. (2007). Toward greater understanding of market orientation and the resource-based view. *Strategic Management Journal, 28*(9), 961–964. https://doi.org/10.1002/smj.620

Keupp, M. M., & Gassmann, O. (2009). Determinants and archetype users of open innovation. *R&D Management, 39*(4), 331–341. https://doi.org/10.1111/j.1467-9310.2009.00563.x

Kianto, A. (2011). The influence of knowledge management on continuous innovation. *International Journal of Technology Management, 55*(1/2), 110–121. https://doi.org/10.1504/IJTM.2011.041682

Kim, T. H., Lee, J. N., Chun, J. U., & Benbasat, I. (2014). Understanding the effect of knowledge management strategies on knowledge management performance: A contingency perspective. *Information & Management, 51*(4), 398–416. https://doi.org/10.1016/j.im.2014.03.001

Kirsch, P., Hine, A., & Maybury, T. (2015). A model for the implementation of industry-wide knowledge sharing to improve risk management practice. *Safety Science, 80*, 66–76. https://doi.org/10.1016/j.ssci.2015.07.009

Kivimäki, M., Länsisalmi, H., Elovainio, M., Heikkilä, A., Lindström, K., Harisalo, R., Sipilä, K., & Puolimatka, L. (2000). Communication as a determinant of organizational innovation. *R&D Management, 30*(1), 33–42. https://doi.org/10.1111/1467-9310.00155

Klincewicz, K. (2012). Cele zarządzania wiedzą. In D. Jemielniak & A. K. Koźmiński (Eds.), *Zarządzanie wiedzą* (pp. 71–104). Wolters Kluwer.

Knight, K. E. (1967). A descriptive model of the intra-firm innovation process. *The Journal of Business, 40*(4), 478–496. www.jstor.org/stable/2351630

Knott, P. J. (2015). Does VRIO help managers evaluate a firm's resources? *Management Decision, 53*(8), 1806–1822. https://doi.org/10.1108/MD-08-2014-0525

Koberg, C. S., Detienne, D. R., & Heppard, K. A. (2003). An empirical test of environmental, organizational, and process factors affecting incremental and radical innovation. *The Journal of High Technology Management Research, 14*(1), 21–45. https://doi.org/10.1016/S1047-8310(03)00003-8

Kogut, B., & Zander, U. (1992). Knowledge of the firm, combinative capabilities, and the replication of technology. *Organization Science, 3*(3), 383–397. https://doi.org/10.1287/orsc.3.3.383

Kogut, B., & Zander, U. (1996). What firms do? Coordination, identity, and learning. *Organization Science, 7*(5), 502–518. https://doi.org/10.1287/orsc.7.5.502

Kohli, A. K., & Jaworski, B. J. (1990). Market orientation: The construct, research propositions, and managerial implications. *Journal of Marketing, 54*(2), 1–18. https://doi.org/10.1177/002224299005400201

Kohli, A. K., & Jaworski, B. J. (1993). MARKOR: A measure of market orientation. *Journal of Marketing Research, 30*(4), 467–477. https://doi.org/10.1177/002224379303000406

Koohang, A., Paliszkiewicz, J., & Goluchowski, J. (2017). The impact of leadership on trust, knowledge management, and organizational performance: A research model. *Industrial Management & Data Systems, 117*(3), 521–537. https://doi.org/10.1108/IMDS-02-2016-0072

Kowalczyk, A., & Nogalski, B. (2007). *Zarządzanie wiedzą. Koncepcja i narzędzia*. Difin.

KPMG (1998). *Knowledge management research report 1998*. www.brint.com/papers/submit/knowmgmt.pdf

Lambooy, J. (2005). Innovation and knowledge: Theory and regional policy. *European Planning Studies, 13*(8), 1137–1152. https://doi.org/10.1080/09654310500336444

Lampón, J. F., & González-Benito, J. (2019). Backshoring and improved key manufacturing resources in firms' home location. *International Journal of Production Research, 58*(20), 6268–6282. https://doi.org/10.1080/00207543.2019.1676479

Lane, P. J., Koka, B. R., & Pathak, S. (2006). The reification of absorptive capacity: A critical review and rejuvenation of the construct. *Academy of Management Review, 31*(4), 833–863. https://doi.org/10.5465/amr.2006.22527456

Lanzolla, G., & Markides, C. (2021). A business model view of strategy. *Journal of Management Studies, 58*(2), 540–553. https://doi.org/10.1111/joms.12580

Lapierre, J., & Hénault, B. (1996). Bidirectional information transfer: An imperative for network and marketing integration in a Canadian telecommunications firm. *Journal of Product Innovation Management, 13*(2), 152–166. https://doi.org/10.1016/0737-6782(95)00111-5

Lau, R. S. M., & May, B. E. (1998). A win-win paradigm for quality of work life and business performance. *Human Resource Development Quarterly, 9*(3), 211–226. https://doi.org/10.1002/hrdq.3920090302

Lavie, D. (2006). The competitive advantage of interconnected firms: An extension of the resource-based view. *Academy of Management Review, 31*(3), 638–658. https://doi.org/10.5465/amr.2006.21318922

Leach, M., Rockström, J., Raskin, P., Scoones, I., Stirling, A. C., Smith, A., Thompson, J., Millstone, E., Ely, A., Arond, E., Folke, C., & Olsson, P. (2012). Transforming innovation for sustainability. *Ecology and Society, 17*(2). www.jstor.org/stable/26269052

Leavy, P. (2017). *Research design quantitative, qualitative, mixed methods, arts-based, and community-based participatory research approaches*. The Guilford Press.

Lee, H., & Kelley, D. (2008). Building dynamic capabilities for innovation: An exploratory study of key management practices. *R&D Management, 38*(2), 155–168. https://doi.org/10.1111/j.1467-9310.2008.00506.x

Lee, J., Kim, C., & Choi, G. (2019). Exploring data envelopment analysis for measuring collaborated innovation efficiency of small and medium-sized enterprises in Korea. *European Journal of Operational Research, 278*(2), 533–545. https://doi.org/10.1016/j.ejor.2018.08.044

Leenders, M. A. A. M., & Wierenga, B. (2002). The effectiveness of different mechanisms for integrating marketing and R&D. *Journal of Product Innovation Management, 19*(4), 305–317. https://doi.org/10.1111/1540-5885.1940305

Leenders, M. A. A. M., & Wierenga, B. (2008). The effect of the marketing–R&D interface on new product performance: The critical role of resources and scope. *International Journal of Research in Marketing, 25*(1), 56–68. https://doi.org/10.1016/j.ijresmar.2007.09.006

Legard, R., Keegan, J., & Ward, K. (2003). In-depth interviews. In J. Ritchie & J. Lewis (Eds.), *Qualitative research and practice. A guide for social science students and researchers* (pp. 138–169). SAGE Publications.

Legler, H., Licht, G., & Spielkamp, A. (2000). *Germany's technological performance: A study on behalf of the German Federal Ministry of Education and Research*. Physica-Verlag.

Leiponen, A. (2006). Managing knowledge for innovation: The case of business-to-business services. *Journal of Product Innovation Management, 23*(3), 238–258. https://doi.org/10.1111/j.1540-5885.2006.00196.x

Leonard, D., & Sensiper, S. (1998). The role of tacit knowledge in group innovation. *California Management Review, 40*(3), 112–132. https://doi.org/10.2307/41165946

Levallet, N., & Chan, Y. E. (2016). Knowledge loss and retention: The paradoxical role of IT. In J. Liebowitz (Ed.), *Successes and Failures of knowledge management* (pp. 97–111). Morgan Kaufmann. https://doi.org/10.1016/B978-0-12-805187-0.00007-3

Li, D. Y., & Liu, J. (2014). Dynamic capabilities, environmental dynamism, and competitive advantage: Evidence from China. *Journal of Business Research, 67*(1), 2793–2799. https://doi.org/10.1016/j.jbusres.2012.08.007

Li, H., & Atuahene-Gima, K. (2001). The impact of interaction between R&D and marketing on new product performance: An empirical analysis of Chinese high technology firms. *International Journal of Technology Management, 21*(1–2), 61–75. https://doi.org/10.1504/IJTM.2001.002902

Li, P., & Bathelt, H. (2018). Location strategy in cluster networks. *Journal of International Business Studies, 49*, 967–989. https://doi.org/10.1057/s41267-017-0088-6

Li, P. C., & Chen, Y. C. (2012). How does social orientation influence R&D-marketing collaboration? *Asia Pacific Journal of Management, 29*, 151–168. https://doi.org/10.1007/s10490-010-9195-7

Li, P. C., & Chen, Y. C. (2016). Exploring interaction-based antecedents of marketing-R&D collaboration: Evidence from the Taiwan's semiconductor industry. *Innovation, 18*(3), 352–372. https://doi.org/10.1080/14479338.2016.1219618

Li, T., & Calantone, R. J. (1998). The impact of market knowledge competence on new product advantage: Conceptualization and empirical examination. *Journal of Marketing, 62*(4), 13–29. https://doi.org/10.1177/002224299806200402

Li, T., & Cavusgil, S. T. (1999). Measuring the dimensions of market knowledge competence in new product development. *European Journal of Innovation Management, 2*(3), 129–146. https://doi.org/10.1108/14601069910289068

Lichtenberg, F. R. (1992, September). *R&D investment and international productivity differences* (National Bureau of Economic Research Working Paper No. 4161). https://doi.org/10.3386/w4161

Lichtenthaler, U. (2009). Absorptive capacity, environmental turbulence, and the complementarity of organizational learning processes. *Academy of Management Journal, 52*(4), 822–846. https://doi.org/10.5465/amj.2009.43670902

Lichtenthaler, U. (2016). Absorptive capacity and firm performance: An integrative framework of benefits and downsides. *Technology Analysis & Strategic Management, 28*(6), 664–676. https://doi.org/10.1080/09537325.2015.1131258

Liebeskind, J. P. (1996). Knowledge, strategy, and the theory of the firm. *Strategic Management Journal, 17*(S2), 93–107. https://doi.org/10.1002/smj.4250171109

Lin, R. J., Che, R. H., & Ting, C. Y. (2012). Turning knowledge management into innovation in the high-tech industry. *Industrial Management & Data Systems, 112*(1), 42–63. https://doi.org/10.1108/02635571211193635

Linder, J. C., Jarvenpaa, S., & Davenport, T. H. (2003). Toward an innovation sourcing strategy. *MIT Sloan Management Review, 44*(4), 43–49. https://sloanreview.mit.edu/article/toward-an-innovation-sourcing-strategy

Liu, K., & Daly, K. (2011). Foreign direct investment in China Manufacturing Industry—transformation from a low tech to high tech manufacturing. *International Journal of Business and Management, 6*(7), 15–27. https://doi.org/10.5539/ijbm.v6n7p15

Liu, M. S., & Liu, N. C. (2008). Sources of knowledge acquisition and patterns of knowledge-sharing behaviors—An empirical study of Taiwanese high-tech firms. *International Journal of Information Management, 28*(5), 423–432. https://doi.org/10.1016/j.ijinfomgt.2008.01.005

López, S. V. (2005). Competitive advantage and strategy formulation: The key role of dynamic capabilities. *Management Decision, 43*(5), 661–669. https://doi.org/10.1108/00251740510597699

López-Nicolás, C., & Meroño-Cerdán, Á. L. (2011). Strategic knowledge management, innovation and performance. *International Journal of Information Management, 31*(6), 502–509. https://doi.org/10.1016/j.ijinfomgt.2011.02.003

Lu, L. Y. Y., & Yang, C. (2004). The R&D and marketing cooperation across new product development stages: An empirical study of Taiwan's IT industry. *Industrial Marketing Management, 33*(7), 593–605. https://doi.org/10.1016/j.indmarman.2003.11.002

Lu, L. Y. Y., & Yang, C. (2005). R&D and marketing integration in Taiwan's IT industry. *International Journal of Information Technology and Management, 4*(1), 68–81. https://doi.org/10.1504/IJITM.2005.006404

Lucas Jr., G. H., & Bush, A. J. (1988). The marketing–R&D interface: Do personality factors have an impact? *Journal of Product Innovation Management, 5*(4), 257–268. https://doi.org/10.1111/1540-5885.540257

Lumpkin, G. T., & Dess, G. G. (1996). Clarifying the entrepreneurial orientation construct and linking it to performance. *Academy of Management Review, 21*(1), 135–172. https://doi.org/10.5465/amr.1996.9602161568
Lundvall, B., & Johnson, B. (1994). The learning economy. *Journal of Industry Studies, 1*(2), 23–42. https://doi.org/10.1080/13662719400000002
Macher, J. T. (2006). Technological development and the boundaries of the firm: A knowledge-based examination in semiconductor manufacturing. *Management Science, 52*(6), 826–843. https://doi.org/10.1287/mnsc.1060.0511
Maier, R. (2004). *Knowledge management systems. Information and communication technologies for knowledge management.* Springer.
Makadok, R. (2001). Toward a synthesis of the resource-based and dynamic-capability views of rent creation. *Strategic Management Journal, 22*(5), 387–401. https://doi.org/10.1002/smj.158
Makkonen, H., Pohjola, M., Olkkonen, R., & Koponen, A. (2014). Dynamic capabilities and firm performance in a financial crisis. *Journal of Business Research, 67*(1), 2707–2719. https://doi.org/10.1016/j.jbusres.2013.03.020
Malik, A., Froese, F. J., & Sharma, P. (2020). Role of HRM in knowledge integration: Towards a conceptual framework. *Journal of Business Research, 109*, 524–535. https://doi.org/10.1016/j.jbusres.2019.01.029
Malik, Z., Hashmi, K., Najmi, E., & Rezgui, A. (2019). Wisdom extraction in knowledge-based information systems. *Journal of Knowledge Management, 23*(1), 23–45. https://doi.org/10.1108/JKM-05-2018-0288
Maltz, E., Souder, W. E., & Kumar, A. (2001). Influencing R&D/marketing integration and the use of market information by R&D managers: Intended and unintended effects of managerial actions. *Journal of Business Research, 52*(1), 69–82. https://doi.org/10.1016/S0148-2963(99)00096-X
Mansfield, E. (1982). How economists see R&D. *Research Management, 25*(4), 23–29. https://doi.org/10.1080/00345334.1982.11756738
Marcinkowska, E. (2017). Wpływ teorii kosztów transakcyjnych i teorii zasobowej na proces decyzyjny outsourcingu. *Studia Ekonomiczne, 341*, 220–229. https://bibliotekanauki.pl/articles/590660.pdf
Mardani, A., Nikoosokhan, S., Moradi, M., & Doustar, M. (2018). The relationship between knowledge management and innovation performance. *The Journal of High Technology Management Research, 29*(1), 12–26. https://doi.org/10.1016/j.hitech.2018.04.002
Marinova, D. (2004). Actualizing innovation effort: The impact of market knowledge diffusion in a dynamic system of competition. *Journal of Marketing, 68*(3), 1–20. https://doi.org/10.1509/jmkg.68.3.1.34768
Marques, J. P. C. (2014). Closed versus open innovation: Evolution or combination? *International Journal of Business and Management, 9*(3), 196–203. https://doi.org/10.5539/ijbm.v9n3p196
Martinelli, E., Tagliazucchi, G., & Marchi, G. (2018). The resilient retail entrepreneur: Dynamic capabilities for facing natural disasters. *International Journal of Entrepreneurial Behavior & Research, 24*(7), 1222–1243. https://doi.org/10.1108/IJEBR-11-2016-0386
Massa, S., & Testa, S. (2008). Innovation and SMEs: Misaligned perspectives and goals among entrepreneurs, academics, and policy makers. *Technovation, 28*(7), 393–407. https://doi.org/10.1016/j.technovation.2008.01.002

Massey, G. R., & Kyriazis, E. (2007). Interpersonal trust between marketing and R&D during new product development projects. *European Journal of Marketing, 41*(9/10), 1146–1172. https://doi.org/10.1108/03090560710773381

Matthias, O., Fouweather, I., Gregory, I., & Vernon, A. (2017). Making sense of Big Data—can it transform operations management? *International Journal of Operations & Production Management, 37*(1), 37–55. https://doi.org/10.1108/IJOPM-02-2015-0084

Matwiejczuk, R. (2011). Zasoby oraz zdolności i kompetencje przedsiębiorstwa w tworzeniu przewagi konkurencyjnej. *Przegląd Organizacji, 855*(4), 32–35. https://doi.org/10.33141/po.2011.04.08

McGuckin, R. H., Abbott, T. A., & Norfolk, L. (1992). Measuring advanced technology products trade: A new approach. *Journal of Official Statistics, 8*(2), 223–233. www.scb.se/contentassets/ca21efb41fee47d293bbee5bf7be7fb3/miscellanea-measuring-advanced-technology-products-trade-a-new-approach.pdf

McKlevie, A., & Wiklund, J. (2004). How knowledge affects opportunity discovery and exploitation among new ventures in dynamic markets. In J. E. Butler (Ed.), *Opportunity identification and entrepreneurial behavior* (pp. 219–240). Information Age Publishing Inc.

Mears, C. L. (2012). In-depth interviews. In J. Arthur, M. Waring, R. Coe, & L. V. Hedges (Eds.), *Research methods and methodologies in education* (pp. 170–176). Sage Publication.

Merriam, S. B., & Tisdell, E. J. (2016). *Qualitative research: A guide to design and implementation.* Jossey-Bass.

Mertins, K., Reisig, P., & Vorbeck, J. (2003). Introduction. In K. Mertins, P. Reisig, & J. Vorbeck (Eds.), *Knowledge management concepts and best practices* (pp. 1–11). Springer.

Mikuła, B., & Oczkowska, R. (2009). Transfer wiedzy między partnerami aliansu strategicznego. *Organizacja i Zarządzanie, 2*(6), 121–137. https://oamquarterly.polsl.pl/wp-content/uploads/2018/01/9-Miku%C5%82a-Oczkowska-KN6.pdf

Mikuła, B., & Stefaniuk, T. (2018). Zagrożenia dla bezpieczeństwa wiedzy w ramach zarządzania wiedzą klienta. *Przegląd Organizacji, 9*, 21–28. https://doi.org/10.33141/po.2018.09.03

Millman, A. F. (1982). Understanding barriers to product innovation at the R&D: Marketing interface. *Management Decision, 20*(3), 10–22. https://doi.org/10.1108/eb001291

Mina, A., Bascavusoglu-Moreau, E., & Hughes, A. (2014). Open service innovation and the firm's search for external knowledge. *Research Policy, 43*(5), 853–866. https://doi.org/10.1016/j.respol.2013.07.004

Ministry of Foreign Affairs and Communications (n.d.). *The Japan Standard Industrial Classification (JSIC) summary of development of the JSIC and its eleventh revision.* Retrieved December 24, 2023, from www.soumu.go.jp/main_content/000315022.pdf

Mitręga, M. (2016). Dynamiczne zdolności marketingowe jako obiekt badań w zarządzaniu. *Prace Naukowe Uniwersytetu Ekonomicznego we Wrocławiu, 422*, 313–321. www.ceeol.com/search/article-detail?id=343325

Moenaert, R. K., De Meyer, A., Souder, W. E., & Deschoolmeester, D. (1995). R&D/marketing communication during the fuzzy front-end. *IEEE Transactions on Engineering Management, 42*(3), 243–258. https://doi.org/10.1109/17.403743

Moenaert, R. K., Deschoolmeester, D., De Meyer, A., & Souder, W. E. (1992). Information styles of marketing and R&D personnel during technological product innovation projects. *R&D Management*, *22*(1), 021–040. https://doi.org/10.1111/j.1467-9310.1992.tb00786.x

Moenaert, R. K., & Souder, W. E. (1990). An analysis of the use of extrafunctional information by R&D and marketing personnel: Review and model. *Journal of Product Innovation Management*, *7*(3), 213–229. https://doi.org/10.1111/1540-5885.730213

Moenaert, R. K., & Souder, W. E. (1996). Context and antecedents of information utility at the R&D/marketing interface. *Management Science*, *42*(11), 1592–1610. https://doi.org/10.1287/mnsc.42.11.1592

Moenaert, R. K., Souder, W. E., De Meyer, A., & Deschoolmeester, D. (1994). R&D-marketing integration mechanisms, communication flows, and innovation success. *Journal of Product Innovation Management*, *11*(1), 31–45. https://doi.org/10.1016/0737-6782(94)90117-1

Monteleone, J. P. (1976). How R&D and marketing can work together. *Research Management*, *19*(2), 19–21. https://doi.org/10.1080/00345334.1976.11756341

Monteverde, K. (1995). Technical dialog as an incentive for vertical integration in the semiconductor industry. *Management Science*, *41*(10), 1624–1638. https://doi.org/10.1287/mnsc.41.10.1624

Moores, T. T., & Chang, J. C. J. (2006). Ethical decision making in software piracy: Initial development and test of a four-component model. *MIS Quarterly*, *30*(1), 167–180. https://doi.org/10.2307/25148722

Moorthy, S., & Polley, D. E. (2010). Technological knowledge breadth and depth: Performance impacts. *Journal of Knowledge Management*, *14*(3), 359–377. https://doi.org/10.1108/13673271011050102

Moos, B., Wagner, H.-T., Beimborn, D., & Weitzel, T. (2011). The role of innovation governance and knowledge management for innovation success. In *Proceedings of the 44th Hawaii International Conference on System Sciences*, Kauai, HI. IEEE. https://doi.org/10.1109/HICSS.2011.429

Morgan, R. E., & Strong, C. A. (2003). Business performance and dimensions of strategic orientation. *Journal of Business Research*, *56*(3), 163–176. https://doi.org/10.1016/S0148-2963(01)00218-1

Mosey, S. (2005). Understanding new-to-market product development in SMEs. *International Journal of Operations & Production Management*, *25*(2), 114–130. https://doi.org/10.1108/01443570510576994

Mulier, K., & Samarin, I. (2021). Sector heterogeneity and dynamic effects of innovation subsidies: Evidence from Horizon 2020. *Research Policy*, *50*(10), 1–16. https://doi.org/10.1016/j.respol.2021.104346

Najib, M., & Kiminami, A. (2011). Innovation, cooperation and business performance: Some evidence from Indonesian small food processing cluster. *Journal of Agribusiness in Developing and Emerging Economies*, *1*(1), 75–96. https://doi.org/10.1108/20440831111131523

Narasimhan, O., Rajiv, S., & Dutta, S. (2006). Absorptive capacity in high-technology markets: The competitive advantage of the haves. *Marketing Science*, *25*(5), 510–524. https://doi.org/10.1287/mksc.1060.0219

Narver, J. C., & Slater, S. F. (1990). The effect of a market orientation on business profitability. *Journal of Marketing*, *54*(4), 20–35. https://doi.org/10.1177/002224299005400403

Neely, A., Adams, C., & Kennerley, M. (2002). *The performance prism. The scorecard for measuring and managing business success*. Prentice Hall.

Nelson, R. R., & Winter, S. G. (1982). *An evolutionary theory of economic change*. The Belknap Press of Harvard University Press.

Nieves, J., & Haller, S. (2014). Building dynamic capabilities through knowledge resources. *Tourism Management*, *40*, 224–232. https://doi.org/10.1016/j.tourman.2013.06.010

Nijssen, E. J., & Ordanini, A. (2020). How important is alignment of social media use and R&D–marketing cooperation for innovation success? *Journal of Business Research*, *116*, 1–12. https://doi.org/10.1016/j.jbusres.2020.04.056

Nikiforou, A., Lioukas, S., & Voudouris, I. (2020). Network structure and firm-level entrepreneurial behavior: The role of market and technological knowledge networks. *Journal of Business Research*, *106*, 129–138. https://doi.org/10.1016/j.jbusres.2019.09.008

Nohria, N., & Gulati, R. (1996). Is slack good or bad for innovation? *Academy of Management Journal*, *39*(5), 1245–1264. https://doi.org/10.5465/256998

Nonaka, I. (1994). A dynamic theory of organizational knowledge creation. *Organization Science*, *5*(1), 14–37. https://doi.org/10.1287/orsc.5.1.14

Nonaka, I., Reinmoeller, P., & Senoo, D. (1998). The 'ART' of knowledge: Systems to capitalize on market knowledge. *European Management Journal*, *16*(6), 673–684. https://doi.org/10.1016/S0263-2373(98)00044-9

Nonaka, I., & Takeuchi, H. (1995). *The knowledge-creating company: How Japanese companies create the dynamics of innovation*. Oxford University Press.

Norman, D. A., & Verganti, R. (2014). Incremental and radical innovation: Design research vs. technology and meaning change. *Design Issues*, *30*(1), 78–96. https://doi.org/10.1162/DESI_a_00250

Norton, J., Parry, M. E., & Song, X. M. (1994). Integrating R&D and marketing: A comparison of practices in the Japanese and American chemical industries. *IEEE Transactions on Engineering Management*, *41*(1), 5–20. https://doi.org/10.1109/17.286321

Obłój, K. (2007). Pułapki teoretyczne zasobowej teorii strategii. *Przegląd Organizacji*, *5*, 7–10. https://doi.org/10.33141/po.2007.05.01

O'Brien, S. F., & Yi, Q. L. (2016). How do I interpret a confidence interval? *Transfusion*, *56*(7), 1680–1683. https://doi.org/10.1111/trf.13635

Ode, E., & Ayavoo, R. (2020). The mediating role of knowledge application in the relationship between knowledge management practices and firm innovation. *Journal of Innovation & Knowledge*, *5*(3), 210–218. https://doi.org/10.1016/j.jik.2019.08.002

O'Dell, C., Grayson, Jr., C. J., & Essaides, N. (1998). *If only we knew what we know. The transfer of internal knowledge and best practice*. The Free Press.

O'Donnell, R. W., O'Malley, J. J., Huis, R. J., & Halt, G. B. (2008). *Intellectual property in the food technology industry. Protecting your innovation*. Springer. https://doi.org/10.1007/978-0-387-77389-6

OECD. (1996). *The knowledge-based economy* (No. OCDE/GD(96)102). https://one.oecd.org/document/OCDE/GD%2896%29102/En/pdf

OECD. (1999). *OECD science, technology and industry scoreboard. Benchmarking knowledge-based economies*. OECD Publishing. https://doi.org/10.1787/sti_scoreboard-1999-en

OECD. (2001). *OECD science, technology and industry scoreboard. Towards a knowledge-based economy*. OECD Publications Service. https://doi.org/10.1787/sti_scoreboard-2001-en

OECD. (2002). *Frascati manual: Proposed standard practice for surveys on research and experimental development*. OECD Publications Service. www.oecd-ilibrary.org/docserver/9789264199040-en.pdf?expires=1682189677&id=id&accname=guest&checksum=C32EA84E7F3B935BC52E39B6DFC6F596

OECD. (2003). *OECD science, technology and industry scoreboard*. OECD Publications Service. https://doi.org/10.1787/sti_scoreboard-2003-en

OECD. (2005). *Oslo manual: Guidelines for collecting and interpreting innovation data, 3rd edition, the measurement of scientific and technological activities*. OECD Publishing. https://doi.org/10.1787/9789264013100-en

OECD. (2015). *Frascati manual 2015: Guidelines for collecting and reporting data on research and experimental development, the measurement of scientific, technological and innovation activities*. OECD Publishing. https://doi.org/10.1787/9789264239012-en

OECD. (2018). *Oslo manual 2018: Guidelines for collecting, reporting and using data on innovation, 4th edition, the measurement of scientific, technological and innovation activities*. OECD Publishing. https://doi.org/10.1787/9789264304604-en

OECD. (2020). *Gross domestic spending on R&D*. https://doi.org/10.1787/d8b068b4-en

Oehmichen, J., & Puck, J. (2016). Embeddedness, ownership mode and dynamics, and the performance of MNE subsidiaries. *Journal of International Management, 22*(1), 17–28. https://doi.org/10.1016/j.intman.2015.11.002

Oh, C., Cho, Y., & Kim, W. (2015). The effect of a firm's strategic innovation decisions on its market performance. *Technology Analysis & Strategic Management, 27*(1), 39–53. https://doi.org/10.1080/09537325.2014.945413

Oke, A., Burke, G., & Myers, A. (2007). Innovation types and performance in growing UK SMEs. *International Journal of Operations & Production Management, 27*(7), 735–753. https://doi.org/10.1108/01443570710756974

Ortega-Argilés, R., Piva, M.-C., Potters, L., & Vivarelli, M. (2009). *Is corporate R&D investment in high-tech sectors more efficient? Some guidelines for European Research Policy* (IZA Discussion Paper No. 3945). https://doi.org/10.2139/ssrn.1332586

O'Shannassy, T. (2008). Sustainable competitive advantage or temporary competitive advantage: Improving understanding of an important strategy construct. *Journal of Strategy and Management, 1*(2), 168–180. https://doi.org/10.1108/17554250810926357

Ozkaya, H. E., Droge, C., Hult, G. T. M., Calantone, R., & Ozkaya, E. (2015). Market orientation, knowledge competence, and innovation. *International Journal of Research in Marketing, 32*(3), 309–318. https://doi.org/10.1016/j.ijresmar.2014.10.004

Palacios, D., Gil, I., & Garrigos, F. (2009). The impact of knowledge management on innovation and entrepreneurship in the biotechnology and telecommunications industries. *Small Business Economics, 32*, 291–301. https://doi.org/10.1007/s11187-008-9146-6

Paliszkiwicz, J. (2019). *Przywództwo, zaufanie i zarządzanie wiedzą w innowacyjnych przedsiębiorstwach*. CeDeWu.

Paliszkiewicz, J., Gołuchowski, J., & Koohang, A. (2015). Leadership, trust, and knowledge management in relation to organizational performance: Developing an instrument. *Online Journal of Applied Knowledge Management, 3*(2), 19–35.

Papa, A., Dezi, L., Gregori, G. L., Mueller, J., & Miglietta, N. (2020). Improving innovation performance through knowledge acquisition: The moderating role of employee retention and human resource management practices. *Journal of Knowledge Management, 24*(3), 589–605. https://doi.org/10.1108/JKM-09-2017-0391

Park, W. G. (1995). International R&D spillovers and OECD economic growth. *Economic Inquiry, 33*(4), 571–591. https://doi.org/10.1111/j.1465-7295.1995.tb01882.x

Parry, M. E., & Song, X. M. (1993). Determinants of R&D—marketing integration in high-tech Japanese firms. *Journal of Product Innovation Management, 10*(1), 4–22. https://doi.org/10.1016/0737-6782(93)90050-Z

Partanen, J., Chetty, S. K., & Rajala, A. (2014). Innovation types and network relationships. *Entrepreneurship Theory and Practice, 38*(5), 1027–1055. https://doi.org/10.1111/j.1540-6520.2011.00474.x

Paschen, J., Kietzmann, J., & Kietzmann, T. C. (2019). Artificial intelligence (AI) and its implications for market knowledge in B2B marketing. *Journal of Business & Industrial Marketing, 34*(7), 1410–1419. https://doi.org/10.1108/JBIM-10-2018-0295

Paswan, A. K., & Wittmann, C. M. (2009). Knowledge management and franchise systems. *Industrial Marketing Management, 38*(2), 173–180. https://doi.org/10.1016/j.indmarman.2008.12.005

Pathirage, Ch. P., Amaratunga, D. G., & Haigh, R. P. (2007). Tacit knowledge and organisational performance: Construction industry perspective. *Journal of Knowledge Management, 11*(1), 115–126. https://doi.org/10.1108/13673270710728277

Pavitt, K. (1984). Sectoral patterns of technical change: Towards a taxonomy and a theory. *Research Policy, 13*(6), 343–373. https://doi.org/10.1016/0048-7333(84)90018-0

Pearson, A. W., & Ball, D. F. (1993). A framework for managing communication at the R&D/Marketing interface. *Technovation, 13*(7), 439–447. https://doi.org/10.1016/0166-4972(93)90027-S

Penrose, E. (1959). *The theory of the growth of the firm.* John Wiley & Sons.

Peretz, H., Fried, Y., & Levi, A. (2018). Flexible work arrangements, national culture, organisational characteristics, and organisational outcomes: A study across 21 countries. *Human Resource Management Journal, 28*(1), 182–200. https://doi.org/10.1111/1748-8583.12172

Perks, H., Kahn, K., & Zhang, C. (2009). An empirical evaluation of R&D–marketing NPD integration in Chinese firms: The Guanxi effect. *Journal of Product Innovation Management, 26*(6), 640–651. https://doi.org/10.1111/j.1540-5885.2009.00689.x

Perks, H., Kahn, K. B., & Zhang, C. (2010). The nature of R&D-marketing integration in Chinese high-tech companies. *International Journal of Innovation Management, 14*(01), 19–40. https://doi.org/10.1142/S1363919610002532

Perraton, J., & Tarrant, I. (2007). What does tacit knowledge actually explain? *Journal of Economic Methodology, 14*(3), 353–370. https://doi.org/10.1080/13501780701562559

Peteraf, M. A. (1993). The cornerstones of competitive advantage: A resource-based view. *Strategic Management Journal, 14*(3), 179–191. https://doi.org/10.1002/smj.4250140303

Peterson, W., Gijsbers, G., & Wilks, M. (2003). *An organizational performance assessment system for agricultural research organizations: Concepts, methods, and procedures.* ISNAR Research Management Guidelines No. 7. International Service for National Agricultural Research. https://doi.org/10.22004/ag.econ.310698

Pham, N. D., Donovan, M., & Pierce, B. (2019). *A comparison of profitability measurements between R&D-intensive and non-R&D-intensive industries.* NDP Analytics. http://dx.doi.org/10.2139/ssrn.3352831

Piening, E. P. (2013). Dynamic capabilities in public organizations: A literature review and research agenda. *Public Management Review, 15*(2), 209–245. https://doi.org/10.1080/14719037.2012.708358

Piñeiro-Chousa, J., López-Cabarcos, M. Á., Romero-Castro, N. M., & Pérez-Pico, A. M. (2020). Innovation, entrepreneurship and knowledge in the business scientific field: Mapping the research front. *Journal of Business Research, 115*, 475–485. https://doi.org/10.1016/j.jbusres.2019.11.045

Podsakoff, P. M., MacKenzie, S. B., Lee, J. Y., & Podsakoff, N. P. (2003). Common method biases in behavioral research: A critical review of the literature and recommended remedies. *Journal of Applied Psychology, 88*(5), 879–903. https://doi.org/10.1037/0021-9010.88.5.879

Pohulak-Żołędowska, E. (2016). Innovation in contemporary economies. *Oeconomia Copernicana, 7*(3), 451–466. www.ceeol.com/search/article-detail?id=459771

Polanyi, M. (1962). *Personal knowledge. Towards a post-critical philosophy.* Routledge & Kegan Paul Ltd.

Popa, C., Holvoet, K., Van Montfort, T., Groeneveld, F., & Simoens, S. (2018). Risk-return analysis of the biopharmaceutical industry as compared to other industries. *Frontiers in Pharmacology, 9*(1108), 1–7. https://doi.org/10.3389/fphar.2018.01108

Popadiuk, S., & Choo, C. W. (2006). Innovation and knowledge creation: How are these concepts related? *International Journal of Information Management, 26*(4), 302–312. https://doi.org/10.1016/j.ijinfomgt.2006.03.011

Prabhu, J. C., Chandy, R. K., & Ellis, M. E. (2005). The impact of acquisitions on innovation: Poison pill, placebo, or tonic? *Journal of Marketing, 69*(1), 114–130. https://doi.org/10.1509/jmkg.69.1.114.55514

Prahalad, C. K., & Hamel, G. (1990, May–June). The core competence of the corporation. *Harvard Business Review.* https://hbr.org/1990/05/the-core-competence-of-the-corporation

Prakash, A., Jha, S. K., Prasad, K. D., & Singh, A. K. (2017). Productivity, quality and business performance: An empirical study. *International Journal of Productivity and Performance Management, 66*(1), 78–91. https://doi.org/10.1108/IJPPM-03-2015-0041

Presenza, A., Abbate, T., Meleddu, M., & Cesaroni, F. (2017). Small- and medium-scale Italian winemaking companies facing the open innovation challenge. *International Small Business Journal, 35*(3), 327–348. https://doi.org/10.1177/0266242616664798

Prieto, I. M., & Revilla, E. (2006). Assessing the impact of learning capability on business performance: Empirical evidence from Spain. *Management Learning, 37*(4), 499–522. https://doi.org/10.1177/1350507606070222

Probert, J., Connell, D., & Mina, A. (2013). R&D service firms: The hidden engine of the high-tech economy? *Research Policy, 42*(6–7), 1274–1285. https://doi.org/10.1016/j.respol.2013.03.004

Probst, G., Raub, S., & Romhardt, K. (2004). *Zarządzanie Wiedzą w Organizacji.* Oficyna Ekonomiczna.

Protogerou, A., Caloghirou, Y., & Lioukas, S. (2012). Dynamic capabilities and their indirect impact on firm performance. *Industrial and Corporate Change, 21*(3), 615–647. https://doi.org/10.1093/icc/dtr049

Rafiq, M., & Saxon, T. (2000). R&D and marketing integration in NPD in the pharmaceutical industry. *European Journal of Innovation Management, 3*(4), 222–231. https://doi.org/10.1108/14601060010352506

Raguseo, E., & Vitari, C. (2018). Investments in big data analytics and firm performance: An empirical investigation of direct and mediating effects. *International Journal of Production Research, 56*(15), 5206–5221. https://doi.org/10.1080/00207543.2018.1427900

Rakthin, S., Calantone, R. J., & Wang, J. F. (2016). Managing market intelligence: The comparative role of absorptive capacity and market orientation. *Journal of Business Research, 69*(12), 5569–5577. https://doi.org/10.1016/j.jbusres.2016.03.064

Ratajczak-Mrozek, M. (2017). *Network embeddedness. Examining the effect on business performance and internationalization*. Palgrave Macmillan.
Raymond, L., Marchand, M., St-Pierre, J., Cadieux, L., & Labelle, F. (2013). Dimensions of small business performance from the owner-manager's perspective: A re-conceptualization and empirical validation. *Entrepreneurship & Regional Development*, *25*(5–6), 468–499. https://doi.org/10.1080/08985626.2013.782344
Razmerita, L., Kirchner, K., & Sudzina, F. (2009). Personal knowledge management: The role of Web 2.0 tools for managing knowledge at individual and organisational levels. *Online Information Review*, *33*(6), 1021–1039. https://doi.org/10.1108/14684520911010981
Rhee, J., Park, T., & Lee, D. H. (2010). Drivers of innovativeness and performance for innovative SMEs in South Korea: Mediation of learning orientation. *Technovation*, *30*(1), 65–75. https://doi.org/10.1016/j.technovation.2009.04.008
Ringle, C. M., Wende, S., & Becker, J.-M. (2015). *SmartPLS 3*. SmartPLS GmbH. www.smartpls.com.
Ritala, P., & Hurmelinna-Laukkanen, P. (2013). Incremental and radical innovation in coopetition—the role of absorptive capacity and appropriability. *Journal of Product Innovation Management*, *30*(1), 154–169. https://doi.org/10.1111/j.1540-5885.2012.00956.x
Ritala, P., Olander, H., Michailova, S., & Husted, K. (2015). Knowledge sharing, knowledge leaking and relative innovation performance: An empirical study. *Technovation*, *35*, 22–31. https://doi.org/10.1016/j.technovation.2014.07.011
Roberts, E. B. (2007). Managing invention and innovation. *Research-Technology Management*, *50*(1), 35–54. https://doi.org/10.1080/08956308.2007.11657418
Rogers, E. (1995). *Diffusion of innovations*. The Free Press.
Rollett, H. (2003). *Knowledge management. Processes and technologies*. Springer Science+Business Media.
Rouse, M. J., & Daellenbach, U. S. (2002). More thinking on research methods for the resource-based perspective. *Strategic Management Journal*, *23*(10), 963–967. https://doi.org/10.1002/smj.256
Rowley, J. (2007). The wisdom hierarchy: Representations of the DIKW hierarchy. *Journal of Information Science*, *33*(2), 163–180. https://doi.org/10.1177/0165551506070706
Rowley, J., Baregheh, A., & Sambrook, S. (2011). Towards an innovation-type mapping tool. *Management Decision*, *49*(1), 73–86. https://doi.org/10.1108/00251741111094446
Rubera, G., Ordanini, A., & Calantone, R. (2012). Whether to integrate R&D and marketing: The effect of firm competence. *Journal of Product Innovation Management*, *29*(5), 766–783. https://doi.org/10.1111/j.1540-5885.2012.00936.x
Rud, O. P. (2009). *Business intelligence success factors: Tools for aligning your business in the global economy*. John Wiley & Sons.
Sáenz, J., Aramburu, N., & Blanco, C. E. (2012). Knowledge sharing and innovation in Spanish and Colombian high-tech firms. *Journal of Knowledge Management*, *16*(6), 919–933. https://doi.org/10.1108/13673271211276191
Saghafi, M. M., Gupta, A., & Sheth, J. N. (1990). R&D/marketing interfaces in the telecommunications industry. *Industrial Marketing Management*, *19*(1), 87–94. https://doi.org/10.1016/0019-8501(90)90033-R
Salavou, H. (2004). The concept of innovativeness: Should we need to focus? *European Journal of Innovation Management*, *7*(1), 33–44. https://doi.org/10.1108/14601060410515628

Sanzo, M. J., Álvarez, L. I., Rey, M., & García, N. (2012). Perceptions of top management commitment to innovation and R&D-marketing relationship effectiveness: Do they affect CSR? *Annals of Public and Cooperative Economics, 83*(3), 383–405. https://doi.org/10.1111/j.1467-8292.2012.00468.x

Sapienza, H., Parhankangasb, A., & Autio, E. (2004). Knowledge relatedness and post-spin-off growth. *Journal of Business Venturing, 19*(6), 809–829. https://doi.org/10.1016/j.jbusvent.2003.06.002

Sarstedt, M., Ringle, C. M., & Hair, J. F. (2014). PLS-SEM: Looking back and moving forward. *Long Range Planning, 47*(3), 132–137. https://doi.org/10.1016/j.lrp.2014.02.008

Sarstedt, M., Ringle, C. M., & Hair, J. F. (2021). Partial least squares structural equation modeling. In C. Homburg, M. Klarmann, & A. Vomberg (Eds.), *Handbook of market research* (pp. 587–632). Springer. https://doi.org/10.1007/978-3-319-57413-4_15

Sarwoko, E., & Nurfarida, I. N. (2021). Entrepreneurial marketing: Between entrepreneurial personality traits and business performance. *Entrepreneurial Business and Economics Review, 9*(2), 105–118. https://doi.org/10.15678/EBER.2021.090207

Scandura, A. (2019). The role of scientific and market knowledge in the inventive process: Evidence from a survey of industrial inventors. *The Journal of Technology Transfer, 44*, 1029–1069. https://doi.org/10.1007/s10961-017-9643-3

Schiuma, G., & Lerro, A. (2008), Knowledge-based capital in building regional innovation capacity. *Journal of Knowledge Management, 12*(5), 121–136. https://doi.org/10.1108/13673270810902984

Schultze, U. (2004). On knowledge work. In C. W. Holsapple (Ed.), *Handbook on knowledge management 1* (pp. 43–58). Springer-Verlag. https://doi.org/10.1007/978-3-540-24746-3_3

Schumpeter, J. A. (1983). *The theory of economic development. An inquiry into profits, capital, credit, interest, and the business cycle.* Transaction Publishers.

Sciascia, S., Alberti, F. G., & Salvato, C. (2009). Firm-level entrepreneurial contents for strategic renewal: A knowledge-based perspective. In G. T. Lumpkin & J. A. Katz (Eds.), *Entrepreneurial strategic content (Advances in entrepreneurship, firm emergence and growth, Vol. 11)* (pp. 41–75). Emerald Group Publishing Limited. https://doi.org/10.1108/S1074-7540(2009)0000011004

Seashore, S. E., & Yuchtman, E. (1967). Factorial analysis of organizational performance. *Administrative Science Quarterly, 12*(3), 377–395. https://doi.org/10.2307/2391311

Seidler-de Alwis, R., & Hartmann, E. (2008). The use of tacit knowledge within innovative companies: Knowledge management in innovative enterprises. *Journal of Knowledge Management, 12*(1), 133–147. https://doi.org/10.1108/13673270810852449

Senker, J. (2008). The contribution of tacit knowledge to innovation. In S. P. Gill (Ed.), *Cognition, communication and interaction: Transdisciplinary perspectives on interactive technology* (pp. 376–392). Springer. https://doi.org/10.1007/978-1-84628-927-9_20

Shang, S. S., Yao, C. Y., & Liou, D. M. (2017). The effects of knowledge interaction for business innovation. *R&D Management, 47*(3), 337–351. https://doi.org/10.1111/radm.12130

Shaw, C. T., Shaw, V., & Enke, M. (2004). Relationships between engineers and marketers within new product development: An Anglo-German comparison. *European Journal of Marketing, 38*(5/6), 694–719. https://doi.org/10.1108/03090560410529295

Shaw, V., & Shaw, C. T. (1998). Conflict between engineers and marketers: The engineer's perspective. *Industrial Marketing Management, 27*(4), 279–291. https://doi.org/10.1016/S0019-8501(97)00060-6

Sheehan, J., & Wyckoff, A. (2003). *Targeting R&D: Economic and policy implications of increasing R&D spending* (OECD Science, Technology and Industry Working Papers No. 2003/08). https://doi.org/10.1787/072772055603

Sheng, M. L., & Chien, I. (2016). Rethinking organizational learning orientation on radical and incremental innovation in high-tech firms. *Journal of Business Research, 69*(6), 2302–2308. https://doi.org/10.1016/j.jbusres.2015.12.046

Shi, S., Wang, Y., Chen, X., & Zhang, Q. (2020). Conceptualization of omnichannel customer experience and its impact on shopping intention: A mixed-method approach. *International Journal of Information Management, 50*, 325–336. https://doi.org/10.1016/j.ijinfomgt.2019.09.001

Shim, D., Kim, J. G., & Altmann, J. (2016). Strategic management of R&D and marketing integration for multi-dimensional success of new product developments: An empirical investigation in the Korean ICT industry. *Asian Journal of Technology Innovation, 24*(3), 293–316. https://doi.org/10.1080/19761597.2016.1253023

Shin, G. C., & Roh, J. J. (2015). Interaction of marketing, R&D and critical innovation: Case study of Korean and Japanese firms. *International Journal of Business Information Systems, 18*(4), 437–450. https://doi.org/10.1504/IJBIS.2015.068480

Shmueli, G., & Koppius, O. R. (2011). Predictive analytics in information systems research. *MIS Quarterly, 35*(3), 553–572. https://doi.org/10.2307/23042796

Shrout, P. E., & Bolger, N. (2002). Mediation in experimental and nonexperimental studies: New procedures and recommendations. *Psychological Methods, 7*(4), 422–445. https://doi.org/10.1037/1082-989X.7.4.422

Shujahat, M., Sousa, M. J., Hussain, S., Nawaz, F., Wang, M., & Umer, M. (2019). Translating the impact of knowledge management processes into knowledge-based innovation: The neglected and mediating role of knowledge-worker productivity. *Journal of Business Research, 94*, 442–450. https://doi.org/10.1016/j.jbusres.2017.11.001

Siegel, D. S., & Renko, M. (2012). The role of market and technological knowledge in recognizing entrepreneurial opportunities. *Management Decision, 50*(5), 797–816. https://doi.org/10.1108/00251741211227500

Silaghi, M. I. P., Alexa, D., Jude, C., & Litan, C. (2014). Do business and public sector research and development expenditures contribute to economic growth in Central and Eastern European Countries? A dynamic panel estimation. *Economic Modelling, 36*, 108–119. https://doi.org/10.1016/j.econmod.2013.08.035

Silva, H. C., & Lima, F. (2017). Technology, employment and skills: A look into job duration. *Research Policy, 46*(8), 1519–1530. https://doi.org/10.1016/j.respol.2017.07.007

Silverberg, G. (2002). The discrete charm of the bourgeoisie: Quantum and continuous perspectives on innovation and growth. *Research Policy, 31*(8–9), 1275–1289. https://doi.org/10.1016/S0048-7333(02)00063-X

Simon, A., Bartle, C., Stockport, G., Smith, B., Klobas, J. E., & Sohal, A. (2015). Business leaders' views on the importance of strategic and dynamic capabilities for successful financial and non-financial business performance. *International Journal of Productivity and Performance Management, 64*(7), 908–931. https://doi.org/10.1108/IJPPM-05-2014-0078

Skrzypek, E. (2013a). Uwarunkowania efektywności organizacyjnej w nowej ekonomii. *Annales Universitatis Mariae Curie-Skłodowska, Sectio H Oeconomia, 47*(1), 167–178. www.ceeol.com/search/article-detail?id=526182

Skrzypek, E. (2013b). Uwarunkowania zarządzania wiedzą w organizacji w społeczeństwie informacyjnym. *Nierówności Społeczne a Wzrost Gospodarczy, 32*, 381–393. https://yadda.icm.edu.pl/yadda/element/bwmeta1.element.ekon-element-000171255365

Skrzypek, E. (2014). Kreatywność a zarządzanie wiedzą. *Zeszyty Naukowe Małopolskiej Wyższej Szkoły Ekonomicznej w Tarnowie, 24*(1). https://doi.org/10.25944/znmwse.2014.01.175188

Slater, S. F., Olson, E. M., & Sørensen, H. E. (2012). Creating and exploiting market knowledge assets. *Journal of Business Strategy, 33*(4), 8–27. https://doi.org/10.1108/02756661211242672

Smith, T. M., & Reece, J. S. (1999). The relationship of strategy, fit, productivity, and business performance in a services setting. *Journal of Operations Management, 17*(2), 145–161. https://doi.org/10.1016/S0272-6963(98)00037-0

Sokolov-Mladenović, S., Cvetanović, S., & Mladenović, I. (2016). R&D expenditure and economic growth: EU28 evidence for the period 2002–2012. *Economic Research-Ekonomska Istraživanja, 29*(1), 1005–1020. https://doi.org/10.1080/1331677X.2016.1211948

Song, L. Z., & Song, M. (2010). The role of information technologies in enhancing R&D–marketing integration: An empirical investigation. *Journal of Product Innovation Management, 27*(3), 382–401. https://doi.org/10.1111/j.1540-5885.2010.00723.x

Song, M., & Thieme, R. J. (2006). A cross-national investigation of the R&D–marketing interface in the product innovation process. *Industrial Marketing Management, 35*(3), 308–322. https://doi.org/10.1016/j.indmarman.2004.09.024

Song, X. M., Montoya-Weiss, M. M., & Schmidt, J. B. (1997). Antecedents and consequences of cross-functional cooperation: A comparison of R&D, manufacturing, and marketing perspectives. *Journal of Product Innovation Management, 14*(1), 35–47. https://doi.org/10.1111/1540-5885.1410035

Song, X. M., & Parry, M. E. (1992). The R&D–marketing interface in Japanese high-technology firms. *Journal of Product Innovation Management, 9*(2), 91–112. https://doi.org/10.1111/1540-5885.920091

Song, X. M., & Parry, M. E. (1993a). How the Japanese manage the R&D–marketing interface. *Research-Technology Management, 36*(4), 32–38. https://doi.org/10.1080/08956308.1993.11670913

Song, X. M., & Parry, M. E. (1993b). R&D-marketing integration in Japanese high-technology firms: Hypotheses and empirical evidence. *Journal of the Academy of Marketing Science, 21*(2), 125–133. https://doi.org/10.1177/009207039302100204

Song, X. M., & Parry, M. E. (1997). Teamwork barriers in Japanese high-technology firms: The sociocultural differences between R&D and marketing managers. *Journal of Product Innovation Management, 14*(5), 356–367. https://doi.org/10.1111/1540-5885.1450356

Song, X. M., Thieme, R. J., & Xie, J. (1998). The impact of cross-functional joint involvement across product development stages: An exploratory study. *Journal of Product Innovation Management, 15*(4), 289–303. https://doi.org/10.1111/1540-5885.1540289

Song, X. M., Xie, J., & Dyer, B. (2000). Antecedents and consequences of marketing managers' conflict-handling behaviors. *Journal of Marketing, 64*(1), 50–66. https://doi.org/10.1509/jmkg.64.1.50.17989

Song, Y. M., & Dyer, B. (1995). Innovation strategy and the R&D-marketing interface in Japanese firms: A contingency perspective. *IEEE Transactions on Engineering Management, 42*(4), 360–371. https://doi.org/10.1109/17.482085

Sopińska, A. (2008). *Wiedza jako strategiczny zasób przedsiębiorstwa. Analiza i pomiar kapitału intelektualnego przedsiębiorstwa*. Szkoła Główna Handlowa w Warszawie—Oficyna Wydawnicza.

Souder, W. E. (1977). Effectiveness of nominal and interacting group decision processes for integrating R&D and marketing. *Management Science, 23*(6), 595–605. https://doi.org/10.1287/mnsc.23.6.595

Souder, W. E. (1980). Promoting an effective R&D/marketing interface. *Research Management, 23*(4), 10–15. https://doi.org/10.1080/00345334.1980.11756612

Souder, W. E. (1981). Disharmony between R&D and marketing. *Industrial Marketing Management, 10*(1), 67–73. https://doi.org/10.1016/0019-8501(81)90029-8

Souder, W. E., & Chakrabarti, A. K. (1978). The R&D/marketing interface: Results from an empirical study of innovation projects. *IEEE Transactions on Engineering Management, EM-25*(4), 88–93. https://doi.org/10.1109/TEM.1978.6447302

Spender, J. C. (1996). Making knowledge the basis of a dynamic theory of the firm. *Strategic Management Journal, 17*(S2), 45–62. https://doi.org/10.1002/smj.4250171106

Spender, J. C. (2015). Knowledge management: Origins, history, and development. In E. Bolisani & M. Handzic (Eds.), *Advances in knowledge management: Celebrating twenty years of research and practice* (pp. 3–24). Springer. https://doi.org/10.1007/978-3-319-09501-1

Spigel, B., & Harrison, R. (2018). Toward a process theory of entrepreneurial ecosystems. *Strategic Entrepreneurship Journal, 12*(1), 151–168. https://doi.org/10.1002/sej.1268

Stabe, M., Rininsland, Æ., & Bernard, S. (2017, May 17). The FT 1000: The complete list of Europe's fastest-growing companies. *Financial Times*. https://ig.ft.com/ft-1000/

Stevens, G. A., & Burley, J. (1997). 3,000 raw ideas = 1 commercial success! *Research-Technology Management, 40*(3), 16–27. https://doi.org/10.1080/08956308.1997.11671126

SubbaNarasimha, P. N., Ahmad, S., & Mallya, S. N. (2003). Technological knowledge and firm performance of pharmaceutical firms. *Journal of Intellectual Capital, 4*(1), 20–33. https://doi.org/10.1108/14691930310455360

Subramaniam, M., & Youndt, M. A. (2005). The influence of intellectual capital on the types of innovative capabilities. *Academy of Management Journal, 48*(3), 450–463. https://doi.org/10.5465/amj.2005.17407911

Subramanian, A. (1996). Innovativeness: Redefining the concept. *Journal of Engineering and Technology Management, 13*(3–4), 223–243. https://doi.org/10.1016/S0923-4748(96)01007-7

Sullivan, D. M., & Marvel, M. R. (2011). Knowledge acquisition, network reliance, and early-stage technology venture outcomes. *Journal of Management Studies, 48*(6), 1169–1193. https://doi.org/10.1111/j.1467-6486.2010.00998.x

Sun, P. (2010). Five critical knowledge management organizational themes. *Journal of Knowledge Management, 14*(4), 507–523. https://doi.org/10.1108/13673271011059491

Suseno, Y., & Pinnington, A. H. (2018). Building social capital and human capital for internationalization: The role of network ties and knowledge resources. *Asia Pacific Journal of Management, 35*, 1081–1106. https://doi.org/10.1007/s10490-017-9541-0

Sveiby, K. E. (1997). *The new organizational wealth: Managing and measuring knowledge-based assets*. Berrett-Koehler Publishers.

Sveikauskas, L. (2007, September). *R&D and productivity growth: A review of the literature* (Bureau of Labor Statistics Working Paper No. 408). www.bls.gov/osmr/research-papers/2007/pdf/ec070070.pdf

Swaminathan, V., & Moorman, C. (2009). Marketing alliances, firm networks, and firm value creation. *Journal of Marketing, 73*(5), 52–69. https://doi.org/10.1509/jmkg.73.5.52

Światowiec-Szczepańska, J. (2012). Renta ekonomiczna a przewaga konkurencyjna przedsiębiorstwa. *Ekonomista, 2*, 203–226. https://bibliotekanauki.pl/articles/701435.pdf

Takayama, M. (2010). Law of success or failure in the high tech driven market—"revenge of success" in the biotech, nanotech, and ICT industry. In I. Fuerstner (Ed.), *Products and services; from R&D to final solutions* (pp. 15–35). InTech.

Tan, L. P., & Wong, K. Y. (2015). Linkage between knowledge management and manufacturing performance: A structural equation modeling approach. *Journal of Knowledge Management, 19*(4), 814–835. https://doi.org/10.1108/JKM-11-2014-0487

Taouab, O., & Issor, Z. (2019). Firm performance: Definition and measurement models. *European Scientific Journal, 15*(1), 93–106. https://doi.org/10.19044/esj.2019.v15n1p93

Tashakkori, A., & Creswell, J. W. (2007). The new era of mixed methods. *Journal of Mixed Methods Research, 1*(1), 3–7. https://doi.org/10.1177/2345678906293042

Teece, D., & Pisano, G. (1994). The dynamic capabilities of firms: An introduction. *Industrial and Corporate Change, 3*(3), 537–556. https://doi.org/10.1093/icc/3.3.537-a

Teece, D. J., Pisano, G., & Shuen, A. (1997). Dynamic capabilities and strategic management. *Strategic Management Journal, 18*(7), 509–533. https://doi.org/10.1002/(SICI)1097-0266(199708)18:7<509::AID-SMJ882>3.0.CO;2-Z

Thames, B., & Webster, D. W. (2009). *Chasing change: Building organizational capacity in a turbulent environment.* John Wiley & Sons.

Theriou, N. G., Aggelidia, V., & Theriou, G. (2009). A theoretical framework contrasting the resource-based perspective and the knowledge-based view. *European Research Studies, 12*(3), 177–190. www.um.edu.mt/library/oar//handle/123456789/32156

Thompson, V. A. (1965). Bureaucracy and innovation. *Administrative Science Quarterly, 10*(1), 1–20. https://doi.org/10.2307/2391646

Tödtling, F., Grillitsch, M., & Hoeglinger, C. (2012). Knowledge sourcing and innovation in Austrian ICT companies—how does geography matter? *Industry and Innovation, 19*(4), 327–348. https://doi.org/10.1080/13662716.2012.694678

Tödtling, F., Lehner, P., & Kaufmann, A. (2009). Do different types of innovation rely on specific kinds of knowledge interactions? *Technovation, 29*(1), 59–71. https://doi.org/10.1016/j.technovation.2008.05.002

Triantis, A. J. (2019). Foreword. In N. D. Pham, M. Donovan, & B. Pierce (Eds.), *A comparison of profitability measurements between R&D-intensive and non-R&D-intensive industries* (p. 1). NDP Analytics. http://dx.doi.org/10.2139/ssrn.3352831

Trott, P. (2021). *Innovation management and new product development.* Pearson.

Tsai, K. H., & Wang, J. C. (2009). External technology sourcing and innovation performance in LMT sectors: An analysis based on the Taiwanese Technological Innovation Survey. *Research Policy, 38*(3), 518–526. https://doi.org/10.1016/j.respol.2008.10.007

Tsoukas, H. (1996). The firm as a distributed knowledge system: A constructionist approach. *Strategic Management Journal, 17*(S2), 11–25. https://doi.org/10.1002/smj.4250171104

Tu, M. (2018). An exploratory study of Internet of Things (IoT) adoption intention in logistics and supply chain management: A mixed research approach. *The International Journal of Logistics Management, 29*(1), 131–151. https://doi.org/10.1108/IJLM-11-2016-0274

Tung, R. L., Walls, J., & Frese, M. (2014). Cross-cultural entrepreneurship: The case of China. In J. R. Baum, M. Frese, & R. A. Baron (Eds.), *The psychology of entrepreneurship* (pp. 265–286). Psychology Press. https://doi.org/10.4324/9781315750989

Tuomi, I. (1999). Data is more than knowledge: Implications of the reversed knowledge hierarchy for knowledge management and organizational memory. *Journal of Management Information Systems, 16*(3), 103–117. https://doi.org/10.1080/07421222.1999.11518258

Tzelepis, D., & Skuras, D. (2004). The effects of regional capital subsidies on firm performance: An empirical study. *Journal of Small Business and Enterprise Development, 11*(1), 121–129. https://doi.org/10.1108/14626000410519155

Ujwary-Gil, A. (2012). Identyfikowanie i klasyfikowanie barier zarządzania wiedzą. *Studia i Prace Kolegium Zarządzania i Finansów, Szkoła Główna Handlowa w Warszawie, 115*, 169–179. https://core.ac.uk/reader/48035700

United States Census Bureau. (n.d.). *Advanced technology product code descriptions.* Retrieved December 24, 2023, from www.census.gov/foreign-trade/reference/codes/atp/index.html

Uppenberg, K. (2009). *R&D in Europe: Expenditures across sectors, regions and firm sizes.* Centre for Europeans Policy Studies.

Urbancová, H. (2013). Competitive advantage achievement through innovation and knowledge. *Journal of Competitiveness, 5*(1), 82–96. https://doi.org/10.7441/joc.2013.01.06

Varis, M., & Littunen, H. (2010). Types of innovation, sources of information and performance in entrepreneurial SMEs. *European Journal of Innovation Management, 13*(2), 128–154. https://doi.org/10.1108/14601061011040221

Venkatraman, N., & Ramanujam, V. (1986). Measurement of business performance in strategy research: A comparison of approaches. *Academy of Management Review, 11*(4), 801–814. https://doi.org/10.5465/amr.1986.4283976

Verbič, M., Majcen, B., Ivanova, O., & Čok, M. (2011). R&D and economic growth in Slovenia: A dynamic general equilibrium approach with endogenous growth. *Panoeconomicus, 58*(1), 67–89. https://doi.org/10.2298/PAN1101067V

Verona, G., & Ravasi, D. (2003). Unbundling dynamic capabilities: An exploratory study of continuous product innovation. *Industrial and Corporate Change, 12*(3), 577–606. https://doi.org/10.1093/icc/12.3.577

Viaene, J., & Januszewska, R. (1999). Towards an integration of R & D and marketing in production development. *Journal of International Food & Agribusiness Marketing, 10*(3), 79–98. https://doi.org/10.1300/J047v10n03_05

Villar, C., Alegre, J., & Pla-Barber, J. (2014). Exploring the role of knowledge management practices on exports: A dynamic capabilities view. *International Business Review, 23*(1), 38–44. https://doi.org/10.1016/j.ibusrev.2013.08.008

Volberda, H. W., Foss N. J., & Lyles, M. A. (2010). Perspective—absorbing the concept of absorptive capacity: How to realize its potential in the organization field. *Organization Science, 21*(4), 931–951. https://doi.org/10.1287/orsc.1090.0503

Volberda, H. W., Van Den Bosch, F. A., & Heij, C. V. (2013). Management innovation: Management as fertile ground for innovation. *European Management Review, 10*(1), 1–15. https://doi.org/10.1111/emre.12007

von Krogh, G., & Roos, J. (1996). Imitation of knowledge: A sociology of knowledge perspective. In G. von Krogh & J. Roos (Eds.), *Managing knowledge: Perspectives on cooperation and competition* (pp. 32–54). Sage Publications.

Voorhees, C. M., Brady, M. K., Calantone, R., & Ramirez, E. (2016). Discriminant validity testing in marketing: An analysis, causes for concern, and proposed remedies. *Journal of the Academy of Marketing Science, 44*, 119–134. https://doi.org/10.1007/s11747-015-0455-4

Vrakking, W. J. (1990). The innovative organization. *Long Range Planning, 23*(2), 94–102. https://doi.org/10.1016/0024-6301(90)90204-H

Wang, C., & Han, Y. (2011). Linking properties of knowledge with innovation performance: The moderate role of absorptive capacity. *Journal of Knowledge Management, 15*(5), 802–819. https://doi.org/10.1108/13673271111174339

Wang, C. L., & Ahmed, P. K. (2004). The development and validation of the organisational innovativeness construct using confirmatory factor analysis. *European Journal of Innovation Management, 7*(4), 303–313. https://doi.org/10.1108/14601060410565056

Wang, C. L., & Ahmed, P. K. (2007). Dynamic capabilities: A review and research agenda. *International Journal of Management Reviews, 9*(1), 31–51. https://doi.org/10.1111/j.1468-2370.2007.00201.x

Wang, C. N., & Lee, Y. H. (2014). Degrees of R&D/marketing integration and firms' economic performance. *Asian Journal of Empirical Research, 4*(1), 65–78. https://EconPapers.repec.org/RePEc:asi:ajoerj:v:4:y:2014:i:1:p:65-78:id:3668

Wang, L. W., Kuang, N. P., & Shu, M. H. (2014). Impacts of R&D-marketing interaction: Market performance of new products. *International Journal of Economics and Statistics, 2*, 137–144. www.naun.org/main/NAUN/economics/2014/a322001-297.pdf

Wang, Q. (1996). The exploitation of a multidisciplinary approach in studying the R&D/marketing interface with some empirical evidence. *International Journal of Technology Management, 11*(3–4), 369–379. https://doi.org/10.1504/IJTM.1996.025439

Wang, Q. (1997). R&D/marketing interface in a firm's capability-building process: Evidence from pharmaceutical firms. *International Journal of Innovation Management, 1*(01), 23–52. https://doi.org/10.1142/S1363919697000036

Wang, Q., & Montaguti, E. (2002). The R&D-marketing interface and new product entry strategy. *Marketing Intelligence & Planning, 20*(2), 82–85. https://doi.org/10.1108/02634500210418491

Wang, Y., & Li, J. (2017). ICT's effect on trade: Perspective of comparative advantage. *Economics Letters, 155*, 96–99. https://doi.org/10.1016/j.econlet.2017.03.022

Ward, K., Gott, M., & Hoare, K. (2015). Participants' views of telephone interviews within a grounded theory study. *Journal of Advanced Nursing, 71*(12), 2775–2785. https://doi.org/10.1111/jan.12748

Warier, S. (2003). *Knowledge management*. Vikas Publishing.

Wernerfelt, B. (1984). A resource-based view of the firm. *Strategic Management Journal, 5*(2), 171–180. https://doi.org/10.1002/smj.4250050207

Wiig, K. M. (2004). *People-focused knowledge management: How effective decision making leads to corporate success*. Elsevier Butterworth-Heinemann.

Wiklund, J., & Shepherd, D. (2003). Knowledge-based resources, entrepreneurial orientation, and the performance of small and medium-sized businesses. *Strategic Management Journal, 24*(13), 1307–1314. https://doi.org/10.1002/smj.360

Wilhelm, H., Schlömer, M., & Maurer, I. (2015). How dynamic capabilities affect the effectiveness and efficiency of operating routines under high and low levels of environmental dynamism. *British Journal of Management, 26*(2), 327–345. https://doi.org/10.1111/1467-8551.12085

Winter, S. G. (2003). Understanding dynamic capabilities. *Strategic Management Journal, 24*(10), 991–995. https://doi.org/10.1002/smj.318

Wojan, T., & Parker, T. (2017). *Innovation in the rural nonfarm economy: Its effect on job and earnings growth,* 2010–2014 (Report No. 238). United States Department of Agriculture. https://doi.org/10.22004/ag.econ.264596

Wong, S. Y., & Chin, K. S. (2007). Organizational innovation management: An organization-wide perspective. *Industrial Management & Data Systems, 107*(9), 1290–1315. https://doi.org/10.1108/02635570710833974

Wong, W. L. P., & Radcliffe, D. F. (2000). The tacit nature of design knowledge. *Technology Analysis & Strategic Management, 12*(4), 493–512. https://doi.org/10.1080/713698497

World Bank Group (2021). *Research and development expenditure (% of GDP).* https://data.worldbank.org/indicator/GB.XPD.RSDV.GD.ZS

Wu, Y., Gu, F., Ji, Y., Guo, J., & Fan, Y. (2020). Technological capability, eco-innovation performance, and cooperative R&D strategy in new energy vehicle industry: Evidence from listed companies in China. *Journal of Cleaner Production, 261.* https://doi.org/10.1016/j.jclepro.2020.121157

Xie, X., Zou, H., & Qi, G. (2018). Knowledge absorptive capacity and innovation performance in high-tech companies: A multi-mediating analysis. *Journal of Business Research, 88,* 289–297. https://doi.org/10.1016/j.jbusres.2018.01.019

Xu, S. (2015). Balancing the two knowledge dimensions in innovation efforts: An empirical examination among pharmaceutical firms. *Journal of Product Innovation Management, 32*(4), 610–621. https://doi.org/10.1111/jpim.12234

Yang, M., Wang, J., & Yang, J. (2021). Boundary-spanning search, knowledge integration capability and sustainable competitive advantage. *Baltic Journal of Management, 16*(3), 446–464. https://doi.org/10.1108/BJM-08-2020-0314

Yao, Q., Xu, M., Song, H., Jiang, W., & Zhang, Y. (2014). R&D-marketing integration and performance—evidence provided by Agricultural Science and Technology Enterprises. *Journal of Service Science and Management, 7*(1), 18–29. https://doi.org/10.4236/jssm.2014.71003

Yin, R. K. (2016). *Qualitative research from start to finish.* The Guilford Press. https://doi.org/10.1111/fcsr.12144

Yongsheng, Z., & Jinjie, X. (2019). The concave relevance between R&D/marketing functional integration and product innovation performance of environmentally friendly enterprises in China. *Ekoloji, 28*(107), 1495–1502.

Yuan Fu, Q., Ping Chui, Y., & Helander, M. G. (2006). Knowledge identification and management in product design. *Journal of Knowledge Management, 10*(6), 50–63. https://doi.org/10.1108/13673270610709215

Zachariadis, M. (2004). R&D-induced growth in the OECD? *Review of Development Economics, 8*(3), 423–439. https://doi.org/10.1111/j.1467-9361.2004.00243.x

Zahra, S. A., & George, G. (2002). The net-enabled business innovation cycle and the evolution of dynamic capabilities. *Information Systems Research, 13*(2), 147–150. https://doi.org/10.1287/isre.13.2.147.90

Zahra, S. A., Ireland, R. D., & Hitt, M. A. (2000). International expansion by new venture firms: International diversity, mode of market entry, technological learning, and performance. *Academy of Management Journal, 43*(5), 925–950. https://doi.org/10.5465/1556420

Zahra, S. A., Sapienza, H. J., & Davidsson, P. (2006). Entrepreneurship and dynamic capabilities: A review, model and research agenda. *Journal of Management Studies*, *43*(4), 917–955. https://doi.org/10.1111/j.1467-6486.2006.00616.x

Zhang, T., Gerlowski, D., & Acs, Z. (2022). Working from home: Small business performance and the COVID-19 pandemic. *Small Business Economics*, *58*, 611–636. https://doi.org/10.1007/s11187-021-00493-6

Zhao, W., & Wang, L. (2015). How knowledge affects resource acquisition: Entrepreneurs' knowledge, intra-industry ties and extra-industry ties. *Journal of Entrepreneurship in Emerging Economies*, *7*(2), 115–128, https://doi.org/10.1108/JEEE-11-2014-0040

Zheng, S., Zhang, W., & Du, J. (2011). Knowledge-based dynamic capabilities and innovation in networked environments. *Journal of Knowledge Management*, *15*(6), 1035–1051. https://doi.org/10.1108/13673271111179352

Zhou, K. Z., & Li, C. B. (2012). How knowledge affects radical innovation: Knowledge base, market knowledge acquisition, and internal knowledge sharing. *Strategic Management Journal*, *33*(9), 1090–1102. https://doi.org/10.1002/smj.1959

Zollo, M., & Winter, S. G. (2002). Deliberate learning and the evolution of dynamic capabilities. *Organization Science*, *13*(3), 339–351. https://doi.org/10.1287/orsc.13.3.339.2780

Index

Note: Page numbers in *italics* indicate a figure and page numbers in **bold** indicate a table on the corresponding page.

Kolibri 360 GmbH
Ferdinand-Jühlke-Straße 7
99095 Erfurt, Deutschland
produktsicherheit@kolibri360.de